DESKTOP PUBLISHING

FOR

LIBRARIANS

DESKTOP PUBLISHING

FOR

LIBRARIANS

Walt Crawford

G.K. Hall & Co. ▪ Boston, Massachusetts

Desktop Publishing for Librarians
Walt Crawford

Copyright 1990
by Walt Crawford.

Published by G.K. Hall & Co.
70 Lincoln Street
Boston, Massachusetts 02111

10 9 8 7 6 5 4 3 2 1

Library of Congress Cataloging-in-Publication Data

Crawford, Walt.
    Desktop publishing for librarians / by Walt Crawford.
       p.   cm—(Professional librarian series)
      ISBN 0-8161-1929-5—ISBN 0-8161-1930-9 (pbk.)
      1. Desktop publishing—Library applications. 2 Libraries—
Publishing—Data processing. 3. Libraries and electronic
publishing. 4. Libraries—Automation. I. Title. II. Series.
Z678.93.D46C7   1990
686.2'2544536—dc20   90-31952
                                                            CIP

The paper used in this publication meets the minimum requirements of
American National Standard for Information Sciences—Permanence of
Paper for Printed Library Materials, ANSI Z39.48-1984.   ∞™

MANUFACTURED IN THE UNITED STATES OF AMERICA

To Linda A. Driver
and the
College of Notre Dame Library

My wife, Linda Driver, tolerates a great deal and encourages my writing in many ways. As director of the College of Notre Dame Library, she has taken advantage of my desktop publishing capabilities to provide the library with printed materials and me with needed experience and ideas. My thanks to her for giving me both the support and the opportunities.

Contents

Figures

Preface

We live and learn. When desktop publishing first became popular in 1985, I felt that it was too expensive for most libraries, particularly because it then required an Apple Macintosh, LaserWriter, and hard disk. On the other hand, it seemed clear that libraries could be more effective by using some of the techniques involved in desktop publishing to produce better and more varied printed products.

I suggested that a lower-cost alternative, which I rather naively called *desktop typesetting*, could offer many of the advantages of desktop publishing at lower cost and without replacement of existing computers. I used desktop typesetting techniques to improve the currency and coverage of the *LITA Newsletter*,[1] wrote about that experience, and prepared a book-length manuscript on desktop typesetting.

The manuscript was rejected. What I had overlooked (or chosen to ignore) was that the methodology required for desktop typesetting was too cumbersome for most users and, more important, that desktop publishing would almost certainly migrate from the Macintosh to other platforms and come down in price.

Thanks to a small software company called Ventura and a surprisingly good marketing decision by Xerox, the migration to the PC happened—in a way that has brought the virtues of a competitive marketplace to the desktop-publishing field. Prices for desktop-pub-

---

1   The quarterly newsletter of the Library and Information Technology Association, a division of the American Library Association.

xiii

lishing systems have come down; the capabilities of medium-priced systems have improved considerably; several digital type foundries offer hundreds of typefaces at varying degrees of cost, ease of use, and typographic precision and quality.

In 1988, I converted the *LITA Newsletter* to desktop publishing, started another desktop-published newsletter (*Information Standards Quarterly*), and used pure desktop-publishing techniques to produce a book, the second edition of *MARC for Library Use*.

That same year, my wife became director of the library at the College of Notre Dame, a small college in Belmont, California. I began to pay more attention to the ways that desktop publishing could serve libraries of all sizes and gained some experience in producing real materials for a real library. I became convinced that all but the smallest libraries could improve their operations, image, and communications with the public through desktop publishing. I also suspected that librarians could use a good introduction to desktop operations, written from a library perspective and with examples of real and potential uses in a library setting. Thus, this book.

Acknowledgments

My wife's needs as a library director and her honest reactions to design suggestions helped me to make this book what it is. My editor at G.K. Hall, Carol Chin, provided invaluable guidance along the way, specifically pointing out where early drafts had gone entirely off one deep end or another.

Without the Library and Information Technology Association (LITA), this book would never have been written, because I would (probably) never have taken the plunge into desktop publishing.

Several companies provided review copies of software or hardware:

- Software Publishing Corporation provided a copy of pfs:First Publisher, together with all nine of the clip-art and font portfolios available for that program in mid-1989;

- Swfte provided the Glyphix Installation Kits and all six of the Glyphix Business Font packages;

- Logitech loaned me a ScanMan handheld scanner and provided a copy of Finesse, Logitech's low-end desktop-publishing program, later replacing the ScanMan with the new ScanMan Plus (which I will purchase rather than return);
- SymSoft provided HotShot Graphics, its screen-capture and graphics editing and cataloging system.

Note that these are *not* companies that responded when others turned me down. Quite the contrary. In each case, I approached the company because its product already had a good reputation in published reviews and would fill a specific void in my coverage of the field and because each product was reasonably-priced, making it a plausible part of a library's desktop-publishing system. In fact, there were no refusals. My requests were limited because space for product analysis in this book is limited, as is my time and capacity for trying new products.

My colleagues James W. Coleman and Jonathan Lavigne at RLG reviewed an earlier version of this manuscript and provided helpful comments.

Thanks to everyone listed above and to all the readers of the *LITA Newsletter* (and, to a lesser extent, *Information Standards Quarterly*), who tolerated the mistakes I made in the course of learning the fundamentals of desktop publishing. I hope that this book helps a few of you along a smoother journey to successful document production.

PART 1

Uses for Desktop Publishing

Librarians acquire, store, and circulate the written word. They also generate documents for a wide variety of purposes. Libraries run on paper, generating everything from memos, manuals, and staff newsletters to lists of new books, subject bibliographies, fliers for special events, and signs announcing holiday schedules.

Librarians have always adopted new techniques and technologies when that adoption could improve library services and made economic sense. Many librarians now use personal computers at work and at home. One of the most common uses of personal computers, for librarians as for all PC users, is word processing. Today, many librarians can also make effective use of desktop publishing.

Desktop publishing techniques can make library-produced printed products more polished, more attractive, and more functional. Desktop publishing can save time (and sometimes money) while helping libraries fulfill their missions effectively. This book should help you to put together a desktop publishing system and establish an effective publishing program.

The next three chapters serve as an extended introduction for the remainder of the book.

- Chapter 1 discusses the nature of desktop publishing, the steps involved in producing documents, and typical varieties of library-produced documents.

- Chapter 2 deals with the benefits and drawbacks of desktop publishing, with some notes on when desktop publishing should be avoided and when it is particularly worthwhile.

- Chapter 3 concerns document planning, the heart of all effective publishing programs.

Production and Examples

This book practices what it preaches. Everything except the title leaf was produced using the system and techniques described herein, including all examples. In other words, this is a desktop-published book on desktop publishing.

Most full-page examples in this book were produced separately, then photoreduced to 53 percent of their original size in each dimension. Some examples represent real documents and signs prepared for the College of Notre Dame (Belmont, California) Library, or alternative versions of such documents. Other examples are taken from my own writing and publishing activities or are prepared for the nonexistent (so far as I know) Halltown City Library.

Appendix B provides details of the methodology used for this book and for the figures and illustrations in each chapter.

1

Introduction

Desktop-publishing systems let the user design and produce type-set documents by working with text and graphics interactively on a computer screen before printing the finished pages.

Graphic artists think of desktop-publishing systems as comput-erized replacements for T squares, layout tables, paste pots, and the other tools of pasteup layout and design. Aldus PageMaker, the program for which Paul Brainerd coined the term *desktop publishing*, works from that perspective—it began as a designer's tool for short printed products, assembled page by page.

Others see desktop publishing in terms of production: estab-lishing typographic controls and document designs and using them to produce documents with as little manual intervention as possible. You might think of this as a typographer's viewpoint, which is reflected in the most popular PC-DOS (IBM-compatible) desktop-publishing program, Xerox Ventura Publisher. Ventura Publisher began as a document-production system, well-suited to books and other lengthy projects where a set of rules handles most details of the printed format.

Some people assert that all desktop publishing involves illustra-tions. That is clearly nonsense. Although one hallmark of any good desktop-publishing system is the *ability* to integrate graphic images into a document and control them together with text, many benefits of desktop publishing apply equally to text-only documents—and some desktop publishers may *never* work with the graphic tools in their desktop-publishing system.

Librarians have many uses for the typographic control and power of desktop publishing. Some librarians will make effective use of the graphics-handling capabilities in desktop publishing. Whether the result is an intricately designed and graphically rich folded flier to promote library services or a monthly new-titles list in a straight-forward format that eliminates the need for page-by-page inspection before printing, library-generated printed products can benefit from desktop-publishing systems and techniques.

Thinking about Documents

This book is designed to help you think about the aspects of document production in libraries and for librarians, and the ways that desktop publishing techniques can help in that process.

My intention is not to convince you that you need to run out and buy a complete desktop-publishing system. My hope is that you will find that this book helps you to produce better printed products, even if you never use desktop publishing.

Desktop publishing works effectively only when you come to it with a view of the complete document-production cycle and a good idea of what you want as a result. The set of tools provided in a good desktop-publishing system will help you to carry out your own ideas, but those tools will no more produce high-quality documents automatically than your word processor will write your text for you.

When you understand the document-production cycle and aspects of design, you can produce more effective documents regardless of the tools at hand. Some contemporary word-processing programs contain substantial elements of desktop-publishing software. You may be able to use the techniques of desktop publishing without actually using desktop publishing.

This book will not make you an expert on desktop publishing, and it will certainly not tell you all you need to know. If I succeed, you will be more aware of the elements of document design and production. You will also know where to get more information and whether you should move forward with desktop publishing, read more about it, or stick with your current techniques.

Word Processing and Desktop Publishing

If you use word processing, you already know that it can make the writing process easier and makes editing and revision much faster and more straightforward. You probably recognize that word processing has its drawbacks as well; however, for most users word processing offers a major improvement in the writing process.

Most modern word-processing programs encourage a shift in the way you think about and work with text. When you use a typewriter, two arbitrary units of measure become significant to the writing process: the line and the page. You may be writing sentences, but you must interrupt that process at least momentarily to start a new line and interrupt it more substantially to start a new page.

Good word-processing software eliminates those interruptions and essentially eliminates the line and page as factors in writing. You work with words, sentences, paragraphs, and other logical divisions of text such as sections and chapters. You move freely within a document to organize, edit, and revise; you need not worry about where lines begin and end except in those cases (such as tables) where you need explicit line breaks.

Desktop publishing moves beyond this view of the document as a whole to deal with the final appearance of the printed product. In a sense, desktop publishing is all about appearance. It gives you control over the layout and typography of a product in a way that was inconceivable in word-processing programs three or four years ago and that is still only partially available in today's word-processing software.

Desktop publishing encourages you to think in terms of design and final appearance—not necessarily as part of the writing process but as a separate process that takes the text (including any graphics) and molds it. Just as word processing gives you greater power to act as editor and indexer for your writing, desktop publishing gives you added power to act as typographer, layout person, and designer for your printed products.

Desktop publishing doesn't do everything. It is not really publishing at all, but rather an important subset of document production. It is only a tool—but when used with thought and realistic planning, it can be enormously effective and productive.

Good desktop-publishing software provides many features and makes them useful. Among other things, a desktop-publishing system will allow you to do the following:

- Define page formats interactively, specifying the number of columns, column width and separation, margins for odd and even pages, and the running text at the tops and bottoms of pages (headers and footers);

- Name and store page designs and designs for portions of text (such as heading levels) so that similar documents can be prepared consistently and rapidly;

- Define all aspects of typography for an entire document and for specific categories of text within the document;

- Import text from different word-processing programs and graphics in a variety of standard formats;

- Modify text and graphics interactively, always seeing what the results will be;

- View the results in fine detail or as complete pages;

- Print the results on a variety of printers, using the full capabilities of the printer.

Drawbacks of Desktop Publishing

Power comes at a price. Desktop publishing demands training and study, and it is neither necessary nor appropriate for every document. Desktop-publishing software typically costs more than word-processing software. Most desktop-publishing programs take longer to learn than word-processing programs. Much of the quality you gain through desktop publishing will be lost in the final product unless you use relatively expensive printers. Some desktop-publishing programs require more powerful computers than most other software, and most such programs require extensive disk space.

You may find that you use word processing for every form of writing other than scribbled notes. You should *not* expect to use desktop publishing for every form of writing. There are many cases in which desktop publishing will add nothing useful to the results of word processing.

You should also be aware of one common danger in desktop publishing: the tendency to spend too much time "making it perfect." Most word-processing users eventually realize that the ease of doing "just one more revision" can be a trap and that there is a time to call a document complete and move on. I believe that most desktop publishers will also reach that point, achieving a satisfactory product and moving on to another project. Chapter 2 goes into more detail on the benefits and drawbacks of desktop publishing.

Document Production

The term *desktop publishing* is a misnomer. Publishing and document production involve many steps; desktop publishing provides control over a few—but only a few—of those steps. The explicit steps involved vary from document to document, and the order in which steps are taken may vary enormously. I would suggest that document production typically includes fourteen steps in some order, setting aside business aspects of publishing. A list of those steps follows; some of the steps will be discussed in more detail in later chapters.

Fourteen Steps of Document Production

- **Need.** No document is ever produced unless somebody has established a need for it. That need may be specific (*We need to post special hours for the Memorial Day weekend*) or vague (*We need to improve staff morale; would a newsletter help?*). It may be unarguable (*A listing of new large-print books, done in large print, would help many of our readers*) or it may be questionable (*I need a publication credit to advance my career, even though I don't have anything to say*).

- **Audience.** It doesn't make much sense to prepare a document before you know who is expected to read it. Knowing the audience for a publication will influence its style, length, schedule, and quite possibly many of the design details. Documents produced with no specific audience in mind tend not to reach *any* audience.

- **Intended Results.** You must be clear about the intended results of a document in order to prepare that document effectively. A library newsletter intended to impress potential donors will differ greatly, both in form and content, from a library newsletter intended to keep the staff well-informed. Many publications serve multiple ends, but those ends should all be recognized before writing and design begin.

- **Overall Design.** Once the need, audience, and intended results of a publication are clear, you are in a position to plan the overall shape of the publication—how it will look, at least in a broad sense. At the very least, you should have a good idea of the amount of text required, whether graphics will be needed, and what the schedule should look like. Think before you write. Early planning for the final product will save time and effort in all later stages.

- **Schedule and Budget.** Every document has a schedule and a budget, even though both factors are frequently implicit. Budget and design must work together. If your budget is $50 and you need 1000 copies of a single-sheet flier, your design options are fairly limited (and if you want typeset appearance, desktop publishing is probably your only option). Note that desktop publishing will usually *increase* the budget and schedule for the first project, but it should reduce both on later projects.

- **Text Preparation.** If there are words, they must be written. Word processing will ease the task, but nothing replaces the mind and skill of the writer.

- **Graphics Preparation.** If you need graphics of any sort, they must be prepared in a way that will work as part of the document. Graphics preparation may be the most complex and difficult part of mixed-document production; computers can help, but only to a degree.

- **Editing and Revision.** It is certainly possible to write the text for a sign correctly on the first try; it's even probable. It is possible to write a very brief document so that it requires no editing or revision, but it becomes less likely as the document becomes longer or must meet a greater variety of needs. Assume that every document with more than one paragraph of text may require editing and revision, quite possibly requiring more time than the original preparation.

- **Typography and Layout.** Once the text and graphics are ready, they must be put together as pages. That may involve typesetting and pasteup or some other combination of techniques. A preliminary layout may be done before the typography is performed, the two may be done in a combined step, or layout may take place after typography is complete or even after all proofreading has been finished.

- **Proofreading and Revision.** It is unusual for a document to be perfect at this point, although not that rare for very short documents. Traditionally, revisions after typography (for typeset documents) were expensive and were to be avoided if possible. With contemporary tools, revisions impose no real penalty and may even be welcomed to improve the finished product. Proofreading and revision may require several cycles, sometimes involving new writing, editing, and graphic preparation steps. Desktop publishing can make revision—even drastic revision—relatively painless. That fact should encourage people to seek improvement, but it should not be used as an excuse to avoid completion.

- **Final Layout.** Once everything is ready, all the pieces must be put in place for the final set of original pages or page equivalents.

- **Production and Replication.** If the document only exists in one copy, this step is combined with final layout. In other cases, it may mean anything from photocopying from an original page to elaborate plate-making, printing, and binding processes.

- **Distribution.** The printed documents do no good if they sit in a heap where they were printed. Document production is not really finished until the documents have been distributed to readers, posted on walls, or otherwise put into use.

- **Patterns and Cycles.** This document is complete. Should other documents follow the same pattern? Will there be new versions of this document periodically? In the first case, intelligent document production means retaining the pattern so that some work can be avoided on later documents. In the latter, the cycle must be established and mechanisms set in place so that deadlines are met regularly and without crisis.

Library Hours: A Simple Example

Sitting down with a marking pen to prepare a sign stating holiday hours for a one-person library involves the same basic steps as producing a 300-page book—although one requires considerably more explicit thought and labor than the other.

When you pull out a marking pen and poster board, you are aware of the need (*making the hours known*) and the audience (*library patrons*). You know the intended results (*patrons will know when they can use the library*) and have an overall design in mind (*big letters that fit on this poster board*). The schedule is probably clear (*we need this posted tomorrow*), as is the budget (*and we're running out of poster board!*).

If you really don't need the sign until tomorrow, you may have the presence of mind to do the text preparation in pencil first, allowing the possibility of editing, proofreading, and revision (*hmm— maybe "Sunday" would be better than "Sun."*). Proofreading and revision will be difficult once you take marking pen in hand: your "typography" will probably establish the final layout. If you only have one door, you've taken care of production, and posting it handles your distribution.

Figure 1.1: Library-Hours Sign

At the College of Notre Dame Library, a special-hours sign might look like a larger version of Figure 1.1.

- *Time required to produce the original sign:* about five minutes.

- *Time required to change the hours and produce a new sign:* about two minutes.

- *Time required to generate four copies of the sign:* less than one minute.

- *Cost:* four or five cents per sign; six, if you use fancy paper.

Desktop Publishing in the Document-Production Cycle

Desktop publishing can control and document overall design and layout; can speed typography, layout, revision, and final layout; and can support cycles and patterns. But nothing can automate the process of establishing needs, audiences, schedules, budgets, and results or writing text.

Word processing usually provides better support for text preparation, editing, and revision than desktop publishing (although some programs combine the two). Similarly, graphics preparation can usually be done more effectively using other programs—and frequently most effectively by adding graphics (particularly photographs) to the pages after they come off the computer. Once the text is in machine-readable form, proofreading may be simplified but can't be eliminated, although you can usually assume that the text that went into the desktop-publishing software is what came out on the printed page. Where desktop publishing shines is in pulling the pieces together and planning them in advance—and in making revisions relatively painless, rapid, and inexpensive.

Later chapters will show how desktop publishing can record and maintain overall design decisions (and offer predefined design models for some publications); how desktop publishing facilitates typography, layout, and revision; the occasions on which desktop publishing can reasonably handle full production; and the ways that desktop publishing works to support patterns of publications, consistency among publications, and cyclic publications.

Library-Produced Documents

Most libraries generate more types of documents than any librarian would initially realize. Libraries need many of the same documents as businesses, but they also need many special documents to serve library goals. Almost every library with more than one or two employees needs to produce some or all of the following:

- Signs for special hours, activities, special events, exhibits, and other purposes;
- Lists of new titles;

- Policy and procedure manuals;
- Internal memos;
- Orientation and instructional materials;
- Fliers to publicize library services;
- Special forms for various purposes;
- Bibliographies and guides.

Beyond those documents common to almost all libraries (but specific to each library), most libraries should produce other forms of documents more specific to the type, size, and special nature of the library. For example:

- Any library with a friends of the library group should have a newsletter for the group, and many libraries might also produce newsletters for their patrons and communities;
- Most libraries will benefit by producing press releases to publicize their activities;
- Most academic libraries need reserved-book lists and can improve services by producing substantial quantities of special bibliographies and finding lists;
- Most public libraries will benefit older readers by producing lists of large-print books, including lists of new titles and cumulative lists;
- Many libraries maintain local-newspaper indexes and can generate overall or selective listings;
- Public libraries should be able to produce community-service directories based on machine-readable information and referral files;
- Many libraries with strong local-history collections may wish to publish materials drawn from or relating to the collections;
- Some academic libraries and libraries in communities with more than a few published authors will find it worthwhile to produce periodic guides to the works of local authors held by the library;
- Libraries with strong children's programs should consider preparing short-run anthologies of stories written by local children;
- Many libraries can effectively produce special publications based on special collections, including periodicals, special-collection newsletters, and even full-scale monographs.

These are but some of the documents that can benefit from desktop publishing; there are doubtless many other categories. Some libraries publish full-scale journals and carry out other special, beneficial publishing programs. Desktop publishing will neither accommodate all publishing needs nor be equally helpful for all projects, but the techniques supported by desktop-publishing systems will prove helpful, even when the systems are not suited to the particular job.

Tips and Reminders

- Every desktop-publishing system allows you to integrate graphics and text, but you don't need to use illustrations in every document.

- You can produce more effective documents by understanding the document-production cycle and aspects of design, even if you don't use desktop-publishing techniques.

- Every library produces a range of printed materials, and desktop publishing can improve many of those publications.

2

Benefits and Drawbacks
of Desktop Publishing

Advance planning improves virtually every publication, from a one-paragraph memo to a 600-page book. Intelligent design will also improve most publications. Desktop publishing supports planning and design and retains decisions for later use—but that doesn't mean that every publication requires or deserves desktop publishing.

If you need to prepare a cost-benefit analysis in order to justify a desktop-publishing system, you should look at every publication your library currently produces. You should also consider the opportunities for new publications to improve the library's service and image. Any library that makes good use of at least two personal computers for internal uses can probably justify some level of desktop publishing.

This chapter includes advanced word processing in the general category of desktop publishing, as does much of this book. I make the distinction between them where it is important, but in many cases the benefits and drawbacks are the same for both.

Benefits of Desktop Publishing

Faster, cheaper, better: those are the fundamental benefits of desktop publishing (and, ideally, of all computing). Don't count on all three benefits for each publication you prepare; however, the improvements can be impressive when everything works out.

The benefits of desktop publishing are not reserved for publications that combine graphics and text or for complex publications. A typical library may derive much more benefit through desktop-publishing its simpler, everyday publications, even as desktop publishing makes more complex publications easier and more practical.

Saving Time: Improving Currency

Desktop publishing should speed up document preparation, making publications more timely. Every publication more formal than a memo requires a series of steps that take an appreciable amount of time. Word processing combines some steps in a way that can make revisions faster and easier, as compared to manual methods. Good desktop-publishing techniques can go much further, particularly for publications that will appear more than once—which include everything from special-hours signs (done many times each year) and newsletters to policy manuals that require periodic updating.

Consider two examples and how they might relate to publications that your library produces or should produce. In the first case, desktop publishing saves time and trouble as compared to manual methods, while producing more consistently professional results. In the second case, desktop publishing saves time and effort as compared to traditional typesetting and layout, without any significant loss in quality.

Special-Hours and Other Signs

Can you produce a new special-hours sign with professional-quality lettering in three or four minutes? You can with desktop publishing. Figure 1.1 in chapter 1 shows a real example of desktop publishing used for the simplest (and, in some ways, most common) library need. Your library has special hours in special cases, and the hours may not be finalized until the last minute. That's a universal case of the need for on-the-spot sign making, but it's far from the only case. Some others:

- Due to sudden illness, your reference desk will be closed this Sunday—and it is now Saturday afternoon.

- A children's author calls and says she'll be in town next Monday; would you like her to do a reading? Of course—but you need to post the event *now*.

- Library closure requires that books be returned two days earlier than usual; you need to alert people to that, since not everyone pays attention to date-due slips.

- The computer club that meets in room A will have twice the usual number of people attending this week; you can move it to room C, but you need to let people know.

Most libraries produce on-the-spot signs using felt-tip pens. Desktop publishing is probably faster, certainly easier, and eminently superior. How fast is it? Once a special-hours "style" has been defined (defining the significance of "HOURNAME" and "HOURS"), it takes only two steps:

- Create a document that contains the heading and the hours, each tagged—for example, the following lines if using Ventura Publisher (where " ↓ " is a forced new line, "→" is the tab key):

@HOURNAME = Spring Break ↓
Library Hours
@HOURS = Mon.-Thurs.→March 20-23→8 a.m.-8 p.m. ↓
Fri.-Sat.→March 24-25→Closed ↓
Sunday→March 26→6-10 p.m.

- Close the document, start the desktop-publishing program, read in the text, and print the sign.

For something as simple as changes in an open-hours sign, you might even eliminate the first step; you could start the desktop-publishing program and modify text from the last sign directly. That is poor strategy for any major document, but for a dozen words it makes good sense. In either case, it would be hard to spend more than five or ten minutes on the whole process. If the library has a logo that has been turned into a graphics file, the signs can include that logo—already set in place within the library-hours document.

The same is true for almost any brief notice. You can set up a general design, then just key in the text and print out the new notice. Without desktop publishing, you would probably use a felt-tip pen— and if you have my artistic skills, it would take four or five tries to get a sign that was legible. With desktop publishing, you can produce a highly legible printed sign in the typeface you have established for library signs—thus using on-the-spot signs to enhance the library's image.

Signs are one case where desktop publishing has a distinct advantage over advanced word processing. The ability to view the finished product as you work on it, so that you can adjust spacing, see whether the borders work well with the type, etc., makes the initial design work easier and revisions much faster.

LITA Newsletter

When the *LITA Newsletter* was typeset, copy had to reach the editor ten weeks before an issue was mailed. That's not an extreme case; many periodicals have much longer lead times. The editor took a week or so to decide which articles to use, put them in shape, retype them if necessary, prepare headline copy, decide on a preferred order of articles, and ship the text off to the headquarters in Chicago. The articles were typeset and proofread. The galleys went back to the editor for a day's worth of checking; then the Chicago staff laid out the pages and sent them off for printing and distribution.

Desktop publishing reduced that lead time from ten weeks to five weeks—and sometimes less. The editor now takes a week to get the copy in shape and sends galleys to Chicago for the executive director to check. At the end of the second week, the editor uses Ventura Publisher to prepare a set of page originals. The page originals are mailed to Chicago and immediately sent out for printing and distribution (a two- to three-week process). In at least one recent case, late-breaking changes were included in the issue only *three weeks* before it was mailed. Since the layout of the *LITA Newsletter* is established as a Ventura Publisher design, page layout and production are nearly automatic, and a new set of sixteen pages requires about half an hour to check and print.

This is not just a savings in *elapsed* time. It is also a considerable savings in total labor, with the editor doing about the same amount of work as before and the Chicago staff doing a lot less. You may not have publications that require production halfway across the country, but any publication that requires typesetting or layout can be done more rapidly with desktop publishing, and without the fear of time-consuming revision.

Planning for Revision

When you need to do something more than once, even if only to revise a single publication, desktop publishing can eliminate most of the production overhead the second time around. That can change your patterns of updating and reissuing publications, improving their timeliness and usefulness.

A library policy or operations manual may require hundreds of hours, not only to gather the material but to put it together in a useful manner. Such manuals are so painful to update that libraries put off overall updates until the scribbled notes and inserted pages make the manual nearly useless. Word processing will improve the situation, as sections of the manual can be constantly maintained in machine-readable form; desktop publishing gives you the support to build an overall design, even including screen images and other illustrations, and produce updated versions with relatively little effort.

Intelligent use of desktop publishing should result in a design for the manual that is settled when the first section is prepared. Each additional section will be easier since the design can be automatically applied. That reduces the complexity of the first version, and an existing design and machine-readable policy files should make updating much easier. Instead of waiting two years and taking another 200 hours to produce a new manual, you should be able to do one every six months, probably taking no more than a day or two to produce an updated version.

Similarly, instructional tools for patrons can be kept up-to-date more readily; new signs to match a stack shift can be professional quality and available the same day the stacks are shifted; lists of new holdings can be produced as soon as the information is available; bibliographies can be generated almost immediately. When a librarian needs to give a presentation on short notice, Ventura can be used to prepare high-quality transparencies in an hour or less.

Increasing Flexibility and Control

You control the final product completely when you use desktop publishing, which provides more flexibility than word processing and more immediacy than traditional typesetting. Good desktop-publishing software provides immediate, interactive control over almost every aspect of the pages you produce. You see how it will look and you see the effects of changes. By working interactively with the page and document design, you can make a wide range of adjustments to suit your needs—typographic and layout adjustments to make the publication more effective and textual adjustments to make everything work. While word processing provides relatively quick results, it may not provide the full range of controls that is available in advanced desktop publishing.

Traditional typesetting and layout always impose a delay between preparation of copy and inspection of possible finished pages, even if you have an in-house typesetting and layout facility. More typically, given the delays and costs of typesetting, the indirect nature of control means that you must make major decisions once (before typesetting) and avoid disruptive changes, even if they would improve the content of the publication.

Assume that you have a sixteen-page newsletter to produce and roughly the right amount of copy. You can't be sure how long the copy will run until it is typeset; your estimates suggest that it might be perfect or it might be one or two paragraphs too long. How will you handle the situation if the results come out two paragraphs too long—sixteen and one-quarter pages rather than sixteen?

If you're paying for typesetting, you will almost certainly cut entire paragraphs or entire articles. But the best way to make the copy fit the space available might well be to remove a few words from each of a dozen articles, retaining all of the significant copy. That is not reasonable for typeset copy, since it might be necessary to reset half of the sixteen pages. With desktop publishing, there is virtually no penalty for making lots of little changes. At worst, you may need another half hour to adjust the results, and printing another set of sixteen pages will cost less than a dollar.

Newsletters produced with a typewriter lack the flexibility of word processing or desktop publishing and take their own toll on control. While you do have control over such a publication, the effort of retyping the entire set of pages to change one or two sentences is sufficient to discourage all but the hardiest editor.

Saving Paper

Desktop publishing can save paper (as compared to typewriting or simple word processing) by putting more information on each page and reducing the number of trial listings needed for a publication. You may be able to reduce the number of pages in a publication by 30 percent, 50 percent, or more by changing from typewriting to desktop publishing. In special cases, where information is used only for brief reference rather than for reading, you may be able to put three times as much information on a page without a severe reduction in legibility, as compared to typewriting or fixed-font word processing.

There are four reasons that desktop publishing puts more information on each page:

- Proportional fonts (such as Times Roman, Palatino, Optima, and Century Schoolbook—fonts in which some letters are wider than others) always use horizontal space more effectively than fixed fonts (such as Courier, Pica, and Elite—fonts in which all letters have the same width) of the same overall size;

- Good proportional fonts are much more readable than fixed fonts, making it possible to use a smaller type size without losing readability;

- Typewritten pages require wide margins in order to avoid lines that are too long for easy reading; desktop publishing makes it easy to use narrower margins and two columns, avoiding the long-line problem;

- Desktop publishing controls spacing (between lines, between paragraphs, above and below headings) more accurately than typewriting, making it possible to reduce some spacing without damaging the overall design.

Consider figures 2.1, 2.2., and 2.3. The difference in size between figures 2.1 and 2.2 results simply from changing typefaces—from 10-point Courier to 10-point Zapf Calligraphic (which is not a particularly space-saving typeface). The *point* is the standard measuring unit for type: there are roughly 72 points to the inch, and type is always specified in terms of vertical points.

```
The amount of reduction possible through desktop
publishing depends on the publication and your de-
sign decisions. If you choose to keep all other
elements of a publication design constant - the
same margins and the same spacing - but change
from a fixed font to a proportional font of
roughly the same characteristics, you should ex-
pect to see a savings of at least 30 percent to
40 percent. You will see greater savings for tex-
tual material composed primarily of long para-
graphs; the least savings will be material that
rarely requires continuation lines. (Naturally,
if the material is strictly tabular with no con-
tinuation lines, you won't save anything at all.)
```

Figure 2.1: Paragraph in Courier 10

Figure 2.2 uses roughly 70 percent as much space as Figure 2.1, putting 40 percent more text in the same space. I would argue that the second figure is more readable than the first.

The amount of reduction possible through desktop publishing depends on the publication and your design decisions. If you choose to keep all other elements of a publication design constant—the same margins and the same spacing—but change from a fixed font to a proportional font of roughly the same characteristics, you should expect to see a savings of at least 30 percent to 40 percent. You will see greater savings for textual material composed primarily of long paragraphs; the least savings will be material that rarely requires continuation lines. (Naturally, if the material is strictly tabular with no continuation lines, you won't save anything at all.)

Figure 2.2: Paragraph in Zapf Calligraphic 10

If the material is for momentary reference purposes, you can reduce the size of proportional type considerably and still retain good legibility, as in Figure 2.3, which is set in 8-point Zapf Calligraphic, four-fifths the height of the type in Figure 2.2. Note that this third version uses only 70 percent as much space as Figure 2.2, and roughly half the space of Figure 2.1. Figure 2.3 is set in two columns, since a single column would be too wide for such small type.

The amount of reduction possible through desktop publishing depends on the publication and your design decisions. If you choose to keep all other elements of a publication design constant—the same margins and the same spacing—but change from a fixed font to a proportional font of roughly the same characteristics, you should expect to see a savings of at least 30 percent to 40 percent. You will see greater savings for textual material composed primarily of long paragraphs; the least savings will be material that rarely requires continuation lines. (Naturally, if the material is strictly tabular with no continuation lines, you won't save anything at all.)

Figure 2.3: Paragraph in Zapf Calligraphic 8

Moving from one wide column to two narrow columns can yield impressive space savings if the results are appropriate for the publication. For example, a bibliography requiring six pages in Courier and four and one-half pages in single-column Times Roman will fit nicely in three pages of two-column Times Roman.

The other paper savings is minor (probably so minor as to be trivial) and is only significant when comparing word processing and desktop publishing for complex publications. Good desktop-publishing software allows you to preview the pages almost exactly as they will appear on paper and modify them while viewing them accurately. As a result, you can be reasonably sure of the format before you print the first trial run, and you can certainly cut the number of versions required to achieve a finished product. That is really more of a time saver than a paper saver; you will definitely avoid frustration by eliminating the need for multiple runs of a lengthy document just to get the format right.

Saving Money

Time, paper, and typesetting all cost money. You can pay for a desktop-publishing system with one big project that would otherwise be typeset or with a year's worth of small ones. Using this method instead of typewriting, you may save enough time over a year to pay for a desktop-publishing system; you will save paper as well, although that may not be a major factor.

Since we have already discussed time and paper, the only point to make about them is that the possible savings can be quite significant. If you save ten hours of staff time each month by moving a particular product from typewriting to desktop publishing, and the staff member earns $15 an hour, you save $1,800 a year.

Typesetting, when you use it, usually adds a significant direct cost to any publication, ranging from $15 to $50 or more per page. If a sixteen-page monthly newsletter costs $25 per page for typesetting, you will have paid for a $4,800 desktop-publishing system in one year—without considering savings in layout and other costs.

Your library may not have any projects big enough so that a single one will pay for the desktop-publishing system—but one 300-page book would suffice.

Improving Effectiveness

Well-designed publications communicate more information more rapidly, improving your effectiveness. Typewriting lacks variety. A long typewritten document—particularly one that uses paper efficiently—becomes a mass of gray, difficult and unrewarding to read.

People read proportional type more rapidly and comfortably than typewriter type. Look back at the comparison of Courier and Zapf Calligraphic in figures 2.1 and 2.2: which would you rather read? Beyond that, desktop publishing supports headlines; textual highlights of various sorts; graphics when they are appropriate; and a variety of other techniques to make publications more effective.

Improving Quality and Consistency

Good form enhances good content. The superior typography and design possible with desktop publishing will enhance your documents and enhance your library's image. When you install desktop publishing and establish designs for your ongoing printed products, you establish a consistent image for your library. If your designs are attractive and your typefaces communicate, that consistency will draw people to your signs, leaflets, bulletins, and other publications.

Handwritten signs fill a need but rarely attract positive attention. Typewritten material must rely on content; the form is familiar but not, in and of itself, interesting or attractive. Output from basic personal computers could actually detract from the content: text printed on less sophisticated dot-matrix printers can turn away the casual reader.

Today's desktop publishing systems offer scores of professionally-designed typefaces, some of them designed specifically for desktop publishing. Used well, those typefaces and other elements of desktop publishing will attract readers to your message and improve your library's image.

Producing New Publications

Have you ever had a good idea for a new library service—one that required printed products—and set it aside because the production effort or expense was too great? When professional-quality publications can be done easily, rapidly, and cheaply, you can expand your range of publications.

Almost any library with alert librarians will have many more possible services than can actually be carried out. The reasons for avoiding new services are many: lack of staff time, lack of funding, complexity of schedules, and others. Desktop publishing can't provide all the answers, but it can reduce some of the obstacles.

Drawbacks of Desktop Publishing

When used effectively, desktop publishing offers enormous advantages to a library or a librarian. When used badly, desktop publishing can be a waste of time, energy, and money. The power of desktop publishing can turn thoughtful prose into garish garbage just as readily as it can make that prose more accessible.

Spending Time

You must spend time to learn desktop publishing, and you can assume that the first example of any type of publication will take extra time. The programs can have a steep learning curve. Each new type of publication requires attention to build the document format.

But you can also get lost in a never-ending cycle of revisions and refinements, just as with word processing. It's tempting to see whether you can tweak the design just a little bit more, trying out a slightly different combination of spacing and fonts. Would a different size look a little better here? Would a little more leading improve the typography there? The search for the perfect design never ends; anyone using desktop publishing must recognize when to stop designing and start producing—when a design is good enough, at least for this time around.

A more serious problem arises when the person using desktop publishing lacks sufficient insight and interest to become comfortable and proficient with the tools. Good writers and editors aren't necessarily good or sensible designers, and they may not be interested in overall document design. A desktop publisher who doesn't like the tools at hand will typically use them awkwardly and badly. Such a problem means many more rounds of revisions and corrections, and it can result in a project taking much more time with a desktop system than with other techniques.

Spending Money

You will spend a few thousand dollars on a complete desktop publishing system—and that's not counting supply costs. Laser cartridges in particular seem to require frequent replacement

Although most popular laser printers actually cost less per page for supplies than most other letter-quality printers, you will almost certainly spend more on supplies for a laser printer.

Why is that? Because you'll do a lot more printing. If you have already moved from typewriters to word processing, you already know this: when it is easier to produce documents, more documents will be produced. Desktop publishing considerably expands your ability to produce high-quality publications; as a result, you will almost certainly go through more paper and cartridges than you originally allocate funds for.

Paper costs money. Cartridges cost money. Software costs money. Desktop publishing has a fairly high start-up cost, particularly for a high-end system. If not used effectively, desktop publishing wastes money. And, as always, if you desktop-publish things that you really should not produce at all, you are wasting money.

Reducing Effectiveness

Desktop publishing can substitute form for content and make publications hard to read. Too many fonts spoil the page. Irrelevant illustrations can detract from communication.

We all remember newsletters and flyers produced with typewriter and press-on lettering, where the person preparing the publication got carried away with variety and produced a jumble of clashing, distracting type. Desktop publishing gives the same people an inexhaustible supply of lettering and the ability to cram even more typefaces on a single page. Who among us has never seen the awful results—results that lead some to regard desktop publishing as the death of style?

It is easy to become enamored of the variety possible with desktop publishing. That's one reason that half of this book deals with design considerations. While good software includes some initial designs to use as starting points, you must provide the taste and judgment to prepare effective publications.

A surprising number of people think that every publication looks better with "art"—whether there's any reason for illustrations or not. The resulting use of meaningless "clip art" and pointless graphs not only consumes space that could better be used for white space and text; it also detracts from the content of the publication. By making it easier to combine text and graphics, desktop publishing encourages the worst instincts of those who demand illustrations.

Losing Quality

One aspect of print quality is resolution, the sharpness and detail of the text and illustrations. For most modern typography, resolution is specified in dots or lines per inch—with higher numbers representing sharper, better-defined print. Most laser printers and photo-typesetters have the same resolution horizontally and vertically, and a single number is given: thus, *1,200 dots per inch* means 1,200 dots per inch vertically by 1,200 dots per inch horizontally—or a total of 1.44 million dots per square inch. If the two resolutions differ, both will be stated.

Indisputably, the output of phototypesetting equipment (1,200 or 2,500 dots or lines per inch) is sharper than the output from a typical desktop laser printer (300 dots per inch). Even lower-density (1,200 dpi) phototypesetting provides sixteen times as much information as laser printing, with a total resolution of 1.44 million dots per square inch as compared to the 90,000 dots per square inch from a Hewlett-Packard LaserJet or Apple LaserWriter.

Any reader using a magnifying glass can spot the imperfections in laser-printed pages. Even without a magnifying glass, some large letters have slight visible imperfections—for example, go back and look closely at the *y* in the word *Library* in figure 1.1. Very small type suffers from the fact that the minimum width of a laser-printed line is $\frac{1}{300}$ of an inch, or roughly $\frac{1}{4}$-point. That makes very small letters thicker than they should be. Some dictionaries are set using six-point type; with desktop publishing, the results would be nearly illegible.

Fortunately, most readers don't read with a magnifying glass, and the printing process smooths out most imperfections in laser type—at least on book paper. As an early printer, Benjamin Franklin might be amused at the hue and cry over the imperfections in laser-printed output. Before the invention of the Linotype, printers rarely had huge supplies of absolutely flawless type, since type had to be reused and tended to wear somewhat. Look at any very old newspaper or book; you'll see imperfections far beyond those of laser printing.

Photographs raise another quality issue. Without special equipment, a photograph reproduced as part of a laser-printed page will be of very poor quality. Special equipment can improve the situation, achieving quality equal to or better than that of newspaper photographs. Any illustrations that use shading may lose detail and quality when converted to electronic form and printed on a laser printer. In this case, the solution is simple: add the illustrations *after* preparing the pages.

The fundamental truth is that desktop publishing is like most other tools and technologies: it will provide benefits or cause problems, depending on how intelligently it is used.

The Balancing Act: Drawing the Lines

When should you definitely use desktop publishing? In some ways, it's easier to establish when you definitely should *not* use desktop publishing. Such cases include:

- Anything that isn't worth the trouble to put into machine-readable form;
- Communications that can be sent electronically (i.e., via electronic mail);
- Brief internal memos and casual correspondence;
- Colorful, large, single-copy posters, particularly when staff have the talent to prepare them by hand.

Any other printed product *may* be a candidate for desktop publishing, depending on your other facilities and needs. There are certain difficult cases, particularly if your desktop publishing system is typical of those discussed here:

- Publications to be produced on slick coated stock or those requiring extremely small type;
- Publications making extensive use of color, particularly color photography;
- Publications larger than 8½ by 14 inches, when other production techniques are available.

Yes, it is possible to produce all of these publications doing much of the work on the desktop; in the first case (where better resolution than 300 dots per inch is required), the solutions are readily available and increasingly affordable. Still, at least for 1990, you probably should not plan to produce such publications entirely through desktop means.

What publications are particularly well-suited to desktop publishing? Just a few of the categories follow:

- Newsletters and other serial publications that follow an established format;

- Manuals, books, and other publications that require headings, sub-headings, organization, tables of contents, and indexes—particularly when the publications require periodic revision;

- Page-size signs for quick posting to alert people of special hours and special situations;

- Bibliographies, pathfinders, and other cases where extensive information must be presented in a readable form without too much preparation or expense.

Conclusion

Word processing should save you money and time as compared to typewriting, while increasing control and flexibility. Desktop publishing and advanced word processing can go further, giving you the tools to produce professional-quality publications on a routine basis, with less effort and cost than would be required to do them far less well.

Desktop publishing can also eliminate much of your typesetting cost, if your library currently uses typesetting for some publications. In doing so, it can pay for itself rapidly—not only in direct savings, but also through indirect savings in time and frustration.

But desktop publishing is not a panacea. It takes time to understand an advanced desktop-publishing program well enough to use it effectively, and a poorly used program may waste time and effort while increasing the frustration of its users.

Advanced word-processing programs with layout capabilities, and the even more advanced facilities present in desktop-publishing systems, offer you remarkable sets of tools with which to take control of your publication program and improve it in many ways. But the programs are nothing more than tools; only when used effectively and thoughtfully will they yield good results.

Tips and Reminders

- Desktop publishing saves time for recurring publications, but only if you don't become trapped in a quest for perfection.

- Desktop publishing can save money—but it does require a significant initial expenditure.

- The greatest benefit of desktop publishing may be the freedom to generate new publications.

- Don't use desktop publishing for everything simply because it's available.

3

Document Planning

Y ou may still be trying to determine whether desktop publishing makes good economic sense for you or your library. You can inform that determination by reviewing your library's or unit's publications for the last six months, seeing how each one might be affected by desktop publishing.

That review is a form of retrospective planning—looking at what each document is or was, how it was produced, and how that process could work better. If you are at all typical, many of your documents may have "just grown" without explicit planning, and you may be surprised at the number and variety of documents published or produced during half a year. Add to that the publications you should have prepared, and you can make a reasonable decision on the economics of desktop publishing.

Use your review of previous publications as a basis for planning future publications—including planning for the predictably unpredictable cases. You certainly can't project exactly what documents will be needed and exactly when, at least not across the board. But you should find that most unplanned documents fall into several categories, and that the categories are predictable. Each category that you can determine in advance becomes better-controlled, providing several advantages over wholly uncontrolled documents.

Many publications—such as special-events calendars, association and staff newsletters, new-title lists, and hours postings, are fully predictable: you know roughly how often they will be needed and roughly how much content they will have, and you can determine in advance what they should look like. Some can be scheduled well in advance, to the day; others can be planned in general, although precise schedules may not be appropriate. These regular categories form the backbone of your document planning and control. Chances are, your library already has some level of document planning for these categories; if it does not, it should. As you improve your publication planning, more categories will appear, such as regularly updated information and referral listings and newspaper indexes.

Predicting the Unpredictable

Predictable categories with unpredictable members offer the chance to avoid crises by advance planning. If you can establish the general design for certain types of "special" publication—as you probably can—that general design helps to eliminate last-minute problems and improve your responsiveness to last-minute needs. Consider, for example, two predictable categories of somewhat unpredictable publications: press releases and bibliographies.

Press Releases

How long does it take you to prepare a press release and send it out—and do your press releases convey a positive image? With advance planning and desktop publishing, you will produce good press releases as soon as you have something newsworthy to write about.

You don't know when the library will have things to publicize in the press, but you know that there will be occasions for press releases. You can certainly plan what a press release looks like and who normally receives it. With a little thought, you can establish a label-preparation dataset, a press-release desktop-publishing format (including your library logo, who to contact, "for immediate release" and the like), and a one-paragraph guide for preparing press releases. When something newsworthy comes up, all you need is someone to write and edit the information; your advance planning will lead to professional releases ready to send out the same day.

If your public or academic library does not currently produce press releases, it probably should, as should most special libraries. Libraries can always use good publicity, and it's a rare library that never does anything deserving public attention.

Bibliographies

Every library should produce special bibliographies; most libraries do. It's unlikely that you can predict a year in advance just what bibliographies will be produced, or exactly how many, but you can certainly establish a common format for all your bibliographies, one that will make them instantly identifiable and easy to produce.

Do bibliographies require desktop publishing? Not necessarily, any more than press releases necessarily do. Desktop-publishing programs will allow you to make that format more elaborate (for example, incorporating a common banner for all library bibliographies), just as you can prepare all the "boilerplate" for a press release in advance as part of a desktop-publishing format. But even if you simply use word processing, it makes sense to set up a format in advance, establishing the series of bibliographies.

Your library probably has several other examples of predictable document categories with unpredictable occurrences, such as job postings. Each category will benefit from advance planning, even though you may not know in advance when you will produce them. Advance planning will provide consistent styles, consistent means of production, and the tools to project costs and other aspects of production.

Control for the Sake of Flexibility

Document planning improves your control over your budget, schedule, and finished products. That improved control should give you the flexibility you need to respond to library, patron, and community requirements as they arise, without crisis.

Money and time are issues in (almost) every library. You may not recognize the amount of time spent preparing documents (particularly those that are not widely distributed), and even the total cost of preparation and publication may be so diffused among budget categories that it is not apparent.

One unfortunate aspect of improved document planning is that you become more aware of the time and money that goes into documents. That awareness may lead you to conclude that the library needs to reduce its publishing program. That should not generally be the case. It may be true that you were wasting money on publications or spending more than could really be afforded—but it may also be true that you are not providing the publications that your patrons and community really need, publications that would improve the effectiveness of the library.

The rest of this chapter goes through some aspects of planning for specific documents. Here as elsewhere, *publish* and *produce documents* are treated as synonymous; a publication need not have more than one copy.

Need

Why do you publish? Generally, to communicate. Specifically, to reach a certain audience and produce certain results. Establishing the specific need for each category of publication—and, in some cases, for each instance of a category—should be the first step in planning your documents.

Explicit need statements clarify the function of specific publications. If a single publication (planned or existing) serves widely differing (and possibly conflicting) needs, you might consider splitting the publication. You can certainly prepare a single newsletter to serve both the staff and the friends of the library, but you might do a much better job for both groups by producing two separate publications.

Needs statements should be as specific as possible. Certainly, a single publication or series can serve many needs; it can serve them best if it is planned according to explicit, specific knowledge of those needs. Consider a common situation for every public library:

- You need to keep your patrons informed of the special programs and activities at the library;

- You want publicity for library programs and events in local newspapers.

Those are certainly related needs—but not actually the same need. They differ both in audience and in intended result. If you try to make one publication serve both needs, you will not be satisfied with the results, for reasons described below.

- Patrons don't want to wade through a dozen double-spaced press releases, and you don't want to produce a thousand copies of each press release. Patrons will be better served by a single monthly sheet presenting activities and highlights in a predictable, attractive, compact format.

- Newspapers aren't inclined to make interesting stories out of items within compact monthly lists of schedules; at best, community papers may simply run the headings in one of those little-read "events" listings. To get news coverage, you need press releases—double-spaced, distinctively formatted, and written to meet newspaper needs.

Suiting the Schedule to the Need: An Example

Your (large) library has a weekly staff newsletter. The newsletter serves a general need—keeping staff morale high and keeping staff informed—but each issue also serves specific needs. One good exercise may be to jot down the need served by each issue during the course of a year or several months, by projection or by review of past issues.

You may well find that during some weeks—for example, the week between Christmas and New Year's Day in most libraries and several weeks in July and August for academic libraries—the only apparent need was "to meet the weekly publication schedule."

Congratulations! You can save a significant amount of time and money by modifying the publication schedule. If there just isn't much to say, why not skip a week? If you must be formal about it, change the publication schedule to "weekly, except fortnightly during summer months, and with the two year-end issues combined." That works for national publications; why not your own newsletter?

Honest Needs Statements

Most needs statements will be short, simple, and specific:

- You need a special-hours sign because patrons need to know about changing hours.

- You need a summary of the commands in the online catalog because people appreciate the "cheat sheet."

- You need to publish multiple, well-formatted copies of a staff-prepared bibliography on a topic of current concern because your patrons will find it useful.

- You need to produce procedure manuals so that staff will be aware of proper procedures.

- You want to produce a quarterly journal of local history because it will make the library a center for local historians.

- You want to produce a child-oriented book of the stories written by children in the library to give pleasure and recognition to the children and their parents.

These are all legitimate needs, easily stated, that will help to guide production planning. Be honest about the need to be served by a publication. There's nothing wrong with a little frivolity, and there's nothing wrong with prestige. On the other hand, putting the specific need down on paper may make the project appear to be pointless. Perhaps you've said it wrong—or perhaps the project really is pointless and should be abandoned. If you find that you can't put down in words why you want or need to produce a publication, how are you going to produce the words for the publication itself?

Producing needs statements helps you to clarify your library goals and to separate real publication needs from imaginary ones; the process can help you to avoid superfluous, wasteful publications.

Audience

Different audiences require different approaches. Knowing your reader should be part of any publication plan. There's more to knowing the audience than knowing who a publication is aimed at. You also need to know, or at least project, how the readers will approach a publication—what they will bring to it. Knowing the readers and their approach should influence the publication design and the style of its content. Consider, for instance, three broad classes of periodicals:

- Some consumer magazines are based on the assumption that readers have short attention spans and must be seduced into reading articles. They use lots of illustrations, large type, relatively short articles, and large margins. The design places great emphasis on attractive appearance, with body text playing a secondary role. Indeed, body text may represent less than half of the editorial space in such magazines. That is particularly true of magazines that depend on newsstand sales for profitability: the reader must be visually enticed to buy the magazine and read the articles.

- Other magazines, particularly specialized magazines primarily sold by subscription, are designed on the assumption that readers bring an existing interest to the magazine and want content. Attraction is still significant, but it is far less critical. The ratio of text to illustration will be much higher; most illustrations will be directly relevant to the article content. Body type is likely to be smaller, with longer articles and fewer graphic intrusions. Margins will be smaller.

- Publishers of scholarly and professional journals such as *Information Technology and Libraries*, typically available exclusively by subscription or with membership, can assume that readers are interested in specific articles purely on the basis of topic and content. Body type may be larger than in some specialized magazines, but it will occupy more of the available space. Illustrations only appear when they are required to support content.

There is definitely a lesson for library publications in the preceding examples:

- If you're producing a publication primarily to attract people, you need to be more concerned with graphics and the overall look of the publication. Text may be secondary, but it should typically be large and well-spaced. Dictionaries use 6-point type—but you would never use 6-point type in a flyer publicizing library services.

- If you're producing a service publication, with readers who use it because they need the information, you can and sometimes should use smaller type and fewer illustrations (if any), paying more attention to content and to a document design that will make the organization of that content clear and easy to follow.

Some other points to consider when addressing the issues of audience and approach for a given document:

- Children and older patrons both benefit from larger-than-normal type. Lists of large-print books should use type as large as that used in the books; publications for the children in the library should use type only slightly smaller. Large type always means more white space within and around the text. Publications intended for children almost always include illustrations as well.

- Subject bibliographies need to attract the reader just enough to recognize the topic and approach. Readers need such publications to use as tools. Type size, spacing, illustrations, and other design elements should clarify and organize the content—but the design should essentially be invisible. Compactness is a virtue in such content-oriented publications.

- The level of formality of page design and production techniques should at least match the formality of the content. A report to the library board produced on a medium-density dot-matrix printer and designed using typical clip art undermines the content.

- Listings of library events should attract readers; a clean, interesting layout is important. But the layout and use of graphics should balance content and space—a single-sheet monthly calendar with a clear, approachable layout will serve you and your patrons better than a multipage publication that requires multiple pages because of irrelevant graphics, lots of headlines, and large body type.

- One good graphic serves brief publications better than numerous less well planned graphics. Clear organization serves publications better than excessive amounts of "visual interest."

The main point is, as usual, basically common sense: think about the audience before you prepare the document—who they are and how they will approach it.

Intended Results

What will success look like? That is to say, what will it mean for this publication to succeed? The final conceptual aspect of preliminary document planning should be the intended results. Need and intended results may be identical, but not for every publication. Intended results may be somewhat more concrete than the specific need for a document.

Every press release you prepare arises from the same basic need: to get some sort of publicity in the press. The intended results may be different for each press release, however.

- An announcement of a new branch or extended hours should result in more patrons making better use of the library system.

- Press releases showing particular successes with specific new library services should result in greater interest in, demand for, and support for those services.

- A story describing record levels of system use should result in greater community support for the library.

- An announcement that the library has won an award or that a librarian has been honored or has published a book should improve the image of the library within the community.

A widely distributed flier announcing an upcoming book sale, designed with big type, bold graphics, and clever wording, serves the same need as a paragraph in a monthly events calendar: both inform library patrons and the community at large of the event. The first is probably intended for a wider audience than the second, however, and has a more specific result. An events calendar keeps library regulars up to date on what's going on; a flier should specifically pull people in for the book sale.

Advance thought about intended results may also help you to prevent unintended results from publications. Perhaps the most common unintended result arises from lack of attention to a "detail" of publishing—getting the words right! A publication that appears with misspelled words, clearly incorrect words, or seriously flawed grammar will cause careful readers to question the professionalism of the librarians. If the guardians of the printed word don't get it right, what hope is there for the rest of us? When you're thinking about typographic details, it's important to keep things in perspective. White space and readable type are important, but good grammar, correct spelling, and clear writing are essential. If you can't write, don't publish.

Other unintended results arise when the form or content of a document are inappropriate to the audience, intent, or need. You wouldn't feature a complex spreadsheet or use 9-point type in a flier aimed at children who use the library. By the same token, you should never see double exclamation points in a library's annual report.

Here is one point to consider when you implement desktop publishing, particularly if your library has an unusually tight budget: in your friends newsletter, trustees report, and similar publications, make it clear how little you spent for the new technology and how much money and time it will save. You will serve your friends well by making their newsletter more attractive and readable, but don't let them think that you're squandering the money they've helped to raise.

Overall Design

Now that the conceptual basis for a publication is clear, you can proceed to plan the overall design of the publication. You should know roughly how long the publication should be, roughly what it should look like, whether you will need graphics (and, if so, what kind of graphics) and roughly how it should be prepared. Once you understand the overall design of a publication, you can and should plan the tools and techniques for the publication.

As your library establishes a pattern of planned publishing, you will find that new publication ideas will often fit into existing molds. Using preestablished overall designs saves time and energy, but it can be taken too far. Be sure that the existing design really does suit the new publication, that you're not simply taking the path of least resistance.

When you're comfortable with the tools at hand, you can try some new ideas—possibly using an entirely different design for an existing publication, purely as a test. There's no special virtue in building a different design for each publication (in fact, it's generally not a good idea), but occasional experiments do provide fresh perspectives on your publishing and can lead you to improvements.

Format

Most of your publications will probably use standard American letter-size paper, 8½ by 11 inches. It's readily available, cheap, and the common paper size for all laser printers and photocopiers. But you can use standard paper in a number of ways:

- Folded in half and printed sideways ("landscape mode") to put four 5½-by-8½-inch pages on each standard sheet;
- Folded in various ways to make fold-out single-sheet brochures of four, six, or eight panels;
- Printed in landscape mode for signs or, possibly using several columns, for special publications;
- Printed with one, two, or three columns per page;
- Cut into two, three, four, or more identical parts after printing for bookmarks, reference cards, bookplates and other special uses;
- Folded differently for different pages to produce interesting brief handbooks at low cost.

Standard paper comes in many colors and weights, further increasing your possible variations. And, while standard letter paper offers your best bet for most short-run publications, it is by no means the only option. Most books use 6-by-9-inch paper (actually printed as signatures on much larger paper). Newsletters can be much more effective if printed on 17-by-11 inch paper, folded and center-stapled; legal-length (8½-by-14-inch) paper can also be useful in some cases.

If you plan to use special paper or special sizes, make your plans well in advance; it will typically cost more and be harder to obtain than standard letter paper. That provision should not rule out use of special stock, but it does underscore the importance of careful preparation. The same is true for coated stock or other special stocks; not only do they require more care in planning production of the original pages, but they require more advance notice. Special folds typically cost more than standard folds; again, that extra cost should be justified as part of the document plan.

Length

You can't estimate the cost of a publication unless you can estimate its length. Sometimes, the length of a publication will substantially influence its success. For example, one of the public libraries I use puts its hours, borrowing policies, circulation periods, overdue charges, and library services on both sides of a card that is one-third of a letter-size sheet, 3½ by 8½ inches. That card works nicely as a bookmark; it's easy to carry away and study at leisure. It is well-organized and clearly typeset, attractive but not flashy, and informative yet not overloaded.

Add 50 percent more copy, and the library would have the choice of reducing the type size or going to a larger form. But a larger form would not work nearly as well. In this case, a longer publication would not be as successful.

I've already mentioned library event calendars and the advantages of single sheets. Going to two sheets will probably cost more than twice as much as using a single sheet because two sheets must be stapled, adding either costs at the printer or time at the library. The two-sheet design also may not work as well; a publication of more than one sheet is often more intimidating to the casual reader. Similarly, brochures always work better if they are brief and to the point. If your library has a weekly column in the local newspaper—which may be easier to work out if you can provide camera-ready copy— you probably have an absolute length requirement: the text must fit in the space allotted, no matter how much more you may have to say.

Sometimes, a publication doesn't work if it is too short. An eight-page scholarly journal would seem ridiculous; likewise, a two-page library newsletter may seem odd. Some publications have customary lengths or need to be planned for a particular length. Most of the time, however, you need to estimate length simply so that you can estimate the cost and effort required for the publication.

Schedule and Budget

Publishing costs money, generally lots of money. Libraries may find that staff salaries represent the largest cost for many publications. That's almost always true for single-copy or photocopied publications such as internal reports and policy manuals. Advance planning will generally save money and time; even when it does not, it will at least alert you to problems with your publishing program.

The most difficult part of the schedule to plan is the most important part of the publication: creating the words and illustrations. Once you've used any publishing system (typewriter, word processor, desktop publishing, or traditional typography) a few times, you can readily estimate how long the layout and production process will take. But you can't produce the words until they're written and edited, and that process can be agonizingly unpredictable.

You already use word processing to support the writing process—if not, you're not even ready to think about desktop publishing. Word processing helps, but it doesn't turn writing from an art into a science. Desktop publishing won't save any time in the writing process, although it can make revisions less painful. Writing takes as long as it takes; there are no magic shortcuts.

Deadlines

You must establish deadlines for the material to be used in a publication, but you must also recognize the difficulty of establishing precise schedules. A deadline essentially says that whatever is done at that point is what will be used; it does not establish the optimum time to produce the ideal words and pictures.

Make schedules sanely, but allow for surprises. Good writing takes time; the amount of time is not always predictable. At this point, I'm a moderately experienced writer, but I can't predict the amount of time required to write something original. I generally allow an hour or hour and a half each day for writing and editing, adding more time when deadlines require it. Some days, that hour results in 1,000 words of useful writing on a new topic. Some days, when it is equally important to keep moving on a project and I feel equally well prepared, two hours will produce no more than 200–300 words—and those words may all prove useless in the long run.

There are writers who can reliably produce x number of words on y topic to a known professional standard in z hours. Newspaper writers and columnists find this to be a crucial job skill; some novelists and other writers can also follow a schedule that readily. I envy them in some ways, but I don't expect to be like them—and you can hardly expect librarians (for whom writing is an important skill but not necessarily a primary one) to be so predictable.

Budget

The cost of a publication depends on the number of copies, how the publication is produced, and how long it takes to prepare. You can control your costs by planning your publications. You should keep an open mind on techniques; sometimes, the "obvious" way to produce a publication is neither the best nor the most economical way.

Don't assume that photocopying is cheaper than printing. That's almost never true above a certain number of copies, and that number may be lower than you think. The fact is, printer's ink is cheaper than toner and probably always will be. That's not the only factor, but it is a significant one—as is the discount that printers (and copy shops) receive by buying paper and supplies in enormous quantities. Of course printers need to make a profit, but that doesn't mean that they will always cost you more. In-house reproduction is certainly not always the best way to go.

When you have problems with the budget for a publication, consider all of its aspects. Does that flier really require a full-color photograph, or would a two-color drawing work just as well? Does a brochure require color printing at all—or would one-color printing on colored stock, with good use of typography and design, be just as effective at a lower price? Do you really need 10,000 copies of a particular publication—or would you do better by printing 1,000 and getting publicity in the local newspaper?

Take care throughout the publication cycle: prepare the copy carefully and check the pages carefully. The second worst waste of money on a publication is a second printing because the first run was wrong.

The worst waste of money is the publication that goes unread and unused. Good planning lays the groundwork for good content to achieve a useful end. Good design and production support good content. Lack of planning and inferior content lead to unread, useless publications that waste time and money while damaging the library's reputation.

Putting It Together

You can only achieve so much through planning. The only way to publish a document is to write the words, prepare the illustrations, design and produce the pages, and arrange for reproduction and distribution.

You've done enough thinking about the publication and planning for its success; now you and others must transform those plans into reality. My hope is that this chapter will help you to think through a solid, workable, and flexible publication plan for yourself, your group, or your library. The rest of this book is intended to help you produce successful publications.

Tips and Reminders

- Planning will make your publication program more effective no matter what tools you use.

- Different kinds of publications—serving different needs and different audiences—require different balances between design and content.

- Good design will establish a consistent appearance for a particular set of publications, with different designs used for publications serving different purposes.

- Good planning includes estimates for length, deadlines, and budgets; the best planning will allow flexibility in all three areas.

PART 2
Document Design and Production

Back when a Selectric was your best output mechanism, there was little point in spending too much time thinking about design. Your options were so limited that the best you could do was use good margins, choose readable type balls, and hope that the text would communicate your message.

Desktop publishing changes all that—and, curiously, changes it in such a way that the designs you used with the Selectric won't work very well. You must pay some attention to design if you are to produce coherent publications that achieve good results and justify the cost of a desktop-publishing system.

The next five chapters introduce aspects of document design. Guidelines appear for many of the design issues. Some guidelines are my own opinion, some represent at least partial consensus in the design community. None are absolute.

You will find many sources of advice on design—some of them good, some of them not so good. If you read widely enough, you will discover that graphics designers almost never agree on design issues. You should also realize, before reading the next few chapters, that you can and should develop your own design sense, rather than relying wholly on the opinions of others.

As Roger C. Parker says in *Looking Good in Print*, "you may already have more design skills than you suspect. In fact, you probably have an inherent but as yet undeveloped sense of good design—often referred to as taste!"[1]

Building Documents

You will probably use word-processing programs to build and revise your documents. This book doesn't deal with that process directly; a later chapter on advanced word processing concerns the use of such programs as substitutes for full-fledged desktop publishing.

Basic editing functions for a good modern word processor should include the following:

- Insertion as the usual text mode, with overstrike as an option. When you insert text, the word processor should move other text as needed to keep your context clear. Most newer word processors will automatically reformat paragraphs as you work.

- Rapid cursor movement in either direction by character, word, sentence, line, paragraph, or screen. Easy movement to the beginning and end of a document. Easy movement to the beginning and end of a line.

- Easy, clearly marked block definition (to delete, move, or copy text) adjustable by character, word, sentence, line, paragraph, or screen, with clear ways to delete, move, and copy blocks and with a single-key restore function for the most recent deletion. A good block definition function will also support use of a search to mark an endpoint for a block. Keystrokes to define the size of a marked block should be consistent with those used to move the cursor in general. A lovely addition is the ability to mark both ends of a block and perform a global replacement strictly within the block.

- Efficient searching in either direction for any text string, preferably without regard to line boundaries within a paragraph. Good search

---

1   Roger C. Parker. *Looking Good in Print: A Guide to Basic Design for Desktop Publishing* (Chapel Hill, N.C.: Ventana Press, 1988), xxii.

functions ignore capitalization by default but allow you to insist on specific capitalization, and they should also allow you to search only for whole words (by choice), not just for strings within words. Good search functions also support a variety of wildcards for special situations, preferably without surprising you by treating a regular character as a wildcard. The best search functions will repeat a search with a single keystroke, and some will let you go to the next or previous occurrence of a string with one or two keystrokes.

- Efficient text-replacement functions, either for the next occurrence or for all occurrences of a given string. Good replacement functions offer the same options as good search functions and will retain the capitalization of a replaced string as an option. Very good replacement functions can replace control characters and other special characters. Very flexible replacement functions offer prompted global replacement, letting you select the occurrences to be replaced in a single pass.

- Good file-management functions, including the ability to merge an entire external file into a current document; the ability to write out a block of text to a new file; the ability to select a file for editing from a visible list (preferably with user control over what is in the list); and some precautions so that files that have been modified are not abandoned unintentionally.

- The ability to view at least two different portions of the same file or portions of two different files simultaneously in two windows on the screen, moving the cursor back and forth between windows with a single keystroke to make editorial changes. Like the ability to undo deletion, two-window capability should be considered basic for any contemporary full-feature word-processing program. More than two windows may occasionally be convenient, but the most important need is for two windows.

In order to work well with desktop publishing, a word processor must also have the option of storing tabs as characters (that is, as decimal 009) rather than expanding them automatically to multiple blanks. Better MS-DOS word processors should also allow the user to key in extended characters such as á, Ç, Æ, and », at least by using the standard MS-DOS Alt-keypad method, and they should preferably show those characters on the screen.

Most contemporary word processors, at least most of those that are document-oriented rather than page-oriented, offer all or nearly all of these editing features. Some additional features may be nice—

for example, the ability to change the capitalization of a marked block, the ability to define sequences of actions or text as macros or glossary entries, the ability to search for text in files other than the open file—but the functions above will provide the editing power you need.

Sensible Editing Options

When you make the logical separation between writing or editing (dealing with the text) and layout (dealing with the design), you can make some choices that may make your software easier and faster to use. A few examples follow.

- Don't use graphics mode, if text mode is available. Text mode always runs faster; graphics mode is irrelevant while you're writing.

- If on-screen justification is at all slower than leaving the text ragged-right, turn off the justification. It will have almost nothing to do with your final output.

- If your word processor supports proportional fonts (as most good modern ones do), it will probably have a mode in which "true" lines are shown, with most lines running off the right edge of the screen. Switch to the other mode, if that's possible, or define margins in such a way that scrolling isn't needed.

- Don't use spaces to line up tables; always use the tab key to separate columns in a table.

- Never use either the tab key or spaces to indent a new paragraph. Better word processing programs may do it for you; if not, leave the new paragraphs at the left margin.

- Never, never, never hyphenate words to break across lines while you're writing. You can, and in some cases should, use soft or optional hyphens to define preferred hyphenation points (and most modern word processors do have an explicit soft-hyphen key, frequently the combination of the Ctrl key and hyphen). If you insert a regular hyphen, that hyphen will always be there—even though the line break may come somewhere else in the printed product.

4

Document Design and Organization

Your library has a style and image, intentional or otherwise. So do you, in your personal and professional dealings. Desktop publications can help to support or modify that style and image—but, intentionally or not, for better or worse, they definitely will influence the way the library is perceived. Thoughtful design will enhance the library's image as well as improving its communications; thoughtless design can diffuse and confuse the image and get in the way of communication.

This chapter explores general considerations in designing a document and various aspects of establishing and maintaining an overall style for your publication program. You should be able to design entire categories of documents, retaining a given design for many individual publications and fine-tuning that design over time. Overall document design includes questions of organization and complexity.

Design, Content, and Expectation

The design of a document should always reflect its content and the needs, audience, and intent related to that content. Sometimes, the design of a document should fall within external guidelines because of the type of document it is—certain documents can be expected to look like others of their kind. Consider, for example, figures 4.1, 4.2, and 4.3, each of which deals (in part or in full) with the same message (Patricia Driver reading from her book).

Sign or Small Poster

Signs such as figure 4.1 (and other examples in other chapters) offer more design freedom than any other document. There are some basic attributes of the content that relate to the design and effectively limit the design. You can't have large amounts of text in a sign and still have it function as a small poster. The content of figure 4.1 consists of four essential elements—who, what, when, and where—all stated in the fewest possible words and all carrying out the underlying message, which is: "Come to this special children's hour."

The sign does include an aspect of continuity (which may or may not be present in signs) in the *Children's Hour* illustration, lower right corner. That illustration presumably appears on each sign announcing a special children's hour.

A library could send that sign to a newspaper, hoping that the newspaper would run a reduced version of it as a public service—but, more realistically, the library should send something like figure 4.2.

Press Release

Like fiction books, press releases fall into a special category of design: one in which the design should follow normal expectations if it is to succeed. While a surprising number of organizations do not seem to recognize norms for press releases, such norms do exist—and you would be well advised to follow them.

Several aspects of figure 4.2 come naturally from its intent and content. For example, the top of the page clearly identifies it as a press release, identifies the organization and provides an address. Conditions on usage appear immediately below the banner, with a specific person's name as a contact point. The story is double-spaced and ends with a source for further information. A standard flag—such as the three pound signs used here, the word "End," or the notation "—30—"—certifies that this is the end of the press release. Finally, the press release is clearly dated.

Figure 4.1: Sign or Poster

Press Release

Halltown City Library

10 City Square
Halltown, North Arizona 94061

For Immediate Release   **Contact: Samantha E. Lyons**

Patricia Driver to Visit Halltown City Library

Halltown, North Arizona ... Noted children's author Patricia Driver, winner of the San Onofre Medal for her 1987 book *A Robin's Spring*, will appear at the Halltown City Library for Children's Hour on Saturday, August 15, from 1-2 p.m. in the Children's Room. Ms. Driver will read from her new book *The Rail's Tale*, the sixth in her series of "stories for the birds."

"We are particularly delighted that Patricia Driver has taken time out from her busy schedule to visit with our children," stated Samantha E. Lyons, director of children's services for Halltown City Library. "In past appearances, she has demonstrated an enthralling spoken delivery that adds even more fascination to her wonderful stories. Parents should join the Children's Hour; you may find yourself reading her books along with your children." The Children's Room is in the main library, just across from City Hall at 10 City Square.

Ms. Driver's reading is only one of this summer's Children's Hour highlights. For more information on Children's Hour, the forthcoming collection of stories or the many other services of Halltown City Library, contact the library at (314) 555-2959.

###

Released: August 1, 1990

Figure 4.2: Press Release

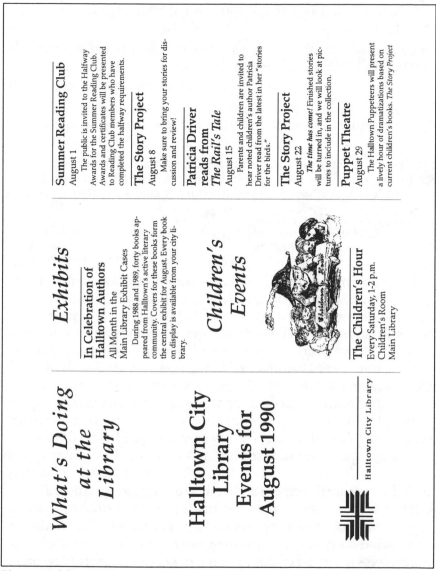

Figure 4.3: Monthly Events Brochure

What's Doing at the Library

Halltown City Library Events for August 1990

Halltown City Library

Exhibits

In Celebration of Halltown Authors
All Month in the
Main Library Exhibit Cases

During 1988 and 1989, forty books appeared from Halltown's active literary community. Covers for these books form the central exhibit for August. Every book on display is available from your city library.

Children's Events

The Children's Hour
Every Saturday, 1–2 p.m.
Children's Room
Main Library

Summer Reading Club
August 1

The public is invited to the Halfway Awards for the Summer Reading Club. Awards and certificates will be presented to Reading Club members who have completed the halfway requirements.

The Story Project
August 8

Make sure to bring your stories for discussion and review!

Patricia Driver reads from
The Rail's Tale
August 15

Parents and children are invited to hear noted children's author Patricia Driver read from the latest in her "stories for the birds."

The Story Project
August 22

The time has come! Finished stories will be turned in, and we will look at pictures to include in the collection.

Puppet Theatre
August 29

The Halltown Puppeteers will present a lively hour of dramatizations based on current children's books. *The Story Project*

Once you design a press-release document, following the general guidelines, you should use the same document format each time you use a press release. It identifies you and lets newspapers know who they are dealing with.

Library Calendar

Unlike press releases, library calendars or monthly events lists have no set or expected form: you can design one that suits your own library and appeals to the tastes of your staff members. Some libraries use pages that are laid out like monthly calendar pages, putting very short events notes in each box, a design that works best for large libraries that regularly sponsor numerous events.

Other libraries might use a style similar to figure 4.3, a single sheet folded in thirds, printed on both sides, thus making five event panels along with the cover panel. Note that figure 4.3 includes the same general content as the other two figures, with more detail than figure 4.1 and less than figure 4.2.

As with press releases, you should prepare a good overall design for your monthly calendars or events lists, then use the same design consistently until you see good reason to change it. That consistent design will serve the content by identifying the document, letting the reader know what to expect, and eliminating any barriers as the reader determines the organization of a new document.

Consistency and Variety

Consider individual documents in terms of overall patterns, but don't rule out special cases or new models. Excessive monotony may be even worse than excessive variety. Experimentation is healthy—if time permits and if the experimenter shows some sense of good design. Experiments may show a better way to present your information, which may make a substantial design change in an ongoing series of documents worthwhile.

More to the point, any active library publication program should involve many different types of document, and they should certainly not all use the same document design, although the different designs may have some similarity.

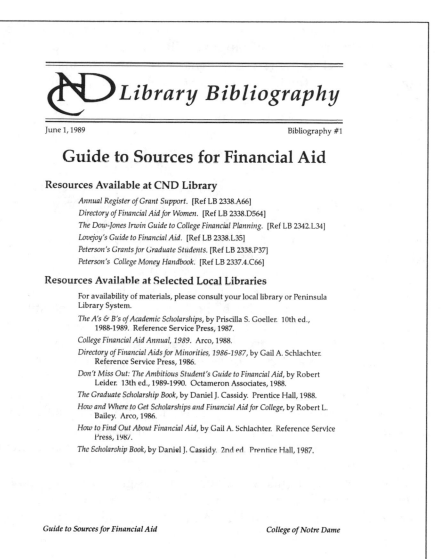

Figure 4.4: Bibliography 1

Figure 4.4 shows a straightforward document design for a bibliography: a single indented column of citations, with a centered title and headings set to the left of the citations. The date and number suggest that this is the first of a series of bibliographies. This particular bibliography is a single sheet, but patrons seeing a stapled five-page (or three-sheet) document with a first page looking like figure 4.5 would recognize it instantly as the same kind of document—even though the date and numbering have been dropped. It has the same page layout, despite the small differences.

But what if the second bibliography began with the page shown in figure 4.6? The design for this document is also workable, and somewhat more compact (it reduces the bibliography from five to four pages). But the banner is differently designed, and there are now two narrow columns of citations, with the headings less distinctly identified. A reader would not subconsciously recognize figure 4.6 as belonging to the same series as figure 4.4; set side by side, the two would clash slightly. If a third bibliography returns to the style of figure 4.4, or moves to another style altogether, the results will be haphazard and possibly confusing for readers.

Figure 4.7 uses a document design similar to figure 4.6—but for an entirely different purpose. There would be no clash with figure 4.4, because this is an entirely different kind of document, serving a different purpose. New title lists are distinctly different publications than bibliographies. There is no good reason that they should use the same overall design, and there may be reasons to make them clearly different.

Establish your families of document design, but don't build a straitjacket around your own creative instincts or those of your staff. Every design can be improved, and some general categories may deserve a different design for each example.

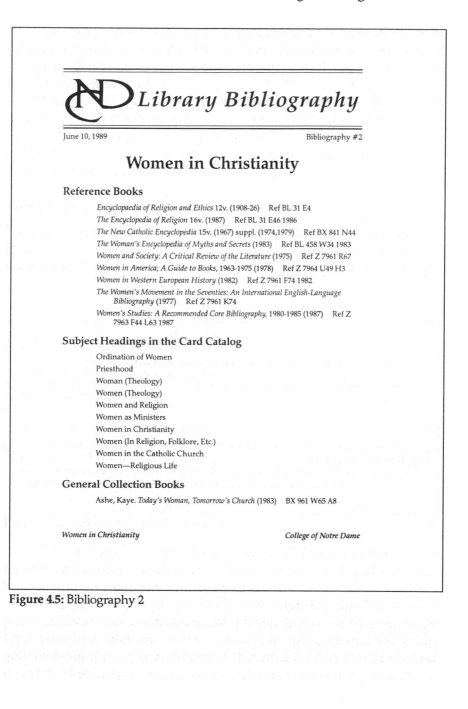

Library Bibliography

June 10, 1989   Bibliography #2

Women in Christianity

Reference Books

Encyclopaedia of Religion and Ethics 12v. (1908-26)   Ref BL 31 E4

The Encyclopedia of Religion 16v. (1987)   Ref BL 31 E46 1986

The New Catholic Encyclopedia 15v. (1967) suppl. (1974,1979)   Ref BX 841 N44

The Woman's Encyclopedia of Myths and Secrets (1983)   Ref BL 458 W34 1983

Women and Society: A Critical Review of the Literature (1975)   Ref Z 7961 R67

Women in America; A Guide to Books, 1963-1975 (1978)   Ref Z 7964 U49 H3

Women in Western European History (1982)   Ref Z 7961 F74 1982

The Women's Movement in the Seventies: An International English-Language Bibliography (1977)   Ref Z 7961 K74

Women's Studies: A Recommended Core Bibliography, 1980-1985 (1987)   Ref Z 7963 F44 L63 1987

Subject Headings in the Card Catalog

Ordination of Women

Priesthood

Woman (Theology)

Women (Theology)

Women and Religion

Women as Ministers

Women in Christianity

Women (In Religion, Folklore, Etc.)

Women in the Catholic Church

Women—Religious Life

General Collection Books

Ashe, Kaye. *Today's Woman, Tomorrow's Church* (1983)   BX 961 W65 A8

Women in Christianity   *College of Notre Dame*

Figure 4.5: Bibliography 2

College of Notre Dame Library Bibliography

Women in Christianity

Reference Books

Encyclopaedia of Religion and Ethics 12v.
(1908-26)   Ref BL 31 E4

The Encyclopedia of Religion 16v. (1987)
Ref BL 31 E46 1986

The New Catholic Encyclopedia 15v. (1967)
suppl. (1974,1979)   Ref BX 841 N44

*The Woman's Encyclopedia of Myths and
Secrets* (1983)   Ref BL 458 W34 1983

*Women and Society: A Critical Review of
the Literature* (1975)   Ref Z 7961
R67

*Women in America; A Guide to Books,
1963-1975* (1978)   Ref Z 7964 U49
H3

Women in Western European History
(1982)   Ref Z 7961 F74 1982

*The Women's Movement in the Seventies:
An International English-Language
Bibliography* (1977)   Ref Z 7961 K74

*Women's Studies: A Recommended Core
Bibliography, 1980-1985* (1987)   Ref
Z 7963 F44 L63 1987

Subject Headings in the Card Catalog

Ordination of Women

Priesthood

Woman (Theology)

Women (Theology)

Women and Religion

Women as Ministers

Women in Christianity

Women (In Religion, Folklore, Etc.)

Women in the Catholic Church

Women—Religious Life

General Collection Books

Ashe, Kaye. *Today's Woman, Tomorrow's
Church* (1983)   BX 961 W65 A8

Bozarth-Campbell, Alla. *Womanpriest: A
Personal Odyssey* (1978)   BX 5995
B665 A38

Cady, Susan. *Sophia: The Future of
Feminist Sprituality* (1986)   BL
625.7 C33 1986

Chittister, Joan. *Women, Ministry and the
Church* (1983)   BX 2347.8 W6 C48
1983

Christ, Carol. *Laughter of Aphrodite* (1987)
BL 458 C48 1987

Christ, Carol and J. Plaskow.
Womanspirit Rising (1979)   BL 458
W657 1979

Clark, Elizabeth. *Women and Religion: A
Feminist Sourcebook of Christian
Thought* (1977)   BT 704 C53 1977

Elizondo, Virgil and N. Greinacher.
Women in a Men's Church (1980)
BV 4415 W63

Women in Christianity   *College of Notre Dame*

Figure 4.6: Bibliography, Different Design

ᴺᴰ New Titles in the CND Library

February-April 1989

B Philosophy, Religion, Psychology

B358.T7 1969	Plato. *The last days of Socrates.* 1969.
B1388.G7	Grean. *Shaftesbury's philosophy of religion.*
B2430.M34G733	Greenburg. *The notion of person ...* 1988.
B3279.H48F7313 1985	Heidegger. *What is a thing?* 1985.
B3279.H48Q47 1977	Heidegger. *The question concerning tech. ...*
BF76.5.H85 1975	Kennedy. *Human rights* 1975.
BF173.F85G377 1988	Gay. *Freud-A life for our times.* 1988.
BF456.R2C52 1979	Clay. *Reading.* 1980.
BF637.S8S467	Sher. *Wishcraft. How to get what you ...*
BF698.6.K55B87 1987	Burns. *Kinetic-house tree ...* 1987
BF1078.S23 1984	Savary. *Dreams and spiritual growth.* 1984.
BF1573,A34 1986	Adler. *Drawing down the moon...* 1986
BF1577.S68S56 1980	Simmons. *Witchcraft in the Southwest.* 1974.
BF1589.S4 1971	Seligmann. *Magic, supernaturalism ...* 1948.
BH221.F8A53 1984	Anderson. *Art in a desacralized world.* 1984.
BL60.B45	Bianchi. *The religious experience of ...*
BL304.C36 1988	Campbell. *The power of myth.* 1988.
BL477.N57	Nitzsche. *The genius figure in antiquity.*
BR65.C46G73	Greeley. *The church as "Body of Christ".*
BR115.A8G57	Glendenning. *The church and the arts.* 1960.
BR1050.U4H44 1988	Lozynsky. *He dwells in our midst.* 1988.
BT314.S33 1987	Schaberg. *The illegitimacy of Jesus.* 1985.
BT367.W34H35	Heil. *Jesus walking on the sea.* 1981.
BV5.S6	Spielmann. *History of Christian worship.*
BV150.U76	Hubbard. *Let's see No. 1.* 1966.
BX1378.2.H3	Hatch. *A man named John.* 1963.
BX2205.K38	Kavanagh. *The shape of Baptism.* 1978.
BX4499.D83	Duchaussois. *Rose of Canada.* 1934.
fBX4700.L6D66	Domenico. *Il volto di Sant' Alfonso.* 1954.
BX4705.M542A3 1988b	Stone. *Thomas Merton.* 1988.
BX4722.S43	Sedgwick. *Jansenism in the 17th century.*

C Auxiliary Sciences of History

CT120.A7 1968	Arendt. *Men in dark times.* 1970.

D History; General and Old World

D1050.F5 1987 Index	*UFSI reports index* 1987.
D1050.F5 1987 no.39	Rusinow. *In re Waldheim.* 1987.
D1050.F5 1988-89	Lesch. *The Palestinian uprising.* 1988.
D1050.F5 1988-89	Sanders. *"Happiness also rises up there".*
D1050.F5 1988-89	Hyden. *Agriculture and development in Africa*

Figure 4.7: New-Title List

The Logical Organization of a Document

Although the figures that have appeared so far show finished designs, such designs (which combine page and text design as well as document design) should not be your concern when you first deal with new document designs. The finished design can (and probably should) come after the first example of a category has been written.

Before writing begins, you can determine the logical organization of a document. Almost every document has such an organization. A document consists of a series of elements; each element can be named. The logical organization of the document consists of the sequence of elements and how they work together.

The discussion of figure 4.2 shows one set of logical elements, those that make up a press release. The body text contains the specific content of the press release, but the remaining elements turn that content into a workable, well-defined document.

Relatively few documents are as unstructured as they may first appear. Most documents do have explicit, nameable structural elements. Consider one of the simplest documents, one that every library produces and that you would typically not use desktop-publishing methods to produce: the business letter.

Business Letters

Secretaries know the elements of simple documents, although they rarely think about them. Consider a standard business letter such as figure 4.8. It includes the following elements, from top to bottom (not including the preprinted letterhead, omitted in the illustration):

- Date;
- Recipient's name and address;
- Salutation;
- Body;
- Signature block;
- List of enclosures (optional);
- Copy list (optional).

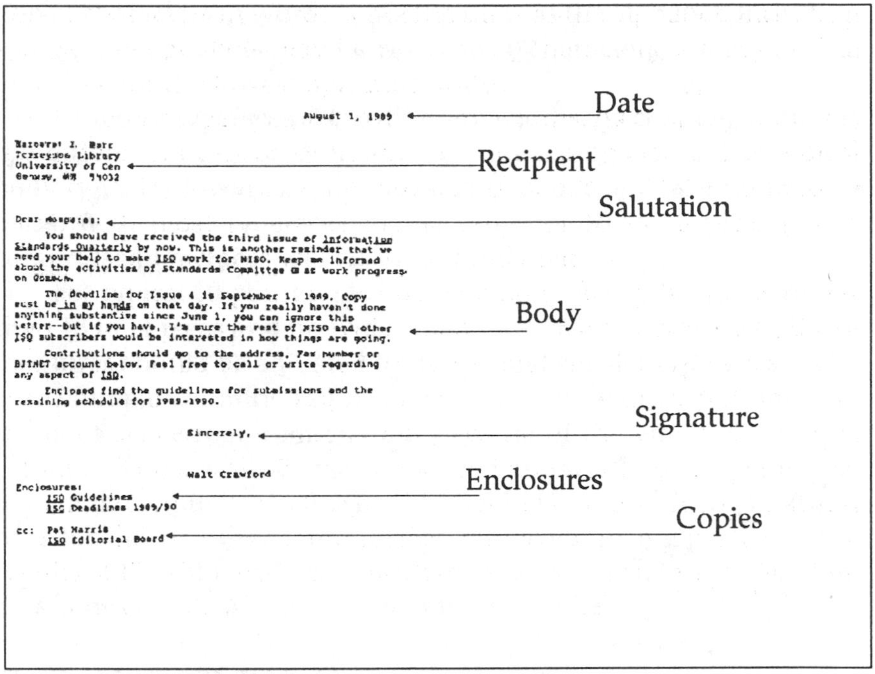

Date

August 1, 1989

Recipient

Marousi I. Marc
Tennessee Library
University of Cen
Germany, WA 99032

Salutation

Dear Mospeies:

You should have received the third issue of Information
Standards Quarterly by now. This is another reminder that we
need your help to make ISQ work for NISO. Keep me informed
about the activities of Standards Committee G at work progress
on Osmah.

The deadline for Issue 4 is September 1, 1989. Copy
must be in my hands on that day. If you really haven't done
anything substantive since June 1, you can ignore this
letter--but if you have, I'm sure the rest of NISO and other
ISQ subscribers would be interested in how things are going.

Contributions should go to the address, fax number or
BITNET account below. Feel free to call or write regarding
any aspect of ISQ.

Enclosed find the guidelines for submissions and the
remaining schedule for 1989-1990.

Body

Sincerely,

Signature

Walt Crawford

Enclosures:
ISQ Guidelines
ISQ Deadlines 1989/90

Enclosures

cc: Pat Harris
ISQ Editorial Board

Copies

Figure 4.8: Business Letter

Every good secretary knows how those elements are placed in standard form (there are several standard forms) and how that form has been modified by a particular organization. The placement of date and address block will typically depend on the design of the letterhead and the design of window envelopes (if those are used); the secretary may even have a reminder card showing the placement of the various elements.

If you rarely prepare business letters directly, you may need advice on proper placement—and if you need to use a window envelope, you may have problems at first. If you use a typically unstructured word processing program, you may need two or three tries to get it right.

Effective document design, as supported either by advanced word-processing programs or advanced desktop-publishing programs, will help you out and assure that letters emerging from your library have a fairly consistent appearance. The elements noted above and in figure 4.8 can take on explicit names, and those names can become part of a style sheet or sample document, depending on your program. After that, the computer will help you to prepare a letter properly.

The notes in Figure 4.9 could, then, become part of a set of note cards or a loose-leaf binder giving the guidelines for each recognized document category that your library deals with. Each category of document should have a series of named elements—even if those names serve only to tell the writers and editors what the elements are.

Letter Style Guide

- DT = *date of letter*
- TO = *addressee, 5 lines*
- SL = *salutation*
- Body text, no special guide.
- AD = *Sincerely, 3 lines, name*
- EN = *enclosures if any, 1 per line*
- CC = *copies if any, 1 per line*

Figure 4.9: Guidelines for Letter

Note that the names say nothing about the actual layout of the letter. The date could be flush right, flush left, or even centered, and could be in almost any typeface. The ending block ("AD") might begin half an inch below the last paragraph and start halfway across the page, or it might begin directly below the paragraph, set at the left margin.

Those decisions are the details of page and text design; the element names and the significance of the elements make up the logic of the document. A coherent set of document designs begins with this explicit recognition of a document's elements; however, with contemporary software, the document design can go much further.

Once you establish the logical elements of a document, writing and illustration can begin, with the elements used and, in some cases, explicitly flagged. That makes sense: while a writer may neither know nor care what the typeface, size, spacing, and position of a subhead will be, the writer does know when he or she is writing a subhead—and, if a document design has been set down as guidelines, what the level of subhead should be called.

The physical design of a document consists largely of page and text design: assigning appropriate physical attributes to each logical element so that they fit together into a workable whole. That process should come after text for the first document has been prepared—but, ideally, that process should not be repeated for any other documents in a category. In other words, once you've produced one issue of a staff newsletter, you should be able to produce consistent following issues just by using the same logical elements; the same should be true for successive bibliographies, new-title lists, and library-events brochures.

Supporting Document Designs

Until recently, the only way to maintain a consistent style in a series of documents was by direct manual effort. You could plan the document and record the planning decisions, but most word-processing programs (and the earliest desktop-publishing programs) were not programmed to recognize the named elements of a document, and would not support your use of those names.

Instead, you designed each document as you went along—establishing overall parameters first, then modifying specific paragraphs or areas to suit your needs. The document design was inextricably linked to the document itself and was largely implicit within individual assignments. In such systems, documents had no established structure as such: overall design consisted of the page size, margins, number of columns, general linespacing, default font for text, and a few related details.

Thoughtful users found that they could reduce the time needed to format the second document in a category by saving a copy of the first, then replacing its text (on an element-by-element basis) with the text for the second. That process is messy and inexact, but it does provide a crude form of stored document design.

Style Sheets and Sample Documents

Some word-processing programs have supported named document segments for years—for example, FinalWord/Sprint and XyWrite have always included such support, as has Microsoft Word. Word used the term "styles" for the names and definitions of individual elements, and "style sheet" for a named collection of such styles. Ventura calls the complete named collection a "style" and each individual definition a "tag." Other programs use other names for the same functions. Most advanced desktop-publishing programs and advanced word-processing programs now support style sheets, in one form or another. Style sheets provide several benefits:

- When you name something, you begin to control it. By naming elements of a document, you can define those elements, and the definitions will be supported by the program.

- The definitions you create for one document can be carried over to similar documents with no new work. A named style sheet provides most of a document definition.

- When you build better designs, those decisions can be reflected in the style sheet without modifying documents.[1]

- You can establish a set of common names for elements—and those names can mean very different things in different contexts.

Although last benefit can also be a trap, it is one of the key benefits of named styles. Those working on the text of a document may only have a list of style or tag names and textual definitions—in other words, a style vocabulary for your operation. A writer will include a tag for a title, first-level heading, or citation—but may neither know nor care what that tag implies for eventual formatting.

---

1   This can be dangerous for existing documents; see the section called "Controlling Change" in this chapter.

Halltown Library Standards Watch

| Volume 12, no. 1 | July 1989 |

CD-ROM Standards: The Fate of Z39.60

NISO's attempt to develop an American National Standard volume and file structure for CD-ROM is a long, complicated story. It is a story in which international settings and actors have played as important a part as American ones, possibly more important. It is also a story in which NISO had to recover responsibility for the standard from a much larger influential American standards development organization, Accredited Standards Committee X3 (Information Processing Systems). Ultimately, from the perspective of NISO's membership and constituency, the story has a happy ending—which can now be told.

From High Sierra to Z39.60

NISO formed Standards Committee EE (Compact Disc Data Format) in July, 1985. Sixteen individuals were named to this committee to insure participation across a broad spectrum of publishers, librarians, information service providers and information technology vendors. SC EE was charged to develop an American National Standard based on a document that had been drafted by a small group of materially-affected parties—the "High Sierra Standard." SC EE held an extended series of meetings over nearly two years. These meetings were open to the public; some of them drew a hundred or more observers. NISO's Voting Members approved the resulting Z39.60, *Volume and File Structure of CDROM for Information Interchange*, on May 28, 1987.

But Wait! What About ECMA?

Normally, NISO would have submitted Z39.60 to the ANSI Board of Standards Review and, in due course, Z39.60 would have been registered as an American National Standard. However, a draft version of Z39.60 had been adopted by the European Computer Manufacturers Association as a regional European standard and submitted to the International Standards Organization (ISO) for immediate processing as a Draft International Standard. NISO suspended Z39.60 processing out of concern that the standard might not be aligned with the corresponding International Standard. The concern was well-founded: IS 9660 (the resulting standard) does, in fact, differ in certain important respects from Z39.60.

ASC X3 Enters the Scene

To make things more complicated, the responsibility for formulating the American position on IS 9660 was assigned to ASC X3 rather than NISO. ASC X3 cast the American vote on ISO ballots leading to the approval of IS 9660—and X3 would have the first option to process IS 9660 as an American National Standard. To explain this unfortunate development we must dive much deeper—undoubtedly too deep—into the ocean of organizational acronyms that characterizes the standards world. In short, the European Computer Manufacturers Association (ECMA) submitted its approved regional European standard to ISO through Technical Committee (TC) 97 (Information Processing) rather than TC 46 (Documentation). The scope and program of work of ECMA and X3 both align with TC 97—just as NISO is aligned with TC 46. This action by ECMA was entirely routine but had the

Figure 4.10: Newsletter

That implication may be very different in different cases. For example, figures 4.10, 4.11, and 4.12 all use exactly the same text files, with exactly the same tags: TITLE, HEAD1, and FIRSTPARA. Thus, in each case, "CD-ROM Standards: The Fate of Z39.60" is a *TITLE*; the paragraph beginning "NISO's attempt to develop..." is a *FIRST-PARA*; and "From High Sierra to Z39.60" is a *HEAD1*. But consider how different the three examples look. The only difference among the three figures (other than page headings and the banner in figure 4.10) is that each figure uses a different style sheet, and each style sheet defines these elements differently.

Thus, the big initial letters in figure 4.10 and the lines over the title are defined by the style sheet; so are the numbers (1., 1.A., 1.B.) in figure 4.11 and the parallel-column headings in figure 4.12. Each style sheet, which should be named to identify the documents it controls, carries forward a standard set of design decisions; it maintains consistency and reduces the effort required to produce new documents.

Controlling Change

Style sheets can lead to accidental changes. Make sure you know what you're changing. Remember that separate style sheets control *all* the documents that refer to them, old as well as new. You may find yourself needing to reprint an old document, for one reason or another—and, if you have modified the style sheet that controls the document, the new printing won't look like the original version.

The rules for controlling change are the same here as in other personal computing. Save the original style and experiment with a copy under a different name. If you're happy with the experiment, you can replace the original at that point, or you can archive the original in case you need to restore it at some later date.

New Designs from Old Beginnings

The ability to save a copy of an existing style sheet under a new name means that you can use your work on one document design as the foundation for a different design. That power can save hours of

CD-ROM Standards:
The Fate of Z39.60

NISO's attempt to develop an American National Standard volume and file structure for CD-ROM is a long, complicated story. It is a story in which international settings and actors have played as important a part as American ones, possibly more important. It is also a story in which NISO had to recover responsibility for the standard from a much larger influential American standards development organization, Accredited Standards Committee X3 (Information Processing Systems). Ultimately, from the perspective of NISO's membership and constituency, the story has a happy ending—which can now be told.

From High Sierra to Z39.60

NISO formed Standards Committee EE (Compact Disc Data Format) in July, 1985. Sixteen individuals were named to this committee to insure participation across a broad spectrum of publishers, librarians, information service providers and information technology vendors. SC EE was charged to develop an American National Standard based on a document that had been drafted by a small group of materially-affected parties—the "High Sierra Standard." SC EE held an extended series of meetings over nearly two years. These meetings were open to the public; some of them drew a hundred or more observers. NISO's Voting Members approved the resulting Z39.60, *Volume and File Structure of CDROM for Information Interchange*, on May 28, 1987.

But Wait! What About ECMA?

Normally, NISO would have submitted Z39.60 to the ANSI Board of Standards Review and, in due course, Z39.60 would have been registered as an American National Standard. However, a draft version of Z39.60 had been adopted by the European Computer Manufacturers Association as a regional European standard and submitted to the International Standards Organization (ISO) for immediate processing as a Draft International Standard. NISO suspended Z39.60 processing out of concern that the standard might not be aligned with the corresponding

| Halltown Library | Annual Report | 1989 |

Figure 4.11: Operations Manual

CD-ROM Standards: The Fate of Z39.60

NISO's attempt to develop an American National Standard volume and file structure for CD-ROM is a long, complicated story. It is a story in which international settings and actors have played as important a part as American ones, possibly more important. It is also a story in which NISO had to recover responsibility for the standard from a much larger influential American standards development organization, Accredited Standards Committee X3 (Information Processing Systems). Ultimately, from the perspective of NISO's membership and constituency, the story has a happy ending—which can now be told.

From High Sierra to Z39.60

NISO formed Standards Committee EE (Compact Disc Data Format) in July, 1985. Sixteen individuals were named to this committee to insure participation across a broad spectrum of publishers, librarians, information service providers and information technology vendors. SC EE was charged to develop an American National Standard based on a document that had been drafted by a small group of materially-affected parties—the "High Sierra Standard." SC EE held an extended series of meetings over nearly two years. These meetings were open to the public; some of them drew a hundred or more observers. NISO's Voting Members approved the resulting Z39.60, *Volume and File Structure of CDROM for Information Interchange,* on May 28, 1987.

But Wait! What About ECMA?

Normally, NISO would have submitted Z39.60 to the ANSI Board of Standards Review and, in due course, Z39.60 would have been registered as an American National Standard. However, a draft version of Z39.60 had been adopted by the European Computer Manufacturers Association as a regional European standard and submitted to the International Standards Organization (ISO) for immediate processing as a Draft International Standard. NISO suspended Z39.60 processing out of concern that the standard might not be aligned with the corresponding International Standard. The con-

Halltown Library   Annual Report   1989

Figure 4.12: Annual Report

repetitive work and help to establish an overall family similarity among different documents.

Chapter 8 discusses different sources for design ideas; one good source is the set of prepared style sheets that will be included along with examples in most packages that support style sheets. As a rule, you should never modify such sheets directly; if you want to use one, always save it under a new name immediately, then make your modifications. That way, the original will always be available as a starting point, and it will always match the description in your program's documentation.

Once you have some fully thought-out document designs of your own, you will find that drastically different designs can be prepared by making a few changes in copies of existing style sheets or chapter definitions. The most drastic changes come from revising the number of columns, the size of the page and its margins, the type family used for body type, and justification decisions—but smaller revisions can also be effective.

In practice, you will rarely start a style sheet or chapter definition completely from scratch; experienced users get so accustomed to working from an existing model that we sometimes do so even when it makes little sense. (The fact is, it doesn't take long to take the essentials from a copied style sheet, and it always seems more cumbersome to start from scratch.)

Summing Up

Even the simplest documents have explicit elements. By naming those elements, you can define them exactly and retain those definitions. In the past, such definitions were reflected in style manuals and other written documents to control final-document formatting. With modern desktop-publishing and word-processing programs, named elements can be combined to make up overall styles that the computer will directly support. To a great extent, the style manual becomes an automatic part of document preparation, not requiring much conscious attention.

Document designs may be reflected in a style sheet alone, in a combination of style sheet and dummy document, or in some other similar device. In any case, the devices provide control without eliminating the opportunity for improvement and creativity, and they enable you to separate the document design process from the actual creation and revision of text itself.

The rest of this chapter addresses a few specific design issues that work at the document level. Most of these design issues primarily affect fairly large, complex documents—but the way that you establish and maintain style sheets will affect the success of your publishing program for all documents, short and long.

Organizing Longer Documents

Single-page documents and other brief publications may not require advance thought about overall organization, but even such short, simple documents benefit from explicit organization. As documents grow longer, and as brief items are incorporated into longer composite publications, more extensive organization will enable readers to use publications more effectively.

The six aspects of document organization discussed in this section all work to break a long document into smaller pieces. That process serves a number of needs:

- Readers can rarely handle a lengthy document in one sitting and may be intimidated by pages of nothing but paragraphs. Explicit break points serve as places to set a document aside and continue it later.

- Many (perhaps most) longer documents serve more purposes than simple beginning-to-end reading. Break points make direct access to specific portions more feasible and can set off the portion of text that may be required for specific access.

- Many publications, including some of those produced by libraries (such as Requests for Proposals [RFPs] and manuals), require updating or responses that can best be handled on a section-by-section basis.

- Composite publications (such as newsletters and journals) require explicit organization to differentiate among the elements.

Chapters and Appendixes

Should a document be divided into chapters? In most cases, the answer will be obvious. Brief and informal documents never require chapters; they would be wholly out of place in a letter, memo, or newsletter. Chapters establish a fairly high level of formality in a document; they only make sense where a document is both fairly long (at least fifteen to twenty pages) and has lengthy, distinct segments.

Chapters serve as abrupt transitions and will be the most obvious places for readers to pause. A chapter typically starts a new page, has a larger-than-normal top margin on that new page, and begins with an explicit name, number, or both. Except in fiction, chapter headings almost always include chapter titles. You would typically use a larger point size and more vertical spacing (primarily above, but also below) for a chapter heading than for any other element except, possibly, a big initial letter.

Chapters in nonfiction publications should always represent meaningful segments of a document. While you may have a goal of ten-page to twelve-page chapters for an operations manual, you should neither split one integral topic into two chapters because it requires twenty pages nor amalgamate several distinctly different topics because each of them only requires two or three pages.

Chapters also serve as a computer management tool: you will typically prepare a separate text file for each chapter. You may even format each chapter separately, linking chapters only to prepare an index or table of contents (if needed). Breaking the document down in this manner makes it possible for more than one writer to work on a document simultaneously. It also makes final processing easier in most cases, with both word-processing and desktop-publishing programs. Not only will most programs perform much faster with a shorter document, but most users can maintain full efficiency better over the shorter period required to handle a single chapter. For that matter, you probably won't want to print drafts of an entire 100-page manual or 60-page RFP at a single sitting.

Chapter headings should be consistent throughout a document. Use the same spacing, justification, typeface, and other design decisions for every chapter heading. An appendix should be treated similarly to a chapter but serves somewhat different purposes. Appendixes contain matter that supplements the main portion of a document. They must be even more self-contained than chapters, since they function as separate entities. You may need appendixes for documents that do not require chapters. Appendix headings in a document with chapters should be consistent with chapter headings, although appendixes will usually have letters or stand alone, rather than having numbers.

Articles as Chapter-Equivalents

Every newsletter and journal should contain more than one article, and every article should begin with a distinctive typographic treatment, which may or may not be the same throughout the newsletter or journal.

Journals may treat articles almost identically to chapters, starting each one on a new page, but they rarely number the article titles. Newsletters should use some other device to let readers know that an entirely different portion of the text is beginning, even though it may not start a new column or page.

Sections and Headings

If you need to break a document down into parts, with more than one paragraph in each part, you need sections, and each section must have a heading. You need to establish how many levels of heading a document requires, the name for each level, and how each level is made distinctive.

At least four different problems can arise when determining section organization and applying those ideas to a given document:

- You may have too few sections or levels, so that the reader is faced with lengthy sections of undifferentiated text;

- You may have too many levels, so that the heading levels become difficult to differentiate, or you may have too many actual sections, so that the document becomes choppy and loses flow within sections.

- Headings may be used inconsistently or may appear to be inconsistent, so that the reader or user finds it difficult to follow the hierarchy of headings.

- The hierarchy of headings may be so complex that portions of the document become too "busy," with more headings and organization than content.

A given heading level must be treated consistently throughout a document: the same typeface, same spacing, and same lines above or below, if those are used.

If a document begins as an outline, a fairly common beginning for a manual or RFP, you may find that there are six or seven levels in the outline. Consider those levels carefully before translating them directly into heading levels: do you really want six or seven levels of organization? It is somewhat difficult to design seven different headings in a way that makes them all distinctive without creating a muddled, confusing overall design; typically, a total of four heading levels below the chapter level is about the most that will work effectively.

Numbered Headings

Every specification (such as an RFP or a contract) should probably have numbered headings, as should most internal manuals. They make it easy to use cross-references (for example "As noted in section 3.A.ii…"). They facilitate responses, if a document requires response. They also facilitate review and revision, since those reviewing or revising can cite specific section numbers.

Beyond that, section numbers can pose a barrier to the reader. They make a document appear formidable; since section numbers appear before headings, the numbers become a dominant factor in the document. I would think twice about using numbered headings in a guide to the online catalog intended for use by readers; such numbers make the material seem "technical" and may discourage readers from using the document effectively.

Note that some programs will assign and maintain section numbers automatically, if you select that option.

Table of Contents

Any document with chapters should probably have a table of contents. Any newsletter with more than eight pages or more than six or seven articles should probably have a table of contents, and such a table can be helpful even in shorter newsletters. In general, any document more than ten or fifteen pages long may work better with a table of contents.

On the other hand, a table of contents usually looks silly in a five-page document and almost always looks odd if it contains only two or three entries. Very simple, very brief documents do not need tables of contents; readers can find their way without the help.

Some programs will prepare tables of contents semiautomatically. You must typically decide how much detail should appear in the table of contents: chapter names only, chapters and first-level headings, or even more detail? Common sense should guide table-of-contents production. A fifty-page document rarely deserves a five-page table of contents; a hundred-page document probably needs more than a quarter-page table of contents.

Make sure that the table of contents is itself legible, and that its format reflects the arrangement of the document. Make sure that readers can relate the page numbers to the appropriate headings, either by using leaders (dots connecting the headings to the page numbers) or some other device. If there are relatively few headings, extra white space between the headings may suffice.

Some documents—even some books—have tables of contents without page numbers. Such a table does tell the reader what topics appear in the document, but otherwise it is useless: it gives the reader no help in locating the information. I find such tables extremely annoying; they suggest that the writer really doesn't care about the reader, at least not enough to do the extra work needed to finish the table of contents. Naturally, your library will always make sure that tables of contents contain page numbers.

What goes for tables of contents also goes for lists of figures and tables. If a document has a fair number of them, and there's some point to providing direct access, it should include a list—and the list should include page numbers. The design used for a table of contents will probably work for such lists, with only slight modifications. Programs that produce tables of contents and lists of figures automatically generally also provide default formats for the tables; those formats will probably provide good starting points for your own designs.

Index

Most long documents will be more useful with an index, and some programs make indexing a little easier. Several programs will build indexes, but only after you key index entries into the text. Some other programs build "indexes" based on all word occurrences; although these are really concordances (not coherent, organized topical indexes) they can still be useful. Some programs allow you to key in a list of key words, then produce an index based on occurrences of those words.

Good indexing requires thought and organization; a good index is more than a list of word occurrences. *The Chicago Manual of Style* contains excellent guidelines for building indexes. It is possible to include too much in an index, making it difficult for readers to locate useful text on a topic—but a more common problem is the index that essentially just recapitulates the table of contents in alphabetic form.

Intermediate-length documents may not require indexes, even though tables of contents may be useful. You would almost never include an index in a newsletter, a bibliography, or a brochure of library services; you might include a topical or name index in a publication listing community-service agencies or an author-title index to an extensive bibliography that is arranged topically.

Notes

Footnotes and endnotes (notes gathered at the end of a chapter or document, rather than at the bottom of each page) always add formality to a document and can easily be overused. Most library publications should not require footnotes or endnotes, but there are always exceptions.

Good word-processing and desktop-publishing programs support notes in some form, usually assigning and maintaining reference numbers automatically. Some programs will support both footnotes and endnotes in a single document—a useful distinction, if you use endnotes for bibliographic citations and footnotes for substantive notes that expand on the text. Other programs will support one or the other, or may allow you to choose which variety to use.

Avoid footnotes in library publications that are not scholarly, if you can. Newsletters should almost never contain footnotes; with careful editing, such supplementary material may be integrated into the text. Some substantive footnotes are really digressions and can be eliminated altogether. If footnotes appear in a public-oriented manual or handbook, consider them carefully: are they needed, or do they represent fine points that need not be made in such a document?

Every footnote[2] inherently interrupts the flow of text and, as a result, causes a slight break in smooth reading and the flow of an argument. A mass of footnotes may intimidate a reader, much as numbered headings do: the document takes on a formidable appearance.

If you must use footnotes or endnotes, use them consistently. If you can avoid them, do.

Organization in Shorter Documents

You would not break a ten-page bibliography into chapters, but you might very well break it down into topical areas or other subdivisions. Even a one-page memo may have more than one heading.

While you will spend less time making decisions about the organization of a short document, those decisions should be no less consistent than for your longest document. If a subordinate section of a brief memo has a larger or more prominent heading than a major section, or if equally significant sections have differently designed headings, you will confuse the reader, albeit slightly.

Every document more than one page long should have running headers or footers, with page numbers on every page (except, possibly, the first page of each chapter). Make sure that the reader always knows where they are and what they are reading—and that the people collating your document don't lose track of the pages!

Think about sections and organization every time a document passes the one-page mark. A new-title list in call-number order may be self-organized, but it will be easier to use if each call-number range has a heading, particularly if the list is five or ten pages long. If your new-title list includes hundreds of items, you might consider the

---

2   Every writer who makes this point seems to be compelled to demonstrate the truth of it by inserting a footnote. I'm no exception.

advantages of adding author and title lists or indexes; that's a service issue more than an organization issue, but it will make the list more useful.

Tracking the Version: Numbers, Dates, and Names

When you need a special-hours sign, you simply prepare it, post it, then discard it. That's appropriate; you don't need to put a date or a name on the sign, since it is so clearly self-identifying.

But if you issue a memo on any aspect of library operations, that memo should contain both an explicit title of some sort and a date. The title and date give you control over the document, and it makes sense to establish consistent placement and style for both as part of your publication plans.

That same principle holds for every publication of any significant size, including single-page bibliographies—perhaps particularly including bibliographies, since they should be revised over time.

Should your documents be numbered? That depends on the type of document and the needs of the library. If you want to establish a useful series of quick bibliographies, it doesn't hurt to number them—but numbers certainly aren't mandatory. Newsletters and other periodicals should always have numbers, but a calendar of library events only requires a date.

It is surprisingly easy to overlook dates and to issue publications that don't include them. That is almost always a mistake. Even though the computer files used to produce the publication will generally be dated automatically (by the operating system), you need a printed date on the document itself to control revision and be sure you have the current version. In some cases, you may prefer a consistent set of codes to explicit dates, particularly for documents that don't change very rapidly.

Make it a simple rule for every multipage textual document that you produce or your library produces: *every document should include either the date on which it was last revised or an equivalent code as part of the printed document.*

Conclusion

As with most aspects of design, overall document design requires more common sense than anything else. You can easily tell whether something has too much organization or too little—just look at it and think about the relationship of content to organization. You know that every publication should have a date and an explicit identity (a name, except for letters)—even though you may forget to date something when you're in a rush.

Pay attention to what you already know and to your own sense and experience; that will keep you out of trouble in most aspects of document organization.

Tips and Reminders

- Document design should always reflect document content.

- Every document has explicit elements; those elements should form the basis of overall design.

- Element names should be known during the writing process, but a name should define the function of an element, not its specific appearance. A title is a title is a title, no matter what typeface or size it will eventually appear in.

- Long documents require explicit organization into chapters and sections or equivalent shorter elements. Provide natural places for readers to pause and resume.

- Numbered headings can be useful for formal documents and manuals, but they should be avoided in less formal documents and user guides.

- If a publication is too long to be read in a single sitting, it should have a table of contents. One good rule of thumb is to include a table of contents if the publication is more than fifteen pages long, but some shorter publications will also benefit from tables of contents.

- Every document should be dated in some manner; almost every multipage document should have page numbers and running headers or footers.

5

Page Design

While content is primary, it is not sufficient for communication. A beautifully written local history serves nobody if it goes unread; a clear, succinct guide to the library's services must be picked up and read if it is to assist library patrons.

For most publications, the first impression of a publication comes from the overall appearance of the first page. The reader perceives the page as a whole before dealing with words and sentences; that perception can influence the success of the text. The first page must do several things:

- *Attract* the reader, so that he or she has some interest in looking at the text;

- *Identify* the publication clearly and unambiguously, so that the reader can determine at a glance whether this particular publication might be worth reading;

- *Organize* part or all of the text, so that the reader can use the publication rapidly and effectively.

Other pages of multipage publications should also achieve several goals:

- Maintain a *coherent design*, with variations as needed to serve the content and to retain the reader's interest;

- Maintain the *identity* of the publication and, as appropriate, of its sections;

- Continue effective text *organization*.

This chapter takes up a few aspects of page design, including page size, orientation, and special considerations; margins and columns; and running heads and feet. Many aspects of page design function directly as part of text design, discussed in the following chapters.

Most measurements in this chapter are stated in terms of inches or *picas*. Like points, picas serve as a typographic measure. A pica is precisely twelve points; there are almost exactly six picas to the inch. Typewriters typically use one-pica line spacing: that is, there are six single-spaced typed lines to each inch.

Page Size and Orientation

Before you can design a page, you must determine the size of the page and the print orientation. Just because the 8½-by-11-inch *portrait mode* (upright style) represents the most common format for word processing and typewriting, don't assume that all your publications need to work that way.

Most library publications do use standard 8½-by-11-inch paper in portrait mode. It's the cheapest and simplest way to go—but it can also cause design difficulties.

When you work with proportional type in a single column, the standard page represents an awkward size. If text fills the space between ordinary margins, the lines will be too long for easy reading. If you use much wider margins, the text may seem lost on the paper, and you will waste much of your paper. You can solve these problems, but they must be faced when working with the standard size.

Portrait and Landscape Orientation

You may never have thought of your typed memos and letters as being in portrait mode, but that's almost certainly what they are. Portrait-mode pages, or portrait pages, are taller than they are wide—like this book. The term derives from art, from the relative dimensions of paintings.

The alternative is *landscape mode*, producing landscape pages or broadsides. Most landscape paintings are wider than they are tall; hence the term.

Contemporary laser printers will print equally well in either orientation, and advanced layout programs (desktop publishing or word processing) will also work either way. In addition, the most important typeface systems (PostScript and Bitstream) work equally well in both modes. Since laser printers have the same number of dots per inch in both directions (with rare exceptions), the equivalence makes sense.

Some publications require landscape orientation to work effectively—for example, a monthly events calendar done within the framework of a calendar matrix, a certificate of appreciation for volunteers, a single-sheet folded brochure, or a special-hours sign. Most multipage textual publications work best as portrait pages, if only because that's what people expect. Except for signs and certificates, think twice before using landscape orientation. It can be effective, but should always be used for good reason.

Standard Sizes

Laser printers typically recognize four standard paper sizes, with different paper trays for each size:

- Executive, 7¼ by 10½ inches;
- Letter, 8½ by 11 inches;
- Legal, 8½ by 14 inches;
- A4, 210 by 297 millimeters (roughly 8¼ by 11¾ inches).

While A4 is the most common size in Europe, American libraries will typically choose between letter and legal sizes. The executive size, while narrow enough so that it represents less of a problem for single-column formats, is far less common, and paper for copying and printing in that size is likely to be considerably more expensive. Your binders, folders, and other support devices probably work best with letter-size paper.

Legal-size paper has its place for special publications, particularly single-sheet publications that require the extra space and publications that will be folded. However, it is too tall for comfortable use in portrait mode, with an awkward width-to-height ratio that makes attractive design even more difficult.

Larger Sizes

You *can* use desktop-publishing techniques to generate publications larger than legal paper, but you will not be able to produce the full-page originals directly. Some desktop-publishing programs include facilities for *tiling* larger pages—producing a large page as a series of smaller pages that can be mounted together for platemaking.

That's not something you're likely to do very often. If you need to do tabloid or other large-format publications on a regular basis, you need more specialized advice than this book can offer.

Note, however, that page size may not be sheet size. If you produce newsletters or periodicals that will be printed rather than photocopied, the printer may very well use 11-by-17-inch sheets, with four pages printed on each sheet. Such sheets, folded in half and center-stapled, present a more professional, finished appearance than a stapled set of letter-size sheets. But the pages are still letter-size; the page originals are combined to make sheets as part of the platemaking process.

Smaller Sizes

The printed page for your final publication may not be the same size as the page that comes out of your printer. Every good word-processing and desktop-publishing program will let you define a smaller effective page; advanced desktop-publishing programs will show that smaller page as the working page on-screen, and may print *crop marks* to indicate that page size—printed marks at or near each corner of the "real" page that guide the platemaking process.

If you prepare a booklike publication, a 6-by-9-inch page will look better and be easier to work with than a standard page. If you prepare booklets or pamphlets—such as guides to the online catalog or guides to local service agencies—smaller pages may make the publication more accessible.

Many multipage publications will work better in a smaller format, but in some cases the economics of smaller pages may be forbidding. Check with the printing agencies that will produce your publications; you will probably find that some smaller pages will be economical, while others will be wasteful.

Consider the section of this chapter on white space. Small pages need white space just as much as standard pages do, even though small pages may avoid the problem of lengthy text lines. If your page size is 5½ by 8½ inches (33 by 51 picas), the text block should probably not be much more than 25 by 38 picas—and anything more than 28 by 43 picas will look cramped and unreadable.

Folded Publications

Why did the previous section mention a size of 5½ by 8½ inches? Because that's the result of folding letter paper in half (landscape mode): each sheet will hold four such pages, with each page being just a little smaller than standard book size.

The letter page, printed in portrait mode and folded in half, is a particularly effective design for pamphlets and other publications that are unwieldy as sets of stapled sheets and too short for book publication. It is also an economical design in the small quantities that most libraries will print. There's nothing cheaper at most offset printers and copy shops than standard letter paper, and the folding and stapling should not be terribly expensive. Additionally, the page size makes single-column design straightforward; with reasonable margins and typography, the text line is an ideal length.

That's far from the only effective folded design. As noted earlier, the best-looking full size newsletters are usually printed on 11-by-17-inch sheets folded in half. Single-sheet brochures can often be effective printed as six panels, with the landscape sheet folded into three 3⅔-by-8½-inch panels (e.g., figure 4.3)—or, using legal paper, three 4⅔-by-8½-inch panels. Some of the best quick guides to online catalogs or collections are in the form of trifold brochures.

Folds need not be identical for each sheet. With careful planning, you can achieve very effective results using different folds. Figure 5.1 shows the front of a two-sheet publication (with lines added below each page edge for emphasis).

This document presents six interior pages of information, with the topics immediately visible for each of the three openings, in addition to the cover and a largely blank rear cover. The document was produced as four pages and printed on both sides of two sheets. The first sheet was folded 4⅔ inches from the top; the second (inner) sheet was folded 5⅓ inches from the top. Figure 5.2 shows one of the original pages—in this case, the page that prints on the back of the inner sheet, providing the second and fifth partial pages of information.

College of
Notre Dame
Library Handbook

General Information	Hours	Circulation Services

Reference	Reserves	Periodicals	Catalog	Music

Special Collections	Miscellaneous Information

Figure 5.1: Folded Brochure

Unfortunately, this design—like any multipage design with *off-set* folds (that is, folds at different points for different sheets)—substantially increases the production cost as compared to using two sheets folded in half (thus losing the topical guide). Most printers have equipment for automatic collating, and stapling, and they can do that with a standard center fold; special folds may require manual collating and stapling. The second edition of the brochure illustrated in figures 5.1 and 5.2 abandoned the special fold after examination of production costs showed that the fold increased those costs by 50 percent. Special folds can be very effective—if you can afford the price.

Archives of
Modern Christian Art

The Archives of Modern Christian Art is located on the second floor balcony next to the Music Library. The Archives was established in 1981 to preserve the record of Christian religious art and architecture in the modern world. The Archives is concerned with publications, personal papers, memorabilia and photographic files of and about those artists, architects and artisans primarily in the United States who have created environments for worship during the past 100 years. Materials in the card catalog with the designation *Special Collections AMCA* are located in the Archives; many of these materials are available for general circulation. The Archives is staffed during the afternoon hours.

Montessori File

The Montessori File is a special collection of papers on Early Childhood Education. This collection is *Library Use Only.*

Media Center

The Media Center is located in the Campus Center building and offers a variety of educational media services to the faculty, staff, and students. Please consult the Media Center brochure for a complete description of hours and services.

Special Collections

Materials located in the Special Collections Room are listed in the card catalog and must be requested from the Library staff. Special Collections contains Californiana, faculty publications, and other materials of special value.

Library Privileges

Access to the library is open to all faculty, students, staff and alumni. Please apply for a library card at the circulation desk. Library cards must be used to check out materials. You are responsible for all materials checked out on your card, so it is inadvisable to lend your card to anyone else. There is a 50¢ replacement fee for lost cards.

Loan Periods

Books may be checked out for three weeks during Fall/Spring semesters, and for one week during Winter/Summer sessions. Periodicals may be checked out for one week. Materials may be renewed if they have not been requested by another borrower. Reference materials do not circulate.

Fines and Fees

Overdue books and periodicals from the circulating collection are fined at a rate of 20¢ per day up to the maximum fine of $5.00 per item. Reserve books are fined at a rate of $1.00 per day. Borrowers who have accrued fines of $5.00 or more will not be permitted to check out materials until all fines have been paid. Borrowers may not renew overdue materials until fines have been paid on those materials.

Lost books and periodicals will be charged to the borrower; charges will include the replacement cost of the item plus a $15.00 processing fee. All overdue materials that reach the maximum fine will be considered lost and will be charged to the borrower. Unpaid fines and fees, if not resolved in person at the library, will be sent to the Business Office for posting on student accounts.

General Information   **Hours**   **Circulation Services**

Figure 5.2: Third Side of Brochure

Preparing Pages for Folded Publications

When you design folded publications, you must decide whether you will produce individual pages on the laser printer and paste them up for final printing or attempt instead to prepare full sheets on the laser printer as they will be printed, with each sheet containing more than one page. As a rule of thumb, most folded publications taking up more than one or two printed sheets should be prepared as individual pages.

Folded publications can become complex in terms of where text goes—for example, in a sixteen-page single-fold pamphlet, pages 3 and 14 are on the same printed side. If you're trying to produce the full-sheet originals from your desktop-publishing program, that means that text must jump backwards—the text on page 14 (part of the third printed side) is on an earlier sheet than the text on page 4 (part of the fourth printed side). Most software doesn't support that process automatically; you'll probably be forced to split the document into many smaller files, each containing the equivalent of one page of text.

The whole process is more trouble than it's worth in most situations. Just because it is possible to do everything with the computer doesn't mean it is the most effective choice. In this case, some physical cutting and pasting will make production faster and easier.

Margins and Columns

Well-designed pages combine intelligent use of white space with sensibly-sized text areas. The clearly defined white areas of a page appear within the text, primarily above and below headings, and around the text, in the form of margins. When dealing with margins, we must also deal with running headers and running footers.

A header is the material that appears above the text block on each page (if any); in this book, it is the page number and name of the book on even-numbered pages, chapter name and page number on odd-numbered pages. A footer is the equivalent material below the text block; this book does not use footers except on the first page of each chapter.

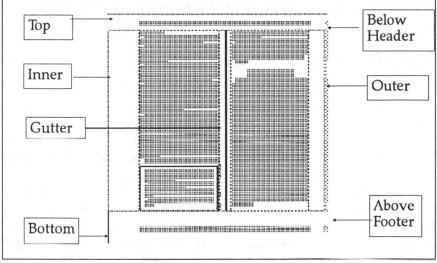

Figure 5.3: Margins

A single page may involve up to eight different margins:

- Top margin, including running header (if any);
- Bottom margin, including running footer (if any);
- Left margin;
- Right margin;
- Margin between header and text block;
- Margin between text block and footer;
- Margin between adjacent columns in a multi-column publication, typically called the gutter;
- Binding margin, an extra margin on the left side of odd-numbered (right-hand) pages and the right side of even-numbered (left-hand) pages.

Figure 5.3 shows all of these margins for a right-hand page. Note that the left margin is also the inner margin; the right margin is the outer margin.

Depending on the software you use and the designs you plan, you may not need to worry about the margins between the text block and running header/footer. Even if you use these elements, the software may well assign default placements and margins that you find acceptable.

Traditional Guidelines

Should you just use one-inch margins all around? That may work for typed manuscripts, but most publications will look better with more varied margins. Placing the text block squarely in the middle of the page works just fine for signs and certificates. Not so for multi-page textual publications. Uniform margins make dull pages and can produce visually unbalanced designs.

Traditional book design, generally a good source of conservative but proven design ideas, does not call for equal margins. One old formula uses ratios of 1½, 2, 3 and 4 for the inner, top, outer and bottom margins respectively—thus, for example, if the inner margin is 3 picas (one-half inch), the top margin would be 4 picas, the outer would be 6 picas and the bottom would be 8 picas. That's not a bad starting point for something like a newsletter or pamphlet, where there is no binding to eliminate some of the inner margin. The inner margins of the two sides combine to make up a space equal to either outer margin, thus creating a balanced two-page spread; the larger bottom margin always seems to work out better in terms of people's sense of apparent balance.

For example, the *LITA Newsletter* uses a (roughly) 3½-pica inner margin, 4-pica top margin, 5-pica outer margin, and 6-pica bottom margin. That is not quite the set of ratios suggested above (and, in fact, relatively few contemporary publications use such extreme ratios), but it does work to create a visually balanced page.

If you don't worry about margins, you'll be in good company. Most publications appear to treat margins as nothing more than leftover space. But if you are willing to do a little thinking and experimenting, your friends of the library newsletter and other publications can be more attractive with very little extra work.

Any librarian who has dealt with binderies and newsletters or magazines knows the frustrations of dealing with inadequate binding margins. Assume that your newsletters and bibliographies will be valuable enough that some people will save them; leave room for three-hole punching or binding. That means that your inner margin must be at least three picas and six points.

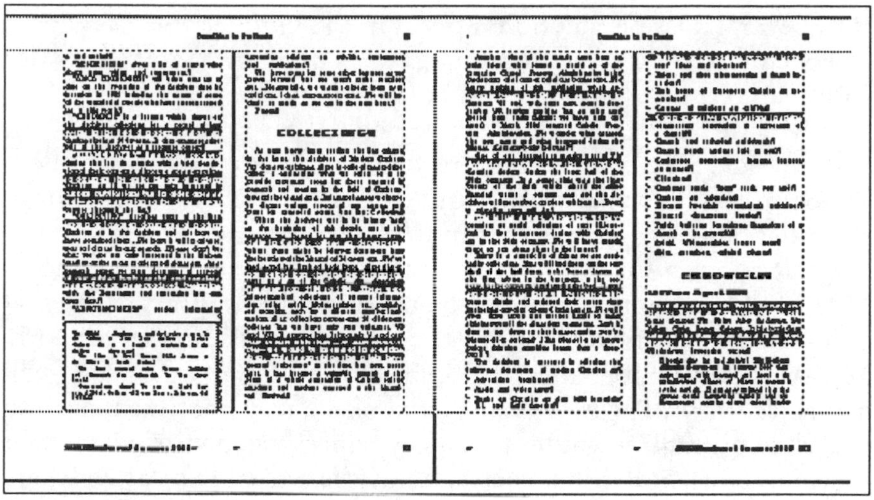

Figure 5.4: The Spread

The Spread

The binding or inner margin works as part of the *spread*, a combination of an even-numbered and an odd-numbered page that appear side by side when a two-sided publication is opened.

Good software will show you side-by-side pages on the screen (as illustrated in figure 5.4) so that you can see what the spread will look like, even if the text is not legible. Good software also supports margins based on the spread. Pay attention to the spread, if you are preparing a publication with visible spreads. For example, if you prepare a newsletter that includes a two-page run of uninterrupted text, try to make sure that the text begins on an odd-numbered page. If it begins near the start of an even-numbered page, you will have a spread with no graphic interest; at that point, you should add sub-headings or some other visual device to break up the gray.

Multiple-Column Pages

When you put together the guidelines for text and appropriate margins, you find that a single text block—while always the easiest to prepare and, in some ways, easiest for the reader to use—is difficult to work with in a letter-size page.

Several possible solutions appear in this chapter and elsewhere; one solution, common to most magazines and newsletters, is to use multiple columns.

Multiple columns can either be newspaper-style ("snaking") or side-by-side. Side-by-side columns only work when your document is structured to make them work—for example, when you have frequent headings that appear in the left column, or when you use the left column for pull quotes, footnotes, and small illustrations. Side-by-side columns need not be equal width; in practice, a good side-by-side design would rarely use two columns of the same width.

Most newspaper-style multiple-column designs do use equal-width columns. For a standard letter-size sheet, that means using either two or three columns. The typefaces needed to make four columns work at all (since each column is less than 12 picas wide) are really too small to work effectively on a laser printer.

Should you use two columns (probably 18 to 22 picas wide) or three columns (probably 12 to 14 picas wide)? Most designers recommend three columns, because such a layout gives you lots of opportunity to break up the page for greater visual interest—two-column photographs or illustrations, double-width text, and so on.

If the publication you're designing has to "grab" people, if you assume that they must be seduced into going through it all, and if you plan to use lots of active design elements, then a three-column layout may work for you. But it poses some serious problems, mostly because the columns are so narrow.

One good rule of thumb says that the optimum width for a text line is twice the point size of the type, converted to picas—with the acceptable range being from 75 to 150 percent of that figure. Even if you use 9-point type, the smallest size normally considered suitable for body text, the acceptable range is 13.5 to 27 picas—just barely fitting into that three-column space. You're out of luck if you want to use a larger, more easily readable typeface: the lines will always be shorter than the optimal range.

If you must use three columns, don't use justified text: the results will probably be disappointing. Justification, discussed further in chapter 6, works less and less well as lines become shorter and shorter. With fewer character spaces per line, the chances of achieving good line breaks diminish, resulting in many more hyphens, more awkwardly large interword spaces, or both.

As a general rule, do not plan a three-column letter-size page unless you plan to do intensive layout work on each page. The advantages of the three-column design serve those who are designing pages directly. They usually become disadvantages if you plan to let most of your text just flow into place.

The Grid

If you plan to prepare design-intensive documents, including almost any three-column document, you should learn to establish and use a grid for your layout work.

A grid is what its name implies—a network of vertical and horizontal lines. The vertical lines may be the text columns—or you may establish more text columns than you actually plan to use, so that you can vary the column widths in an orderly fashion. One popular style uses five columns, with either two or three actual text columns superimposed on the narrow grid.

The horizontal lines will usually be the default baselines, that is, where standard body text would fall if the page were full of such text. You may establish larger vertical zones, such as a third of the text block for each zone, but the software may not enforce such zones.

Good desktop-publishing software will use the grid; when you establish new frames, you can specify that they align automatically with the nearest line and column edge.

As with three-column layouts, grids work best for publications that will be designed page by page and grid section by grid section. For the production-oriented publications that I believe make up the bulk of library needs, the grid is far less relevant.

Forms Design

Grids become particularly useful when you design forms using desktop-publishing software. When you design a form, page design is everything—since there is usually only one page and the primary purpose of text is to define the areas where information will be entered.

In this case, the vertical grid should be set to equal the line-spacing needed to use the form—typically either 12-point, 18-point or 24-point spaces (equaling single-space, one-and-a-half space, or double-spaced typing); if forms are to be filled out by hand, 18-point and 24-point spacing will work. Figure 5.5 shows part of a page set up with a 6-pica-by-18-point grid.

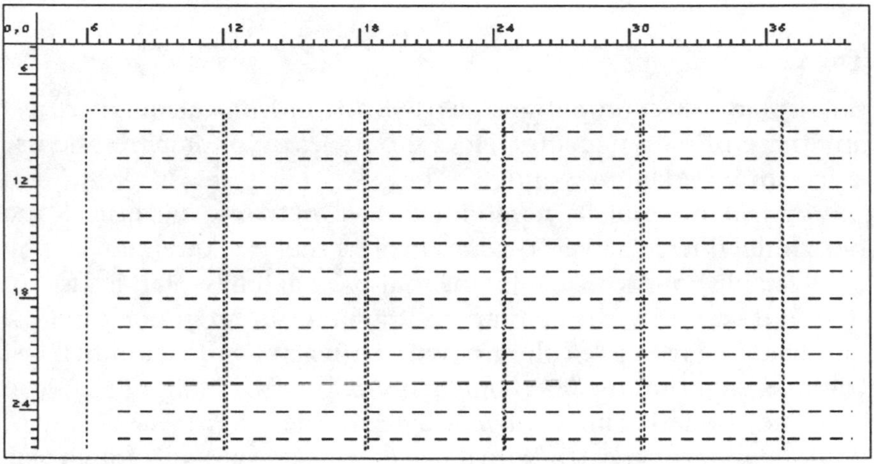

Figure 5.5: Grid

The horizontal grid, in this case, might be better defined as tab stops for the basic styles, indicating the places that labels will begin and lines will end. Some forms may work well with predefined columns, but others will be easiest to prepare using a single-column layout and tabs.

Organizing the Page

How would you react if the largest headline on a newsletter's front page was in the right-hand column, two-thirds of the way down the page? If you're typical, you would find it a little unsettling; the large headline should indicate the most important element on the page, but in this case it's not in the usual location.

You don't need to think about this for most simple publications. Single-column text publications and signs simply read top to bottom.

It would be odd to have a headline in the lower part of the first page that is larger than the headline at the top, but that's simple common sense. By and large, the hierarchy of headlines will provide all the organization you need.

Left to Right, Top to Bottom

When you produce multicolumn publications, specifically newsletters, you should generally follow the normal pattern. Western readers typically follow a standard pattern in looking at a page. You should usually follow that pattern, not fight it. People look at a page the same way they read text: left to right, top to bottom. Designers refer to the Z pattern used in looking at a page, as illustrated in figure 5.7. The most important element should typically appear upper left on the first page.

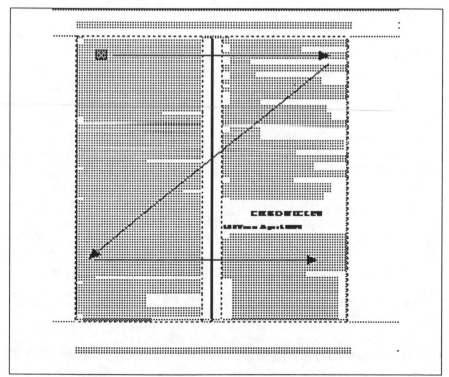

Figure 5.6: Typical Scanning Pattern

That's not an absolute rule, of course. If you prepare a twelve-page newsletter, you will probably include a table of contents. While that table—which is really secondary material—could go in the bottom right-hand corner of the first page, it could also work very well as the left column of the first page, particularly if the contents column includes one-sentence abstracts for the articles.

If the page is set up that way, be sure that the headline for the first article is larger than the heading for the contents. In that manner, the right-hand column (or second column, for a three-column page) becomes the "first" column, with the distinctly formatted left column turning into supporting material.

What if you only have half a column of contents? In that case, do not put the contents upper left—unless, for some reason, the table of contents is the most important thing in the newsletter. The article that begins below the contents table will be buried, having nowhere near the prominence that a lead article deserves. Far better to drop the contents down to the lower right-hand corner.

The same principles apply for other pages, although the format of other pages is typically driven by text. Still, if you use boxed items or other interjections, it is normally reasonable to assume that important boxed items should appear toward the top of the page, with less important boxes appearing toward the bottom. For items appearing on even-numbered pages, the left column is more prominent. For inner odd-numbered pages, placement is more difficult: while people still scan left to right, the outer (right) placement has more visual prominence.

Visible Importance

When you design a publication that uses more than one or two type sizes, do a trial run, then set out the pages and step back a foot or two. Look at the pages, from far enough back that you can't read the text itself.

You should see a clear hierarchy of headings and other elements. You should be able to say, "This is a major change, this is secondary, this is minor," without any reference to the text itself.

If you can't determine the hierarchy, your page is badly organized. If you think you can, but when you look at the text, the hierarchy is not what it appeared to be, you need to rethink the style of your headings and spacing.

Graphic placement serves content much as text placement does. If a newsletter includes a photograph taking up a major portion of the top half of the left column of the first page, that photograph should be important—not simply a minor illustration. If you use clip art and other secondary graphics in ways that give them prominence over headlines and text, you may undermine the coherence and impact of your design.

Simplicity and Consistency

Keep it simple. If one page of your publication has six different type sizes, four different typefaces, half a dozen illustrations, or large capital letters on every paragraph, you're overdoing it. It's like using bright letters, reverse video, underlining, colors, and blinking on the same video screen: there are so many effects that none of them have any meaning. A few special devices used clearly and consistently will serve you well; too many devices will clutter the layout and confuse the reader.

Good page organization is generally simple page organization. The reader should be able to recognize new articles at a glance. The user of a manual should understand the levels of organization whether or not the headings are numbered. One or two highlighting techniques will help to break up the page and call attention to items; a dozen highlighting techniques will negate the usefulness of each one.

Every coherent publication design maintains consistency. Good word-processing and desktop-publishing software supports that consistency through styles, tags, and other devices. But you must work with the software support to carry out a consistent design. By maintaining consistency, you will be able to use occasional differences effectively, to call attention to special elements of the publication.

Identification and Location

Make sure the reader always knows *what* the publication is and *where* he or she currently is within the publication.

Three elements of page design specifically work to maintain identification and location: titles and banners; headings and sub-headings; and running headers and footers.

Titles and Banners

Signs and certificates are self-naming, but you would never produce a bibliography or newsletter without an explicit identification. The first level of identification, either a title (for a single piece) or a banner (for a continuing publication), should usually be the most prominent element on the first page.

Figure 4.4 uses a banner, thus identifying a series of bibliographies and placing the individual publication within that series. The specific title appears below the banner; it is the second most prominent graphic element on the first page, as is appropriate.

This particular chapter has a title—and, aside from the single large capitals starting the first paragraph, the title uses the largest type size in the book.

That's all common sense—but, when you're designing an unusual publication, you may forget that it needs a name and a distinctive style for identification. Put the name up front, make it big, let the reader know what he or she is picking up.

Headings and Subheadings

Designers abhor pages of unbroken text, but such pages make perfectly good sense in many cases. You would not enhance a major novel by adding subheads every few paragraphs.

However, most nonfiction will benefit from consistent use of headings and subheadings. That usually means two or three levels, possibly four. Except for special forms such as annual reports and quick guides, it usually does not mean a heading every paragraph or two, but it may mean a heading at least once every page or two.

Headings help the readers to work through a publication and to locate where they left off if they choose not to read the complete work in one sitting. Headings also provide white space and elements of graphic interest.

Heading levels should follow and support the hierarchy of the content. More important heading levels almost always use more white space above and below the heading; frequently, it also makes sense to use larger type sizes for each higher heading level. If you use larger type, make the difference noticeable: one rule of thumb is that each level should be two points larger than the next. If you choose not to use different sizes for each level—and there are good arguments not to—you should use placement and type style to differentiate levels. One common style, used in this book, takes centered, large, bold headings as the first level (below chapters); flush-left bold headings as a second level; and flush-left italic as a third level.

The basic rules for headings and subheadings are all common sense.

- Don't use so many headings that the text becomes lost; however, some documents require headings for almost every paragraph.

- Make sure each level of heading is distinctly less prominent than the next higher level.

- Use enough heading levels to organize your text effectively, and no more.

- If a trial run looks muddled or confusing, rethink the heading design or the actual headings.

Running Headers and Footers

Have you ever picked up a twenty-page publication with no page numbers? Remember your irritation at trying to find your place when you went back to it, and resolve that your library will never make a similar mistake.

Most publications use either running headers or running footers—for page numbers, to maintain the identification of a serial, to repeat the overall title or a section title, or to establish the explicit location within a reference work. (Imagine using an unabridged dictionary without page headers.) You should use them, too—for whatever cases are appropriate. Some publications should have dates as part of the running information; almost every publication should include page numbers.

The Importance of White Space

Just as music only works by contrast with silence, print only works by contrast with unprinted space. White space should be considered in every publication, but it serves particularly important roles in text-only publications and in single-column publications using standard letter-size paper.

Consider the page illustrated in figure 5.7. No matter how important the text on that page, people will not willingly pick it up and will have difficulty reading it if they do. There are several problems with figure 5.7, but the first problem is that the page is completely filled, with no space except for the one-third inch on each side that represents the minimum margin for laser printers.

That is far too much text coverage for the page. It is not an efficient use of paper, because it does not communicate. The page is simply a mass of type—visually, a gray, nearly uniform whole. The second page, consisting of entirely textual material (unlike the tables of hours and telephone extensions), would be even worse.

Library users would never be attracted to a handbook looking like figure 5.7—and, even if it was forced on them, they would find it exceedingly difficult to read and use. The four primary problems with the page are as follows:

- Lack of white space outside the text and within the text, to provide a frame for the material and make the page visually inviting;

- Lack of apparent organization within the text itself, since there is no extra vertical spacing or changes in typography;

- Text lines that are too wide for comfortable reading. These lines include as many as 78 characters;

- Typewriter type [1] with uniform spacing for each letter, generally less readable than proportional type.

---

1   Actually a laser-printed version of Prestige, a pica type.

```
College of Notre Dame Library Handbook
History
     The College of Notre Dame Library, established in 1922, was housed on the
second floor of Cuvilly Hall until 1952.  The collection was then moved to the
Greenan Library opposite St. Mary's Hall.  Our current library opened in 1975.
Purpose
     The College of Notre Dame Library is committed to providing materials and
services that support and expand the College's undergraduate and graduate
academic programs.  In addition to a collection of approximately 100,000
volumes, 560 current periodical subscriptions, and over 7,500 sound
recordings, the library offers a variety of services, including reference
assistance and advisory services.  Lectures and tours are available upon
request.
Hours
Fall/Spring Semesters
     Mon.-Thurs. 8 a.m. - 10 p.m.
     Fri.        8 a.m. - 4 p.m.
     Sat.        12 p.m. - 4 p.m.
     Sun.        2 p.m. - 10 p.m.
     Exceptions: Holidays and exam periods; changes in hours will be posted on
the library door.
Winter/Summer Sessions
     Mon. - Thurs.    8 a.m.-8 p.m.
     Fri.        8 a.m.-4 p.m.
     Sat.        Closed
     Sun.        Closed
Telephone Numbers: (415) 593-1601
     x346    General Services
     x342    Archives of Modern Christian Art
     x343    Media Center
     x344    Music Library
Library Privileges
     Access to the library is open to all faculty, students, staff and alumni.
Please apply for a library card at the circulation desk.  Library cards must
be used to check out materials.  You are responsible for all materials checked
out on your card, so it is inadvisable to lend your card to anyone else.
There is a 50 cent replacement fee for lost cards.
Loan Periods
     Books may be checked out for three weeks during Fall/Spring semesters, and
for one week during Winter/Summer sessions.  Periodicals may be checked out
for one week.  Materials may be renewed if they have not been requested by
another borrower.  Reference materials do not circulate.
Fines and Fees
     Overdue books and periodicals from the circulating collection are fined at
a rate of 20 cents per day up to the maximum fine of $5.00 per item.  Reserve
books are fined at a rate of $1.00 per day.  Library Use Only books, which
require written permission from the instructor in order to be taken out of the
library, are charged at $1.00 per day.
     Lost books and periodicals will be charged to the borrower; charges will
include the replacement cost of the item plus a $15.00 processing fee.  All
overdue materials that reach the maximum fine will be considered lost and will
be charged to the borrower.  Unpaid fines and fees, if not resolved in person
at the library, will be sent to the Business Office for posting on student
accounts.
Reference Services
     The Reference area contains an extensive collection of encyclopedias,
dictionaries, directories, biographies, bibliographies, indexes, abstracts and
yearbooks.  Librarians are available to help with research problems and
explain the use of reference materials.  At the request of faculty members,
reference librarians also prepare bibliographies and/or bibliographic
instruction lectures for library research assignments.  If there is no
```

Figure 5.7: Page with No Spacing

College of Notre Dame Library Handbook

History

The *College of Notre Dame Library*, established in 1922, was housed on the second floor of Cuvilly Hall until 1952. The collection was then moved to the Greenan Library opposite St. Mary's Hall. Our current library opened in 1975.

Purpose

The College of Notre Dame Library is committed to providing materials and services that support and expand the College's undergraduate and graduate academic programs. In addition to a collection of approximately 100,000 volumes, 560 current periodical subscriptions, and over 7,500 sound recordings, the library offers a variety of services, including reference assistance and advisory services. Lectures and tours are available upon request.

Hours

Fall/Spring Semesters
Mon.-Thurs.	8 a.m. - 10 p.m.
Fri.	8 a.m. - 4 p.m.
Sat.	12 p.m. - 4 p.m.
Sun.	2 p.m. - 10 p.m.

Exceptions: Holidays and exam periods; changes in hours will be posted on the library door.

Winter/Summer Sessions
Mon. - Thurs.	8 a.m.-8 p.m.
Fri.	8 a.m.-4 p.m.
Sat.	Closed
Sun.	Closed

Telephone Numbers: (415) 593-1601

x346	General Services
x342	Archives of Modern Christian Art
x343	Media Center
x344	Music Library

Library Privileges

Access to the library is open to all faculty, students, staff and alumni. Please apply for a library card at the circulation desk. Library cards must be used to check out materials. You are responsible for all materials checked out on your card, so it is inadvisable to lend your card to anyone else. There is a 50 cent replacement fee for lost cards.

Loan Periods

Books may be checked out for three weeks during Fall/Spring semesters, and for one week during Winter/Summer sessions. Periodicals may be checked out for one week. Materials may be renewed if they have not been requested by another borrower. Reference materials do not circulate.

Fines and Fees

Overdue books and periodicals from the circulating collection are fined at a rate of 20 cents per day up to the maximum fine of $5.00 per item. Reserve books are fined at a rate of $1.00 per day. *Library Use Onl*

Figure 5.8: Proportional Text, No Margins

The last problem is almost irrelevant because the others are so overwhelming. Note that this figure is not justified; that would make a bad situation even worse. (One good rule of thumb, although irrelevant for most desktop publishing, is that monospaced type—for example Courier and Pica—should never be justified.)

Changing the typography won't solve the problems entirely. Figure 5.8 is a little better, but not all that much.

The improvement in figure 5.8, such as it is, comes from internal spacing above and below headings and from the different type sizes used for the headings. Thus, the first problem with figure 5.7 is slightly alleviated: since there are many headings, there is quite a bit of internal white space. The second problem disappears: while this design is still neither attractive nor ideal, the organization is clear. The fourth problem is also taken care of, since figure 5.8 does use proportional type. But the third problem becomes even worse—as a direct result of using proportional type. Some lines in figure 5.8 have as many as 115 characters—almost twice the generally-accepted ideal of 50 to 70 characters per line.

Naturally, both figures 5.7 and 5.8 are entirely hypothetical. No single-column publication should ever use the minimum margins for laser-printed pages. We all learned long ago that typewritten documents should have at least one-inch margins on all four sides, and the default settings for most word-processing and desktop-publishing programs will leave margins at least that wide.

For typewritten material or when (for some reason) monospaced fonts make sense, one-inch margins may be sufficient. Consider figure 5.9, another version of figure 5.7, using the same typeface but adding reasonable margins on all four sides and around headings.

This page still is not wonderful, but it is workable. A student would be able to identify the document immediately and would not find the first page repelling. The student would be able to spot topics of interest immediately—the page is clearly organized—and the line width is reasonable for this typeface, with no more than 65 characters per line.

The margins in figure 5.9 will not work, however, for a typical proportionally spaced typeface, such as those you will use for almost all desktop publishing. The average of 30 to 40 percent more text within each line means that 6½-inch lines will contain up to 85 to 100

```
            COLLEGE OF NOTRE DAME LIBRARY HANDBOOK


                          History

    The College of Notre Dame Library, established in 1922, was
housed on the second floor of Cuvilly Hall until 1952.  The
collection was then moved to the Greenan Library opposite St.
Mary's Hall. Our current library opened in 1975.


                          Purpose

    The College of Notre Dame Library is committed to providing
materials and services that support and expand the College's
undergraduate and graduate academic programs.  In addition to a
collection of approximately 100,000 volumes, 560 current
periodical subscriptions, and over 7,500 sound recordings, the
library offers a variety of services, including reference
assistance and advisory services.  Lectures and tours are
available upon request.


                           Hours


Fall/Spring Semesters
    Mon.-Thurs. 8 a.m. - 10 p.m.
    Fri.        8 a.m. - 4 p.m.
    Sat.        12 p.m. - 4 p.m.
    Sun.        2 p.m. - 10 p.m.
    Exceptions: Holidays and exam periods; changes in hours will
be posted on the library door.

Winter/Summer Sessions
    Mon.-Thurs. 8 a.m.-8 p.m.
    Fri.        8 a.m.-4 p.m.
    Sat.        Closed
    Sun.        Closed


               Telephone Numbers: (415) 593-1601

    x346   General Services
    x342   Archives of Modern Christian Art
    x343   Media Center
    x344   Music Library
```

Figure 5.9: Typewritten, Moderate Margins

College of Notre Dame Library Handbook

History

    The College of Notre Dame Library, established in 1922, was housed on the second floor of Cuvilly Hall until 1952. The collection was then moved to the Greenan Library opposite St. Mary's Hall. Our current library opened in 1975.

Purpose

    The College of Notre Dame Library is committed to providing materials and services that support and expand the College's undergraduate and graduate academic programs. In addition to a collection of approximately 100,000 volumes, 560 current periodical subscriptions, and over 7,500 sound recordings, the library offers a variety of services, including reference assistance and advisory services. Lectures and tours are available upon request.

Hours

Fall/Spring Semesters

Mon.-Thurs.	8 a.m. - 10 p.m.
Fri.	8 a.m. - 4 p.m.
Sat.	12 p.m. - 4 p.m.
Sun.	2 p.m. - 10 p.m.

Exceptions: Holidays and exam periods; changes in hours will be posted on the library door.

Winter/Summer Sessions

Mon. - Thurs.	8 a.m.-8 p.m.
Fri.	8 a.m.-4 p.m.
Sat.	Closed
Sun.	Closed

Telephone Numbers: (415) 593-1601

x346	General Services
x342	Archives of Modern Christian Art
x343	Media Center
x344	Music Library

Library Privileges

    Access to the library is open to all faculty, students, staff and alumni. Please apply for a library card at the circulation desk. Library cards must be used to check out materials. You are responsible for all materials checked out on your card, so it is in-

Figure 5.10: Proportional, Wide Margins

College of Notre Dame Library Handbook

History

The College of Notre Dame Library, established in 1922, was housed on the second floor of Cuvilly Hall until 1952. The collection was then moved to the Greenan Library opposite St. Mary's Hall. Our current library opened in 1975.

Purpose

The College of Notre Dame Library is committed to providing materials and services that support and expand the College's undergraduate and graduate academic programs. In addition to a collection of approximately 100,000 volumes, 560 current periodical subscriptions, and over 7,500 sound recordings, the library offers a variety of services, including reference assistance and advisory services. Lectures and tours are available upon request.

Hours
Fall/Spring Semesters

Mon.-Thurs. 8 a.m. - 10 p.m.
Fri.   8 a.m. - 4 p.m.
Sat.   12 p.m. - 4 p.m.
Sun.   2 p.m. - 10 p.m.
   Exceptions: Holidays and exam periods; changes in hours will be posted on the library door.

Winter/Summer Sessions

Mon. - Thurs. 8 a.m.-8 p.m.
Fri.   8 a.m.-4 p.m.
Sat.   Closed
Sun.   Closed

Telephone Numbers:
(415) 593-1601

x346   General Services
x342   Archives of Modern Christian Art
x343   Media Center
x344   Music Library

Library Privileges

Access to the library is open to all faculty, students, staff and alumni. Please apply for a library card at the circulation desk. Library cards must be used to check out materials. You are responsible for all materials checked out on your card, so it is inadvisable to lend your card to anyone else. There is a 50 cent replacement fee for lost cards.

Figure 5.11: Proportional, Side-by-Side

characters per line. That is too much text, making the material hard to read. Consider figure 5.10—again, the same material, with slightly different margins than figure 5.9 and with a proportional typeface.

This style reduces text lines to 6 inches, with headings hanging off to the left edge. That improves the clarity of organization. If space was at a premium, the hanging headings would allow for less vertical space above and below headings. The text lines are still too wide, however; some lines have as many as 90 characters.

You should treat white space as an important design element in every publication. You must make especially intelligent use of white space for single-column letter-size pages.

Several techniques will solve the wide-line problem without going to multiple columns. Figures 4.4 and 4.5 show one solution: wider side margins and a very wide indent for text paragraphs, leaving a 5-inch text line. That's still a little wider than the ideal, but perfectly workable for bibliographies and other publications intended more for quick reference than continuous reading.

Figure 5.11 shows another solution, one that actually makes more efficient use of space than figure 5.10 in a publication with frequent headings. This style uses a 4-inch text column, which is within the ideal range. Rather than using extremely wide outer margins—which would look peculiar and result in a tall, ungainly strip of text on the page—the design reserves a 2½-inch column for headings, placed beside the text.

This technique requires a little more work during formatting, and is most effective for publications with many headings and relatively little text for each heading.

The 50 Percent Guideline

How much white space should you use on a page? That depends on many factors, including the number of columns on the page, the balance of internal and external white space, the number and importance of illustrations, and limitations imposed for financial reasons or other external reasons.

One good starting point may seem extreme, but it works out fairly well in practice: the primary text block for a single-column publication should take up roughly half (50 to 55 percent) of the page.

The remainder should be margins (including running headers and footers).

That rule of thumb applies to well-designed, open publications more often than you might expect. The text block in figure 5.11 takes up 55 percent of the page; the same is true for the text block in figures 4.4 and 4.5. The text block in this book uses 55 percent of the page; you will find similar ratios in most books that appear to have good margins and reasonably open pages.

Remember that 50 percent of the page does not mean 50 percent of the height and 50 percent of the width; that would be 25 percent of the page. A letter-size page measures 51 picas by 66 picas (8½ by 11 inches), or 3,366 square picas. Half of that is 1,683 picas. If the text block is 54 picas (9 inches) high, with running header and footer in the margins, it would be 31 picas wide—just over 5 inches. That's effectively what you would have with a deeply indented text area and hanging headings. Alternatively, if the type size is large enough to justify a 36-pica width, you could use a larger bottom margin and slightly larger top margin, leaving a 47-pica body-text area (just under 8 inches).

You rarely need to concern yourself with the 50 percent guideline, but if you are working on a design and find that the page seems too crowded, you might consider measuring the text block and the overall page. If a single-column text block uses much more than 60 percent of the page, it is probably too crowded to be attractive.

Newsletters and Other Exceptions

Naturally, you can find hundreds of counterexamples to the 50 percent guideline. Many magazines and newsletters use as much as 75 percent of the page for text, and mass-market paperbacks use 70 percent, sometimes more. (You will almost never find a publication that uses more than 75 percent of the page for a text block; the results are almost sure to be unworkable.)

Multicolumn publications can, indeed, use more of the page effectively—but you will rarely see a front page or the lead page of an article with a 75 percent text density. For that matter, if you encounter a typical newsletter or magazine with a two-page spread that has no subheadings, illustrations, or other matter to break up the text, you probably (if subconsciously) regard it as unusually heavy going.

Newsletters use extensive headlines and subheadings to break up the space; promotional newsletters feature many illustrations and reduce the amount of text in other ways. Magazines put more space, more illustrations, and less text into early pages of articles to draw you into the articles; only after you have decided to read an article will you face such dense pages—and even then, better-designed magazines will use pull quotes, subheads, and other devices to keep the text from becoming too dense. Open, inviting page layouts will encourage people to pick up, read, and use your publications; the increased impact should justify the increased use of paper.

The 50 percent rule works surprisingly well for most publications, particularly if applied in its narrower sense. That is to say, the area actually devoted to body text—paragraphs, exclusive of headings, subheadings, and illustrations—should rarely be more than 50 to 55 percent of the total area on a page. If the text portion is more than 60 percent, the page is almost certainly too dense for anything but quick reference.

Internal White Space

Consider the differences between figure 5.7 and figure 5.8. Poor as both examples are, the second would be far more inviting and workable than the first. The major reason is not the use of proportional type; it is, rather, the use of internal white space. Internal white space helps to establish the organization of a document and can make it more accessible.

You may find peculiar, almost random uses of internal white space in publications—particularly in publications that stress visual innovation over functionality. Odd spaces at the bottoms of columns (not related to widow and orphan control); paragraphs with both indents and vertical spacing; odd blank columns within multicolumn pages—these are all largely useless internal spaces.

Internal spaces in good publication designs usually serve very clear purposes. Vertical space helps to establish the hierarchy of headings: more important headings typically have larger spaces above and below. Special horizontal spaces, in addition to paragraph indentations and tables, call material out for special attention of one sort or another, such as citations, pull quotes, or special guidelines.

Internal space also helps to open up a page if used intelligently. We'll get back to some aspects of intelligent internal spacing in later chapters, but the basics can be stated fairly simply:

- Extra space before paragraphs always suggests some form of pause or logical break, and it should not be used unless that is intended.

- Extra space between lines within a paragraph should generally be avoided, except in those cases (such as press releases) where material must be double-spaced. Appropriate linespacing enhances legibility; extraneous linespacing detracts from the flow of text.

- While internal spacing does open up a page, it should always serve the logical organization of the material.

In one sentence: if internal space does not serve an intended logical purpose, it may cause an unintended reaction.

Tips and Reminders

- The first page of a publication is the most important page; make sure it attracts readers and identifies and organizes the text.

- Consider folded publications as an alternative to the standard sizes, but be prepared to pay a price for unusual folds.

- Be aware of all eight margins on a page and the ways that they serve to make the page attractive. Consider the appearance of facing pages, not just how a page looks by itself.

- Beware of columns that are too narrow or too wide; most body text should be set in columns of 14 to 30 picas (depending partly on the type size used).

- A grid of columns and vertical sections can establish consistent zones to help you plan pages; this can be particularly helpful for forms and three-column designs.

- People usually scan a page from left to right, top to bottom, in a Z pattern; your page design should assume that pattern.

- Make sure the visual importance of elements in a page matches their intended importance.

- Keep it simple and consistent: don't use too many different illustrations, typefaces, or type sizes on a single page or in a single publication.

- Use titles, headings, and running headers or footers to make sure your reader always knows what the publication is and where he or she reader is within the publication.

- White space makes publications work. As a starting point, plan to leave 40 to 50 percent of the page as white space.

- Even if your publication design uses small margins, it should make ample use of space and other visual elements. A publication that consistently has more than 50 to 55 percent of each page taken up with body text (excluding headings, subheadings, and illustrations) is probably too dense for comfortable reading, but it may be acceptable for bibliographies or other reference-only uses.

6

Design for Reading

Words form the basis of most publications. Good textual design encourages the reader to read a publication and stays out of the way of the words. Except for those cases where a sign or brochure is intended to startle rather than communicate an extended message, good textual design is always *design for reading*.

Design for reading can be summed up in a few basic principles:

- Typefaces used for text should be both legible and readable, so that letters combine into words and words combine into sentences. Spacing between words should never be so narrow that adjacent words collapse into one, nor so wide that the flow of a sentence is interrupted.

- Text should be large enough for easy reading by the audience for a publication and small enough to be economically sound.

- Readers should be aware of the message (the text) rather than the medium (the typography); thus, typography should be consistent except when a change is necessary to convey a particular message.

- Lines of text should be narrow enough so that readers can keep their places, but not so narrow that the text becomes disjointed.

- Lines within a paragraph should be spaced far enough apart so that the text is open and attractive, but not so far apart that the eye must make an abrupt jump from one line to the next.

This chapter discusses and illustrates some specific aspects of textual design that can play a part in fulfilling those principles.

Selecting Typefaces

First, a few definitions. Desktop publishing seems to have muddled the normal language of typography when it comes to talking about type, and this book probably includes instances of the confusion. In accurate terms, a *typeface* is a particular design and style of type, including all sizes but only one style. Thus, for example, Times Roman Medium is a single typeface, Times Roman Italic is a different typeface, and Times Roman Bold is yet a third. A *font* is a single typeface in a single size. Thus, 8-point Times Roman is one font; 9-point Times Roman is another. Generally, a *type family* is a group of related typefaces—for desktop publishing, usually regular (medium), bold, italic, and bold italic faces with the same basic name and design.

Frequently, however, *font* is now used in place of *typeface*: thus, for example, most PostScript printers are described as "including thirty-five fonts." Those thirty-five fonts are actually thirty-five typefaces in ten or eleven different families; an almost infinite number of fonts can be generated from the set of typefaces.

You also need to know about a second measure besides point size: namely, *leading* (the space between lines of type) expressed either as a percentage or as points. Both are used in this book. The descriptions "Times Roman 10-point with 120 percent leading" and "Times Roman set 10 on 12" both mean the same thing: 10-point Times Roman, set so that adjacent lines of type are 12 points (120 percent of 10) apart.

Type can be either *serif* or *sans serif*. Serif type, such as the type you're reading now, is distinguished by the small lines or curves at the edges of some letters that help to define the letters and pull them together into words. Sans serif type, such as the Bitstream Swiss illustrated in figure 6.1, lacks these lines or curves.

Finally, type can be either *body type* or *display type*. Body type is type used for normal text. Display type is any type used in larger sizes for heading and display purposes. While every typeface suitable for body type is, at least potentially, useful for display type, the reverse is not true. Many typefaces are only suitable for display purposes, being far too unusual to work well in normal text.

The Basics and Beyond

You will probably start out with Helvetica and Times Roman—or Swiss and Dutch, or some other pair of names. They're everywhere; many programs include them and nothing else, and they are the most readily available proportional typefaces in cartridges and other devices. These days, you may wind up with Bitstream Charter as well (or instead): many word processing and other programs include that face as part of the initial Bitstream support that comes free.[1]

For some of you, Times and Helvetica may be all you ever need. Their omnipresence stems from widespread usefulness. Both typefaces work well in a variety of situations. Times is one of the most economical and readable typefaces—economical in that it "sets narrow," with more letters fitting in a given space than most other typefaces. Helvetica works well as a headline typeface when used with Times—and, in its own right, it is very popular for body text in European publications and in advertising. Figure 6.1 shows samples of Bitstream's equivalents for Times Roman and Helvetica.

The only real drawback to Times and Helvetica is that they are perhaps too commonplace in laser-printed material. To some extent, they go beyond the supporting role that typefaces should play to become nearly invisible.

You can avoid that sameness, if you have the option of generating your own sizes or have a wide range of sizes. Try using Times for headlines as well as body type; in larger type sizes, a good Times Roman is interesting and full of character.

Many of you will go beyond the two standards to try a wider range of typefaces. If you use PostScript, you start out with a fairly broad range of choices, with hundreds of additional typefaces available. For the LaserJet, you need to make your choices carefully, since each new typeface will involve some amount of money and, probably, a large amount of disk space.

---

1   Bitstream is one of the two most important "digital type foundries," creators of typefaces for electronic printing. Many desktop-publishing and word-processing programs now include Bitstream installation software and starter sets of typefaces.

Bitstream Dutch (similar to Times) 10 on 12

While typefaces used for body text should not call attention to themselves, this is not to say that the subtle differences among such typefaces are meaningless. Even among the best typefaces for body type – which are, generally, clear serif faces with open, readable designs – the differences will influence the overall look of text.

Bitstream Swiss (similar to Helvetica) 10 on 12

While typefaces used for body text should not call attention to themselves, this is not to say that the subtle differences among such typefaces are meaningless. Even among the best typefaces for body type—which are, generally, clear serif faces with open, readable designs—the differences will influence the overall look of text.

Figure 6.1: Swiss and Dutch

Chapter 13 shows a small sampling of the hundreds of typefaces available for desktop publishing and word processing. That chapter also discusses the arguments for and against serif and sans serif typefaces for body text and the distinctions between body typefaces and display typefaces. I have a strong preference for serif typefaces in body type, but it would be absurd to say that you could never select a sans serif typeface for body text. Sans serif does give a modern look—but, at least to my eye, at some expense in sheer readability.

Figure 6.2 shows the same paragraph in two newly redesigned typefaces, both set at the same size, width, and leading. The first paragraph is in Zapf Calligraphic; the second is in Zapf Humanist. Both typefaces were created by the same master designer, Hermann Zapf; both offer high readability with some distinctiveness. Zapf Humanist may be as good a possibility for sans serif body type as you can find. You can draw your own conclusions; if you (and those that you ask for opinions) find that a long run of the second text would be preferable to the first, who am I to argue?

If the content is worthwhile and the layout clear, I would read a publication set in Zapf Humanist or Optima without grimacing. The American norm is serif text, however, and I regard it as a good norm.

Zapf Calligraphic 10 on 12

While typefaces used for body text should not call attention to themselves, this is not to say that the subtle differences among such typefaces are meaningless. Even among the best typefaces for body type—which are, generally, clear serif faces with open, readable designs—the differences will influence the overall look of text.

Zapf Humanist 10 on 12

While typefaces used for body text should not call attention to themselves, this is not to say that the subtle differences among such typefaces are meaningless. Even among the best typefaces for body type—which are, generally, clear serif faces with open, readable designs—the differences will influence the overall look of text.

Figure 6.2: Zapf Calligraphic and Zapf Humanist

Signature Typefaces and Institutional Typefaces

If you plan to use desktop publishing for your personal and professional activities, or if your library is part of a larger institution with an established publishing program, you may have good reason to select one particular typeface to be used in most of your documents.

If it is a personal choice, that typeface becomes your desktop-publishing signature—one you will share with many others, but nonetheless a recognizable aspect of your desktop publishing. In that case, the crucial rules are simple:

- Make sure that the typeface will work for all the types of documents you plan to prepare. Avoid typefaces that are so distinctive that they are distracting.

- Make sure that you really do like the typeface—you'll be seeing a lot of it.

I did not originally set out to select a signature typeface. Rather, Zapf Calligraphic selected me—possibly because it is straightforward enough to be universally useful and highly readable, but distinctive enough to be enjoyable. You might come to the same decision—or you might prefer another distinctive yet widely useful typeface such as Amerigo, Baskerville, Cheltenham, Clearface, Galliard, Goudy, Korinna, Souvenir, Stone Serif, or Tiffany.

If your institution already has established typographic standards, using typefaces that work well and that are available for the desktop, those typefaces should probably be high on your list. Alternatively, you may be establishing a typographic identity for your institution.

I am lucky; the college at which my wife is library director uses Palatino for many of its documents, so my use of Zapf Calligraphic for library publications fits into the established pattern. If they were using Baskerville as a college typeface, it would make sense to acquire the typeface outlines so that the newly typeset library publications would be consistent. (A new set of typeface outlines from the best foundries typically costs about $100 to $150.)

Many institutions lack established typefaces. Chances are good that you won't have such standards either to guide you or to fall back on. In that case, you will be establishing typefaces as you go. It never hurts to be a bit conservative, but you can certainly venture beyond Times Roman.

Guidelines for Typeface Selection

Some suppliers of typefaces, and some writers on design and desktop publishing, offer sets of guidelines for the typefaces they consider most suitable for certain types of publications. As you might expect, the guidelines don't always agree.

Bitstream offers one such guide. For example, it suggests that Zapf Calligraphic is ill-suited to office correspondence, financial reports, invitations, labels, forms, and directories, but well-suited to catalogs, books, fliers, proposals, instructional materials and newsletters; Tiffany, by contrast, is considered well-suited only for presentation materials, fliers, and invitations. Some guides even suggest which typefaces work well with other typefaces. All such guides can be useful, but none of them should be considered absolute.

Mixing and Matching Typefaces

So you've selected a group of typefaces. How do you combine them in documents? The basic rule is that they must look right together; that can be expanded into a few key points:

- Never use more than one body typeface in a given article—and, except for special inserts, stick to a single body typeface for an entire publication.

- Never use more than two different typefaces in a given article; headlines should all be in the same typeface as the body, a single contrasting typeface, or some combination of the two.

- Don't choose similar typefaces for headlines and body text: they will clash. If you use a different typeface, make it distinctly different.

- You may not need a second typeface for headings.

The first point may not require additional commentary. Any shift in body typeface upsets the look of the publication, almost certainly not for any good reason. High-style magazines may use different typefaces for different articles—but even there, you would not find different body typefaces within a single article.

There are always exceptions. An annual report might use a different typeface for the fine print of budget and footnotes than for the prose account of the library's year. Boxed items within a newsletter, which call out for special attention in any case, might properly use a distinctive body typeface and a heading typeface that differs from the rest of the newsletter. But these are exceptions, and they should be recognized as such.

The other exception, discussed in the next chapter, is the pull quote, a portion of text repeated as a graphic element. This textual highlight might well use a typeface distinct from regular body text—although, more often than not, you will find a larger version of the same typeface (possibly set in italic or bold) to be just as effective and more agreeable to the eye.

The rule for headings is almost absolute. If your body text is Times Roman, you should not have a title in Helvetica, first-level headings in Korinna, and second-level headings in Hammersmith: the results will be bizarre. Any one of the three will produce distinctive, effective headlines that contrast nicely with Times—but you should only use one of them, and larger sizes of Times, within a given article (and, typically, a given publication).

Selecting a distinctly different typeface just makes good sense. If you're going to use a second typeface at all, it should be distinctly different. If it is similar to the body type, you don't gain the sharp break of a distinctive difference but you lose the consistency of a single typeface. That's one reason that the traditional combination is a sans serif headline type with a serif body type: the two are always distinctly different, and only clash if they simply don't work together at all.

Finally, consider the possibility that your body text may provide the ideal headline typeface. Many body typefaces make attractive, distinctive characters at larger sizes. Some do not; for example, Bookman and Century Schoolbook would probably create fairly boring headlines. Still, it's worth a try. Before you settle on a two-typeface design for a given publication, try switching to a single typeface; you may like the results.

Font Size

Once you decide which typefaces to use for specific publications, the choice of size becomes relatively simple—at least for body text. Normal body text basically comes in four sizes: 9-point, 10-point, 11-point and 12-point type.

Figure 6.3 shows the same paragraph in the four common sizes of body type. Nine-point type, usually considered to be the smallest size that is easy to read for continuing passages, may be ideal for lengthy directory-type publications where space is at a premium, such as printed listings of information and referral agencies. You may not want to use type this small for newsletters, brochures, and reference manuals: it is on the small side for continuous reading.

The two most common sizes for desktop publishing are 10-point type, used in most typeface examples in this book, and 11-point type, used for most of the book itself. Twelve-point type takes up significantly more space without adding substantially to readability; you find it used less often, except for brief publications where the body text is really intended for instant recognition and for publications to be used by children.

Zapf Calligraphic 9 on 10.8

While typefaces used for body text should not call attention to themselves, this is not to say that the subtle differences among such typefaces are meaningless. Even among the best typefaces for body type—which are, generally, clear serif faces with open, readable designs—the differences will influence the overall look of text.

Zapf Calligraphic 10 on 12

While typefaces used for body text should not call attention to themselves, this is not to say that the subtle differences among such typefaces are meaningless. Even among the best typefaces for body type—which are, generally, clear serif faces with open, readable designs—the differences will influence the overall look of text.

Zapf Calligraphic 11 on 13

While typefaces used for body text should not call attention to themselves, this is not to say that the subtle differences among such typefaces are meaningless. Even among the best typefaces for body type—which are, generally, clear serif faces with open, readable designs—the differences will influence the overall look of text.

Zapf Calligraphic 12 on 14.4

While typefaces used for body text should not call attention to themselves, this is not to say that the subtle differences among such typefaces are meaningless. Even among the best typefaces for body type—which are, generally, clear serif faces with open, readable designs—the differences will influence the overall look of text.

Figure 6.3: Standard Sizes for Body Text

You will find that some typefaces are more readable at smaller font sizes than others. If you're planning to use 9-point type, or you want to use 10-point and expect a publication to be particularly comfortable to read, print out a long document and see whether the font performs well.

Large-Print Requirements

If your library serves the public, you probably have a large-print collection—and you may be preparing lists of that collection using an Orator type ball on an electric typewriter, or some similarly inelegant way to achieve a larger type. With desktop-publishing techniques, you can give your large-print users the lists they deserve: lists done in type the same size as the books' type.

Zapf Calligraphic 16 on 18

While typefaces used for body text should not call attention to themselves, this is not to say that the subtle differences among such typefaces are meaningless. Even among the best typefaces for body type—which are, generally, clear serif faces with open, readable designs—the differences will influence the overall look of text.

Figure 6.4: Typical Large Print

Figure 6.4 is set using the most common large print specifications: 16-point type on 18-point leading. The classic large-print combination uses Plantin as a typeface; in the absence of that particular face, any good serif body type should be a usable substitute. Since serifs are known to make letters more readable as text, large print should always use serif typefaces.

Remember your large-print users when preparing other materials. Do you have a large-print brochure to introduce special services? Do you prepare large-print bibliographies on subjects such as aging, retirement activities, and the like? How about a special list of the local agencies that specifically serve the elderly, or an invitation for library volunteers?

Whether you use word processing or desktop publishing, it makes sense to generate a 16-point size of your clearest body type and use it for a range of materials. You will please a growing portion of the library users—a community that appreciates the special service and can show that appreciation effectively.

Small Type

Font generators will typically turn out type as small as 6 points—or, in some cases, as small as 3 point! You can find ready examples of type set smaller than 6 points: just open *Webster's Ninth New Collegiate Dictionary.*

Zapf Calligraphic 7 on 8.4

While typefaces used for body text should not call attention to themselves, this is not to say that the subtle differences among such typefaces are meaningless. Even among the best typefaces for body type—which are, generally, clear serif faces with open, readable designs—the differences will influence the overall look of text.

Zapf Calligraphic 8 on 9.6

While typefaces used for body text should not call attention to themselves, this is not to say that the subtle differences among such typefaces are meaningless. Even among the best typefaces for body type—which are, generally, clear serif faces with open, readable designs—the differences will influence the overall look of text.

Figure 6.5: Small Print: 7- and 8-Point Body Text

Figure 6.5 shows Zapf Calligraphic set at 7 and 8 points; figure 6.6 shows Glyphix Palatine and Eterna set at 3, 4, 5 and 6 points. Should you ever use any of these sizes?

Well, yes—although probably not anything smaller than 6 points, at least from a standard laser printer. If you use 10-point body type, your footnotes and any superscript or subscript text will probably be 8-point type; that 2-point differential is fairly standard. And if you need to include extensive textual annotations in a publication, but you know that those annotations won't really be read, you might choose to print them in small type—a particularly good way to characterize 6-point and 7-point type.

Figure 6.6: Very Small Proportional Print

Note that, as discussed in the next section, you really need to set 7-point type at a much narrower line width than 10-point or 11-point type and with proportionally more leading. Otherwise, it becomes nearly impossible to read, even for the brief uses that it is suitable for.

Very small type suggests that you're trying to hide something from the readers. Given the resolution of laser printers, you will succeed in hiding the text. A single dot on a normal laser printer is $\frac{1}{300}$ inch, or roughly $\frac{1}{4}$ point. Thus, 3-point type only occupies twelve dots vertically, from the bottom of the lowest descender to the top of the highest ascender—and a capital M (the widest letter) is only twelve dots wide. That's really not enough to form a legible character, as figure 6.6 shows.

For most work, the difference between laser printing and the highest-resolution phototypesetting may not be that important. At extremely small type sizes, the difference in resolution—eight to one in each direction, or sixty-four times as many elements per character—makes an enormous difference.

In extremely small type sizes, Courier is more legible than most other typefaces. It is an extremely simple typeface; all lines have exactly the same width and all characters are the same size. It also has broad serifs, so that it retains the readability advantages of serif type under difficult conditions. Figure 6.7 shows a version of Courier set at 3, 4, 5, and 6 points; while it certainly is not handsome or even very readable, it is not totally hopeless. Even as small as 6 points, however, a more interesting face like Palatine or Eterna may be preferable. Note, also, that Courier is not "economical": because it is monospaced, it sets wider than almost any proportional type. That's why the 6-point Courier paragraph requires ten lines, where the 6-point Palatine and Eterna require seven; all three are set to the same width.

Courier 3 point
While typefaces used for body text should not call attention to themselves, this is not to say that the subtle differences among such typefaces are meaningless. Even among the best typefaces for body type—which are, generally, clear serif faces with open, readable designs—the differences will influence the overall look of text.

Courier 4 point
While typefaces used for body text should not call attention to themselves, this is not to say that the subtle differences among such typefaces are meaningless. Even among the best typefaces for body type—which are, generally, clear serif faces with open, readable designs—the differences will influence the overall look of text.

Courier 5 point
While typefaces used for body text should not call attention to themselves, this is not to say that the subtle differences among such typefaces are meaningless. Even among the best typefaces for body type—which are, generally, clear serif faces with open, readable designs—the differences will influence the overall look of text.

Courier 6 point
While typefaces used for body text should not call attention to themselves, this is not to say that the subtle differences among such typefaces are meaningless. Even among the best typefaces for body type—which are, generally, clear serif faces with open, readable designs—the differences will influence the overall look of text.

Figure 6.7: Very Small Monospaced Print

Of course there are good reasons to use such extremely small type in special circumstances: if you're required to add large quantities of largely useless text to some publication, you can print a little more than three times as much text in the same space using 6-point type as you can using 11-point type. But if you go smaller than 5 points on a laser printer, you're really not publishing the text in any meaningful sense: you're just putting smudges of toner on paper.

Line Width and Linespacing

When computer users first switch to proportional type, one natural tendency is to leave the rest of the format as it is. The results tend to be hard to read, simply because each line of proportional text contains too many words and therefore is too long for comfortable reading.

Perhaps no area of text design is now so full of conflicting and confusing advice as are guidelines for line width and linespacing. You will see an incredible variety of advice, much of it contradictory—and much of the recent advice contradicting all earlier advice that was based on studies of readability.

Traditional Rules for Line Width

Almost all books on typography and style prior to the days of desktop publishing offer guidelines that fall within a reasonably narrow range. The five guidelines that follow are paraphrases of some of these published guidelines, offered in no particular order.

- An optimal line width accommodates ten to twelve words, or 60 to 70 characters.

- The optimum line width is 1½ times the lowercase alphabet length. The minimum is 25 percent narrower, the maximum is 50 percent wider. A less exact but frequently adequate formula: the optimum line width is twice the point size, expressed in picas.

- Factors of visual comfort suggest a maximum of about 70 characters per line. Fewer characters is better, down to about 50. The ideal is probably between 55 and 60 characters.

- Generally, 10-point type is most legible in widths of 17 to 27 picas; 12-point, in widths of 17 to 37 picas.

- Good lines contain from seven to ten words.

The last bit of advice, from a magazine article, goes on to add a flatly contradictory "that is, from 30 to 40 characters"—which would only be seven to ten words of baby talk!

The second, third, and fourth guidelines recognize the reality of publication design: you can't always use what might be theoretically optimal. Incidentally, 1½ lowercase alphabets is *not* the same as 40 characters (if you include spaces as characters). The typical distribution of characters in words is not the same as the alphabet. Including spaces, 1½ alphabets may be closer to 50 characters, a fairly typical guideline for the lowest optimum width.

Different typefaces set to different widths. As chapter 13 shows, the differences can be dramatic for unusual typefaces. For typical body type, 1½ lowercase alphabets at 10 points will take up 15 to 19 picas, with most typefaces in the range of 16 to 18 picas (some compressed typefaces will be significantly narrower).

For typical 10-point type, lines should probably be no narrower than 13 to 14 picas and no wider than 24 to 26 picas. Naturally, those measures should be adjusted for larger and smaller type sizes.

Multiple columns require narrower line widths, not only because of space requirements but because of the effect of multiple columns. Thus, while 27 picas is a good line width for 11-point type in a single column (as in this book), it would be too wide for a column of a tabloid or other large-format multicolumn publication. Line widths of 17 to 21 picas make much more sense for such a publication, and fit nicely into a two-column letter-size page.

The Problem with Wide Lines

If you leave 1-inch margins on both sides of letter-size paper, the remaining line width is 39 points. That is simply too wide for comfortable reading, based on all the readability studies that have been done and any experiments you might like to try. It becomes difficult to stay on a line from beginning to end, and very easy to put down the document. The guidelines above suggest that you could get by with a 36-pica line using 12-point type, and you can—but it is still uncomfortably wide.[2]

Other chapters of this book show several possible solutions to that problem, in that large number of cases where the only reasonable way to produce a publication is at standard letter size. For newsletters, the solution is obvious: use two columns. For book lists

---

2   The exception, of course, is large print; while 39 picas is still wide for 16-point type, it may not be *too* wide.

and bibliographies, you can either put call numbers in a separate column or use a wide left margin with headings out in the margin area. For manuals and reports, use a wide left column for headings, notes, figures, pull quotes, or some combination of devices. In most of these cases, the "marginal" column should not be as wide as the text column; that asymmetry will lend interest to the page design.

If you must use a very wide line, you should take three measures to minimize the problems it causes:

- Use 12-point type with lots of headings to break up the mass of type;

- Use additional leading (discussed below)—that is, leave a little more white space between lines. Setting the text 12 on 15 or 12 on 16 will help to make the page more readable; even 12 on 17 may be worthwhile. (Note, however, that after adding extra leading you will have lost any space efficiencies purchased by using a wide text column. A 30-pica column set 11 on 13 will carry as much text as a 39-pica column set 12 on 17 and will produce a more open, inviting page.)

- Don't justify the text. Note that the same advice appears below for very narrow columns. While I find justified text more finished and pleasant in general, extremely wide or narrow text seems to benefit from ragged-right setting.

Dealing with Narrow Lines

Earlier in this section, I noted one guideline for line width as "seven to ten words, or 30 to 40 characters." The person writing that guideline probably knew that you can't fit ten words in 40 characters—but that person was also trying to follow the latest fashion in desktop publishing, one that has caused some people to assert suddenly that 30 characters is an optimum line width, in the face of clear evidence to the contrary.

That fashion is the three-column layout, which designers like because it allows so much flexibility for special effects in page design. This design, however, can cause problems: the copy may be legible but not readable. *Legibility* is the ease with which characters can be recognized. *Readability* is the ease with which a document or page can be read. They are not at all the same thing. If you become more concerned with the look of a page than with the text on it, you may easily fail to distinguish between the two qualities—but it's a trap you should avoid.

Narrow columns can be quite legible—if they are set ragged-right, thus avoiding excessive hyphenation and awkward spacing. If you expect a publication to be scanned for highlights, rather than read at any great length, narrow columns may be quite workable; for example, they have a clear place in brochures and pocket guides to library services.

But when a line contains fewer than six or seven words, it is too choppy for comfortable continuous reading. It may be legible, but it is not comfortably readable. That doesn't matter in a brief guide to library services, but it does in any newsletter that contains articles more than two paragraphs long.

For desktop publishers—and, indeed, for all publishers—the main problem with narrow lines is that there are too few places to break the line, too few chances for words to fill out a line normally. The results? Either extremely wide spaces between words, awkward spaces between letters, too many hyphens, or (set ragged-right) extreme variations in the line width.

You probably see any number of 8½-by-11-inch magazines that feature three-column layouts. Typically, those layouts use 9-point type, with columns roughly 13 picas wide. That is not too narrow for 9-point type; it is just within the optimum range. But the magazines also use phototypesetting, probably at 2,500 lines per inch; their 9-point type is much sharper and clearer than the 9-point type you can produce on a laser printer.

Thirteen picas is very narrow for 10-point type, and really too narrow for 11-point type. If you use those sizes, avoid three-column layouts. If you do plan three-column layouts, make sure you avoid the worst problems:

- Don't use anything larger than 10-point type for body text, and use a typeface that sets relatively narrow.

- Don't use too much leading. Anything over 120 percent will break up the text and make it hard to read. If the typeface allows, you might consider cutting the leading down to 110 percent (see below and figure 6.10).

- Set your text ragged-right, since that's probably the only way to avoid excessive amounts of hyphenation and awkward blank spaces. Do use some hyphenation, however—otherwise, you'll have excessively jagged right margins.

Leading

I have tried to drum in the message that white space is important, urging you to be lavish in your use of white space. There is an exception to that general guideline. While white space within paragraphs is important, it is easy to overdo it.

The space between lines of a paragraph is called *leading* because typesetters originally used thin strips of lead to add the space when they were setting type by hand. The metal may be gone in desktop typesetting, but the term remains.

Leading is usually specified in terms of the total space between baselines (the bottoms of lowercase characters that lack descenders), either as a total point size or as a percentage of the type size. Thus, typical leading for 10-point type can be expressed as 10 on 12 or 120 percent—in both cases meaning that two points of extra space are allotted between lines. The most common guideline for normal leading is 120 percent; in many (perhaps most) cases, that's all you need to know about leading.

Automatic Leading

Many word-processing and desktop-publishing programs will set automatic leading values, typically 120 percent of type size. Thus, 11-point type may be set 11 on 13¼ (rounding to the nearest possible increment on a LaserJet or LaserWriter), and a 15-point headline may be set 15 on 18.

Most of the time, that's quite appropriate—but not always. Sometimes you may wish to use less than 120 percent leading in order to conserve space, and sometimes you may need to use more than 120 percent leading because of wide lines. Headings represent a special problem, which we'll get to in a moment.

This book is set 11 on 13, just under 120 percent leading—that's because Zapf Calligraphic can work successfully with less leading. Figure 6.8 shows 10-point Zapf Calligraphic set *solid* (with no extra leading) and with a single point extra (10 on 11); the latter will work very well for two-column newsletters, either as 10 on 11 or 11 on 12. For example, both the *LITA Newsletter* and *Information Standards Quarterly* use 11 on 12 Zapf Calligraphic for normal body text.

Zapf Calligraphic 10 on 10 ("set solid")

While typefaces used for body text should not call attention to themselves, this is not to say that the subtle differences among such typefaces are meaningless. Even among the best typefaces for body type—which are, generally, clear serif faces with open, readable designs—the differences will influence the overall look of text.

Zapf Calligraphic 10 on 11

While typefaces used for body text should not call attention to themselves, this is not to say that the subtle differences among such typefaces are meaningless. Even among the best typefaces for body type—which are, generally, clear serif faces with open, readable designs—the differences will influence the overall look of text.

Figure 6.8: Zapf Calligraphic, Less Leading

Setting type solid or with single-point leading can be dangerous or successful, depending on the typeface. Figure 6.9 shows Glyphix Baskerton set both solid and 10 on 11; because of the design of the type, neither example works very well, and the paragraph set solid loses legibility.

Glyphix Baskerton set 10 on 10 ("set solid")

While typefaces used for body text should not call attention to themselves, this is not to say that the subtle differences among such typefaces are meaningless. Even among the best typefaces for body type – which are, generally, clear serif faces with open, readable designs – the differences will influence the overall look of text.

Glyphix Baskerton set 10 on 11

While typefaces used for body text should not call attention to themselves, this is not to say that the subtle differences among such typefaces are meaningless. Even among the best typefaces for body type – which are, generally, clear serif faces with open, readable designs – the differences will influence the overall look of text.

Figure 6.9: Baskerton, Less Leading

If 20 percent leading is good, would 40 percent or 50 percent be better? Generally not, with the possible exception of very wide lines. Once the white space between lines expands beyond a certain point, the reader stops moving smoothly from one line to the next. The lines are no longer perceived as parts of a paragraph, but as individual, distinct lines. It only takes 2 or 3 extra points of leading to turn a paragraph into an apparent list of single-line items. Figure 6.10 shows Zapf Calligraphic set 10 on 14, 10 on 15, and 10 on 16; as you can see, the paragraph begins to lose definition or, at best, appear double-spaced.

Zapf Calligraphic set 10 on 14

While typefaces used for body text should not call attention to themselves, this is not to say that the subtle differences among such typefaces are meaningless. Even among the best typefaces for body type—which are, generally, clear serif faces with open, readable designs—the differences will influence the overall look of text.

Zapf Calligraphic set 10 on 15

While typefaces used for body text should not call attention to themselves, this is not to say that the subtle differences among such typefaces are meaningless. Even among the best typefaces for body type—which are, generally, clear serif faces with open, readable designs—the differences will influence the overall look of text.

Zapf Calligraphic set 10 on 16

While typefaces used for body text should not call attention to themselves, this is not to say that the subtle differences among such typefaces are meaningless. Even among the best typefaces for body type—which are, generally, clear serif faces with open, readable designs—the differences will influence the overall look of text.

Figure 6.10: Zapf Calligraphic, Excessive Leading

Adjustments for Headlines

Headings and subheadings need vertical space to set them off from body text, but if a heading runs to more than one line, it must not have too much vertical space between lines.

The default 120 percent leading may well leave too much white space in larger type sizes. Figure 6.11 shows a 19-point headline with 20 percent leading (19 on 23); although it is not terrible, it looks better with less space between lines, as in the second example (set 19 on 20). Many larger headline sizes look best with no additional leading.

Headline set 19 on 23

Make The Most of Your Multiline Headlines, Lest They Disrupt Your Document

Headline set 19 on 20

Make The Most of Your Multiline Headlines, Lest They Disrupt Your Document

---

Figure 6.11: Headline Type, 20 and 5 percent Leading

Proper spacing for headlines may require some experimentation. It will depend on the page layout, the typeface being used, possibly even the length of each line of the headline.

Note one other point about headlines that require more than one line: you should always be sure that the line breaks make sense. That means looking at each headline as it will be broken in the printed product and putting in explicit line breaks (if needed) so that the lines work reasonably well when read independently.

To sum up: the most effective use of white space is around text, not within paragraphs. Use enough leading in text and headlines to make the text easy to read, but don't use so much space that the lines become separated.

Hyphenation, Justification, Kerning, and Tracking

You need to consider one final aspect of body text: how the text fits into the line, and what you can do to make it fit better. Copyfitting, the job of making copy fit well into the space allotted for it, can involve decisions in five areas: hyphenation, justification, letterspacing, kerning, and tracking. It can also involve rewriting, but that's an editorial matter.

Three of those terms may be new: letterspacing, kerning, and tracking. They are defined more fully in the sections that follow, but briefly:

- *Letterspacing* is the addition of small spaces between letters within a word in order to justify a line, as opposed to adding all space between words;

- *Kerning* is the process of moving certain pairs of letters closer together so that words appear to be visually balanced;

- *Tracking* is the process of setting a portion of text either tighter (letters closer together) or looser (letters farther apart).

You won't worry about all five for any given document; you may not have any choice in some areas, and you may properly decide never to worry about other areas. But you should understand what each area involves, so that you can decide whether to think about it. In at least one case—tracking—you may find that a technique with little general application can be enormously useful in one or two special cases.

To Justify or Not to Justify?

Any good word-processing or desktop-publishing program will let you set text in one of four alignments or justifications:

- Left-aligned, also called left-justified or ragged-right, with the text lined up at the left margin and ragged (not aligned) at the right margin;

- Center-aligned or centered, with text distributed evenly around the center of a column;

- Right-aligned, also called right-justified or ragged-left, with the text lined up at the right margin and ragged at the left margin;

- Justified, also called fully justified, with the text aligned evenly at both margins.

Figure 6.12 shows the same paragraph treated each of the four ways—but with the only two plausible treatments together for close comparison. You would never center-align or right-align text except for very special occasions.[3] Like *shaped text*—text that runs on a slope or takes the shape of some object—centered and right-aligned text is so foreign to normal expectations that it substantially interferes with legibility.

Your real choice, in almost every case, is between ragged-right and justified text. You will not find a simple or universal guide for that choice, here or anywhere else: it is one of the most confounding choices in publishing.

Readability and Appearance

A number of writers assert that ragged-right text is inherently more readable. Theoretically, that should be true. Unlike justified text, ragged-right text always has exactly the same space between adjacent words, and hyphenation can usually be kept to a minimum. Both factors should make for easier reading—and definitely make for a more uniform "color" on the page, something that interests graphic designers a great deal more than it does readers.

---

3   If you're preparing a Hebrew document, you might very well right-align the text.

Centered

> While typefaces used for body text should not call attention to themselves, this is not to say that the subtle differences among such typefaces are meaningless. Even among the best typefaces for body type—which are, generally, clear serif faces with open, readable designs—the differences will influence the overall look of text.

Flush-Right

> While typefaces used for body text should not call attention to themselves, this is not to say that the subtle differences among such typefaces are meaningless. Even among the best typefaces for body type—which are, generally, clear serif faces with open, readable designs—the differences will influence the overall look of text.

Flush-Left or Ragged-Right

While typefaces used for body text should not call attention to themselves, this is not to say that the subtle differences among such typefaces are meaningless. Even among the best typefaces for body type—which are, generally, clear serif faces with open, readable designs—the differences will influence the overall look of text.

Justified or Fully-Justified

While typefaces used for body text should not call attention to themselves, this is not to say that the subtle differences among such typefaces are meaningless. Even among the best typefaces for body type—which are, generally, clear serif faces with open, readable designs—the differences will influence the overall look of text.

Figure 6.12: Alignment Options

But centuries of practice suggest that these theories are wrong. Tom Lichty notes that "for over 500 years printers, with the evident support of their readers, have determined that the sense of orderliness conveyed by justified type is preferable to consistent word spacing and ragged right margins."[4] He regards justified type as preferable for long works that require continuous reading and concentration; I agree.

Informal reports of readability studies suggest that neither ragged-right nor justified text is more readable—but that readers tire of ragged-right text more rapidly. Justification adds a finished look to a publication and a touch of formality; ragged-right publications appear more casual—but also, to some extent, unfinished.

For many library publications, there is no good reason to achieve that finished, formal look, but you may still find that you prefer justification for most documents. Should you justify a bibliography? There is absolutely no reason that you should—but, with today's best programs for handling justified type, there is also no good reason not to.

Designers who argue for ragged-right tend to do so primarily on the basis of appearance. Some assert that only professional typesetting equipment can do hyphenation and spacing accurately enough to produce adequate results with justified type. That was probably true in years past; it is almost certainly not true now, at least for the best desktop-publishing programs.

The Quality of Justification

Good-looking justified type—which involves all the remaining topics in this chapter except tracking—places heavy demands on software. It is one of the ways that the best desktop-publishing programs distinguish themselves from lesser desktop-publishing and most word-processing programs.

The most sensible approach in deciding whether a given class of publication should be justified is to get reactions from people who did not help to design the publication. Do a sample version two ways, with the only difference being justification. Show people both versions; ask which they like better—preferably without mentioning

---

4   Tom Lichty, *Design Principles for Desktop Publishers* (Glenview, Illinois: Scott, Foresman, 1989), 63.

what the difference is. That's what I did in preparing the final style for one newsletter, after an outside designer had recommended ragged-right text. In that case, I got the same reaction from everyone who looked at the samples: they weren't quite sure why, but they preferred the justified version.

Frankly, I'd be surprised if you don't get the same reaction—unless your reviewers are up on current design trends, of course. But if the people who look at the samples do find the ragged-right version more pleasing or more readable, then by all means use a ragged-right design.

Hyphenation

Justification requires hyphenation. If you do not hyphenate some words and your line widths are reasonable, you will certainly have lines that are much too short, requiring too much space to be added.

Any good word-processing program should provide some help with hyphenation, although the help may be as crude as pointing to the last character that will fit on a line and letting you determine the right place to break a word. Somewhat more helpful are word processors that incorporate simple algorithms for hyphenation; the suggested break points will usually be right, although they sometimes can be not only wrong but damagingly wrong (for example, algorithms will suggest hyphenating *therapist* before the *r*).

Of course, hyphenation help in your word processor won't help at all if you use desktop publishing—the breaks won't come at the same places. High-end desktop-publishing programs will do automatic hyphenation, but you still need to check the results; even the best hyphenation routines can make mistakes.

The best hyphenation comes from hyphenation dictionaries—either exception dictionaries (specific words that don't follow the algorithms) or relatively complete dictionaries. The latter methodology should be nearly 100 percent accurate, except that it won't include all the words you may use (particularly trade jargon).

You should be able to control the extent of hyphenation. Most typographers frown on text that shows more than two hyphens in a row (that is, more than two consecutive lines ending in hyphens). In some programs, you can determine the *zone* in which hyphenation is attempted—that is, how many letters can be missing from a line before the program attempts to break a word.

If you will be setting long documents fully justified, make sure you understand the hyphenation methodology your program uses. How closely do you need to check the results? Will the program show you problem lines, so that you can use additional hyphens if needed?

Any time you check hyphenation, you should have a good dictionary at hand and use it in questionable cases; that will assure that your hyphenation is consistent. You will probably make some mistakes or let some automatic mistakes get through—but those mistakes probably won't begin to compare with hyphenation errors in the daily newspaper.

Hyphenation rules are not universal. British practice for hyphenation follows derivation; American practice follows pronunciation. That makes a difference on quite a few words. Use an American dictionary if you are publishing for an American audience.

Hyphenation in Ragged Text

While ragged-right text reduces the need for and amount of hyphenation, it does not completely eliminate the need for it.

Many library publications will include quite a few long words along with the short. If a publication uses relatively narrow lines, totally unhyphenated text may sometimes yield lines that are absurdly short relative to adjacent lines. While the informality of ragged-right text may be desirable, that extreme jaggedness is never desirable in normal body text.

Wordspacing and Letterspacing

You can ignore this topic entirely if you choose ragged-right text. The space between adjacent words should always be a standard space— probably about ¼ em for a typical program. An *em* for any given font equals the point size; the name is based on the tradition that a lowercase *m* is as wide as the font is high. Letters should always be spaced in a manner determined by the width tables for the typeface, possibly modified by kerning tables (discussed later in this chapter).

Justified text requires adding space somewhere within most lines. That's one reason that justified Courier and other monospaced text frequently looked so awful: all that some programs and printers could do was add full spaces, so that some words had double or triple spaces between them while others were normal.

No good-quality contemporary program justifies proportional type in that manner. If you don't specify anything else, the extra space should be apportioned evenly among all the words, so that the space between each word pair is almost exactly the same size. The spaces between words on one line will be a different width than the spaces in the lines above or below, but each line's wordspacing should be internally consistent.

That, incidentally, is one reason that you are always told not to leave two spaces between sentences when you use proportional type and justification. The program will add extra space to each blank, thus making the space much too wide.

Avoiding the White Rivers

The worst effects of justification are "rivers of white," wide spaces on adjacent lines that appear close enough together to create patterns of white in the midst of text. These rivers interrupt the flow of text and introduce a foreign element that can be disruptive.

You can generally avoid rivers by careful hyphenation, particularly if your program signals which lines are *loose*—that is, which lines have blanks wider than a predetermined width. You may be able to specify that width, possibly by specifying the minimum, standard, and maximum wordspaces.

One other technique will also avoid rivers of white, but it must be used carefully. That technique is *letterspacing*—adding space between the letters within a word as well as between words.

Figure 6.13 shows a troublesome paragraph—one where it is not possible to make lines fit well through hyphenation—with and without letterspacing. The first (left) version does wind up with awkward spaces between words; the second, with letterspacing, eliminates the widest spaces.

Letterspacing has a bad name among most designers, but typographers have used it as a last-ditch solution for decades if not centuries. Programs that do letterspacing should use the smallest available increment, $\frac{1}{300}$ inch, for spacing between letters. That increment will rarely be noticeable, and certainly not as noticeable as the wide wordspaces. If you use Bitstream typefaces or others with similarly tight spacing, modest letterspacing will be even more acceptable; typefaces with looser normal spacing may not work so well. This book, incidentally, does use letterspacing—although it is very rarely needed with a 27-pica line.

Wordspacing

While typefaces used for body text should not call attention to themselves, this is not to say that the subtle differences among such typefaces are meaningless. Even among the best typefaces for body type—which are, generally, clear serif faces with open, readable designs— the differences will influence the overall look of text. Think through your text.

Letterspacing

While typefaces used for body text should not call attention to themselves, this is not to say that the subtle differences among such typefaces are meaningless. Even among the best typefaces for body type—which are, generally, clear serif faces with open, readable designs— the differences will influence the overall look of text. Think through your text.

Figure 6.13: Wordspacing and Letterspacing

Kerning

When proportional typefaces first became available for microcomputer use, traditionalists argued—as some still do—that no laser printer or microcomputer could ever produce truly professional output. One reason for that, in the beginning, was that word-processing packages did not kern letters—and most still don't.

Kerning is (generally) the process of moving letters so that they look better within a word. The most common current meaning, however, is specifically the process of moving certain letters closer to certain other letters so that the letter-to-letter spacing is visually consistent. The name derives from the *kern* in metal type, the portion of a character that extends beyond the type body—such as the descender in the italic letter *f*.

Phototypesetting systems include two categories of spacing information for specific typefaces: width tables, showing the width of each character, and kerning pairs and tables, showing the pairs of letters that should be kerned and how much the second letter should be moved left.

Many desktop-publishing programs can also now read and use kerning tables. Most PostScript typefaces and all Bitstream typefaces include kerning tables—and the tables for Bitstream typefaces are quite complete.

In some cases, the kerning done on a microcomputer will be better than through average-quality traditional typesetting. (I became aware of this because of the name *LITA*—in which the *T* and *A* should be kerned. A quick check of LITA publications, produced traditionally, showed that although kerning had definitely been used in the typesetting, the *TA* pair had not been kerned.)

If the program you use supports kerning and the typefaces include kerning information, you can probably decide whether or not to kern, and then the software will handle it all automatically. That's the only realistic way to kern body text; doing it manually takes too long for too little gain. If your software supports manual kerning but not automatic kerning, your best bet is not to worry about it except in headlines.

Figure 6.14 shows the same paragraph with the first version kerned—as is all Bitstream text in this book—and the second version not kerned. The paragraph includes some words for which kerning makes a significant difference. In most ordinary text, the lack of kerning will never disturb a reader. Kerning is a nicety, not a necessity. Note that the Glyphix examples in this book do not include kerning—but the letters are set so tight that they sometimes give the same effect as kerning. Some letters appear to be kerned regardless of kerning tables; for example, both *j* and *J* in figure 6.14 tuck under the previous letter even if kerning is turned off.

Should you ever turn kerning off? Yes, for the screen display of body text. If on-screen kerning is supported at all, it probably slows down the software and does not really tell you much. But I can't imagine why you would prefer to leave any printed text unkerned if you have the choice. Some writers say that kerning doesn't matter for body text. While they are right to the extent that it isn't critical, they are otherwise wrong. Like other niceties, kerning does slightly improve the readability of text. Your best bet is to turn kerning on globally, if you can, and then not worry about it for body text.

Kerned Type

Fonts vary widely in design and quality. Tests for legibility require not only "character-set runs," e.g. [ABCDE FGHIJ KLMNO PQRST UVWXYZ abcde fghij klmno pqrst uvwxyz 12345 67890 :;?{} !@#$% ^ &*()], but also difficult words—such as LITA, Two and Wave or WAVE. Add a Proper Name such as Johannes Gutenberg or François Cézanne and a sentence such as The quick brown fox jumps over the lazy dog.

Same Type without Kerning

Fonts vary widely in design and quality. Tests for legibility require not only "character-set runs," e.g. [ABCDE FGHIJ KLMNO PQRST UVWXYZ abcde fghij klmno pqrst uvwxyz 12345 67890 :;?{} !@#$% ^ &*()], but also difficult words—such as LITA, Two and Wave or WAVE. Add a Proper Name such as Johannes Gutenberg or François Cézanne and a sentence such as The quick brown fox jumps over the lazy dog.

Figure 6.14: Kerned and Unkerned Text

Tracking

This last aspect of pure text design can also be safely ignored most of the time, but it may occasionally come in handy. Tracking is like letterspacing—but it is uniformly applied to a specified area of text, and it can move letters either closer together or further apart. Tight tracking moves all letters in a defined area closer together. Loose tracking moves them further apart.

Why would you want to adjust the tracking? Normally, you would not—at least not for body text. (Tracking for headlines is discussed briefly in the next chapter.) One exception might be if you find that a particular typeface is "set loose"—that is, that the letters are generally not close enough together. If you don't know enough to modify the width table—and if you do, you're far more expert than most desktop publishers (including me)—you might consider defining paragraphs in that typeface for slightly tighter tracking. Try it first; it may not work well. By some people's standards, Glyphix typefaces and some Bitstream typefaces may already be set too tight;

slightly looser tracking would open up the text in a manner that some people might prefer.

Neither of those cases is particularly likely. Realistically, the only time you will use tracking for body text (unless you really need a special visual effect) is if you must adjust the amount of space taken up by some text and have no better way to do that. For example, say that you have a list of contributors that you need to publish, including the city and state in which each contributor lives. On your first trial, you find that the list runs just two lines longer than the page— and that two or three contributors' name/address listings require a second line, with the state abbreviation being the only text on the second line.

This is a case for specific tracking. By selecting the complete name and address for each such case and tracking it very slightly tighter, you may be able to fit the state into the first line without seriously affecting the legibility or appearance of the list. If you can do that twice, you can fit the whole list on a single page.

Figure 6.15 shows the same paragraph three times, each time set in Zapf Calligraphic 10 on 12. The three examples use progressively tighter tracking. The first example, tracked $\frac{1}{50}$ em tighter (or 2 percent tighter), is acceptable by most standards and can solve some spacing problems. The second and third examples show the effects of excessively tight tracking: letters begin to collapse into one another.

Figure 6.16 shows looser tracking. By the last example, the text is "falling apart"—substantially reducing readability. Loose tracking does have special uses, primarily for headlines; it rarely has any use in body text.

If your software supports tracking on a paragraph-by-paragraph level, you might want to define one paragraph version that tracks text slightly tighter. If a particular paragraph leaves just one word on the last line, or a piece of text runs slightly longer than the space available, or a paragraph seems to have terrible hyphenation problems—try tracking it a little tighter and see if the problems go away. (A few paragraphs in this book are tracked 2 percent tight.)

Text Set Tight (Tracked -2%)

While typefaces used for body text should not call attention to themselves, this is not to say that the subtle differences among such typefaces are meaningless. Even among the best typefaces for body type—which are, generally, clear serif faces with open, readable designs—the differences will influence the overall look of text.

Text Set Very Tight (Tracked -6%)

While typefaces used for body text should not call attention to themselves, this is not to say that the subtle differences among such typefaces are meaningless. Even among the best typefaces for body type—which are, generally, clear serif faces with open, readable designs—the differences will influence the overall look of text.

Text Set Too Tight (Tracked -10%)

While typefaces used for body text should not call attention to themselves, this is not to say that the subtle differences among such typefaces are meaningless. Even among the best typefaces for body type—which are, generally, clear serif faces with open, readable designs—the differences will influence the overall look of text.

Figure 6.15: Tight Tracking

Conclusion

This chapter points out some of the factors you should consider in designing the ordinary text of a publication. Fortunately, you can ignore most of these factors after an initial decision. Some, such as tracking, you can most often ignore entirely.

When you read in a book or magazine that you *must* have a large collection of typefaces in order to do effective desktop publishing, remember the writer's intended audience—most probably, people doing advertising and similarly design-intensive work. For a typical library publishing program, a collection of three or four good type families will probably meet all of your needs; two may even be sufficient. I have never seen a publication that looked bad simply because it used too few typefaces (as distinguished from styles and

Text Set Loose (Tracked +2%)

While typefaces used for body text should not call attention to themselves, this is not to say that the subtle differences among such typefaces are meaningless. Even among the best typefaces for body type—which are, generally, clear serif faces with open, readable designs—the differences will influence the overall look of text.

Text Set Very Loose (Tracked +6%)

While typefaces used for body text should not call attention to themselves, this is not to say that the subtle differences among such typefaces are meaningless. Even among the best typefaces for body type—which are, generally, clear serif faces with open, readable designs—the differences will influence the overall look of text.

Text Set Absurdly Loose (Tracked +10%)

While typefaces used for body text should not call attention to themselves, this is not to say that the subtle differences among such typefaces are meaningless. Even among the best typefaces for body type—which are,

Figure 6.16: Loose Tracking

font sizes). On the other hand, I've seen hundreds that look bad because they use too many.

The next chapter deals with aspects of text design that enrich the page. Many of those aspects require more conscious effort than the items in this chapter. The decisions discussed in this chapter, however, will determine the overall readability of your document.

Tips and Reminders

- All body text within a publication should usually be a single serif typeface. Headings should either use the same typeface or a distinctly different typeface.

- Body text should be no smaller than 9 points and no larger than 12 points, except that large-print publications should use 16 point type. Text smaller than 9 points should be reserved for footnotes and text that won't be read at length.

- The best designs for reading comfort contain 50 to 70 characters per line; that usually means that a column (measured in picas) is 1½ to 2½ times the type size (measured in points).

- Most typefaces work well with 120 percent leading for body text, but some typefaces work equally well with slightly less leading. Multiple-line headlines almost always look better with less leading, and frequently they look best with no leading at all. Excessive leading can destroy the continuity of text.

- Justified text appears more formal than ragged-right text and may be more comfortable to read over the long term. Flush-right and centered text should never be used except for special effects.

- Justified text requires good hyphenation; selective hyphenation will also improve ragged-right text.

- Use wordspacing and letterspacing carefully, to avoid awkward white space within text and to maintain readability.

- Kerning makes text look better, but it isn't worth doing manually. If your software supports it, use it.

- Tracking can be useful for special effects or to solve spacing problems, but it should be used very carefully, since it can destroy readability.

7

Finishing the Document

After you establish the overall document design, the margins and general layout, the proper choice of typefaces and suitable font sizes, leading decisions, and other aspects of textual typography, you must give some thought to the way that those elements become a publication.

Textual design elements that add overall clarity to a document include the identification of paragraphs; use of headings; control of widows and orphans; the relation of headings to text; and special elements within the text itself, such as lists and quoted material. A number of typographic special effects can serve graphic roles similar to illustrations; examples include big initial letters, pull quotes, reverse type, rules, borders, and shading.

All of these elements must be considered in combination as part of a unified document. A series of individually reasonable decisions about styling the text can result in a muddled overall design, just as a combination of half a dozen individually useful special graphic effects can ruin the readability of a publication. Just as for graphics, the general rule for adding finishing touches to text is to use a few design elements well.

The last section of this chapter mentions some aspects of the final steps in desktop publishing: putting it on paper and, for all but single-copy publications, getting that paper reproduced. Most decisions on reproduction techniques depend heavily on your own setting, but a few words here may be generally useful.

Some key points in this chapter should be stated up front.

- Paragraphs and other groupings of text should be recognizable.
- Most lengthy documents need variety to break up long stretches of text.
- Special effects, used sparsely and carefully, can increase interest without decreasing readability.
- Special papers can yield better printed products than standard paper, and laser printers can print directly on a variety of special papers.

Ransom Notes

Remember some of the documents you probably received in the last few years that were generated by enthusiastic Macintosh owners, particularly new Mac users? Freed from the tyranny of Courier and boring dot-matrix typefaces by all those strikingly different typefaces on the Mac screen (with the ImageWriter ready to reproduce them all), many new users went a little overboard. You'd see half a dozen different typefaces in a simple announcement, and wildly inappropriate typefaces used for minutes and reports. One name for that overuse of typefaces is "ransom-note typography."

Times have changed. With desktop publishing and the spread of downloadable typefaces for word processing, MS-DOS owners can now go just as crazy with typefaces as Mac owners did.

Figure 7.1, while certainly not in the style of a ransom note, illustrates what would currently be considered ransom-note typography. It uses far too many typefaces, combined in ways that make no sense typographically. This figure also shows the other problem common to early extremes of Mac output: the fonts are defined at screen resolution and look coarse on the page.

Yes, your publications should be interesting; yes, they should show variety. Variety and interest come from a few good devices used carefully and from interesting material presented well—not from throwing new typefaces and sizes onto the page for each new story. That results in confusion and irritation, not variety and interest.

Staff Comings and Goings

PDC to SCPL

Congratulations to Pat Cross on her new position as Interlending Coordinator at South City Public Library. Pat began her career at Halltown in Public Services, and has been in the A/V Department since September 1983. The Interlibrary Loan staff is looking forward to having a long time friend available as a colleague at SCPL for support and help.

Jack Takes a Trip

For nearly four years, Jack Donagan has officially been secretary to the director and unofficially our Main Man for information, explanation, guidance and cheer. Jack has left Halltown to work for an outfit much closer to his new home, the Halltown Transit Authority. Jack, we wish you friends and colleagues in your new environment who will appreciate your extraordinary qualities of charm and grace, efficiency and thoughtfulness as much as we have. Farewell friend.

Serials Librarian Appointed at West Branch

Samantha Cook was recently named Serials Librarian in charge of the Serials Department at West Branch Library. Prior to her appointment, Samantha was an original cataloger at Halltown Main. Samantha has been part of HCL since 1975, when she received her MLS from the California State University at San Jose. She continues to be active in the HCL Crosstown Cycling Association; her new extension is 745.

Farewell to Shere Granados

With her retirement at the end of April, Shere Granados brought to a close more than 15 years of service to Halltown City Library. While at HCL, her primary responsibility was the processing of audiovisual materials—first 16mm films and vinyl sound recordings, now videocassettes and compact discs. Shere witnessed first-hand HCL's transition from manual to computer-supported systems -- and, after our slight problem with the Vendor Who Shall Be Unnamed, the transition back to manual. She has, indeed, seen many changes.

Inside Look at Hall Corporation Oral History Project

The Hall Corporation Oral History Project at HCL, funded by Hall Corporation and the National Endowment for the Humanities, is an effort to document the people and effort that made Hall Corporation what it is today, not only the largest employer in Halltown but one of the shiny spots in an otherwise rusty economy.

The HCL Staff Association invites you to a behind-the-scenes look at the challenges and rewards to librarians working on the Project. Jenna Connan will speak on

Figure 7.1: "Ransom Note" Design

Staff Events

PDC to SCPL

Congratulations to Pat Cross on her new position as Interlending Coordinator at South City Public Library. Pat began her career at Halltown in Public Services, and has been in the A/V Departments since September 1983. The Interlibrary Loan staff is looking forward to having a long time friend available as a colleague at SCPL for support and help.

Jack Takes a Trip

For nearly four years, Jack Donagan has officially been secretary to the director and unofficially our Main Man for information, explanation, guidance and cheer. Jack has left Halltown to work for an outfit much closer to his new home, the Halltown Transit Authority. Jack, we wish you friends and colleagues in your new environment who will appreciate your extraordinary qualities of charm and grace, efficiency and thoughtfulness as much as we have. Farewell friend.

Serials Librarian Appointed at West Branch

Samantha Cook was recently named Serials Librarian in charge of the Serials Department at West Branch Library. Prior to her appointment, Samantha was an original cataloger at Halltown Main. Samantha has been part of HCL since 1975, when she received her MLS from the California State University at San Jose. She continues to be active in the HCL Crosstown Cycling Association; her new extension is 745.

Farewell to Shere Granados

With her retirement at the end of April, Shere Granados brought to a close more than 15 years of service to Halltown City Library. While at HCL, her primary responsibility was the processing of audiovisual materials--first 16mm films and vinyl sound recordings, now videocassettes and compact discs. Shere witnessed first-hand HCL's transition from manual to computer-supported systems--and, after our slight problem with the Vendor Who Shall Be Unnamed, the transition back to manual. She has, indeed, seen many changes.

Inside Look at Hall Corporation Oral History Project

The Hall Corporation Oral History Project at HCL, funded by Hall Corporation and the National Endowment for the Humanities, is an effort to document the people and effort that made Hall Corporation what it is today, not only the largest employer in Halltown but one of the shiny spots in an otherwise rusty economy. The HCL Staff Association invites you to a behind-the-scenes look at the challenges and rewards to librarians working on the Project. Jenna Connan will speak on May 31, 12:15-1:30 in the West Conference Room, on "The HCOH Project." All staff are invited to bring a bag lunch and join us.

Attention New Staff

The Library Personnel Office has scheduled a new employee orientation which includes a slide show and discussion about the Halltown City Library. The orientation is scheduled for Friday, May 26, 9011 a.m. in East Conference Room. Please reserve a space by contacting Judy Dallas, acting secretary for the director, at extension 121.

Performance Evaluation of Reference Librarians

"Performance Evaluation of Reference Librarians: A Model, Dialogue, and Discussion" is the topic of the May 19 workshop sponsored by the Northwest Regional Academic Reference Librarians Discussion Interest Group. Featuring Anne Kreitz, Head of General Reference Services at Northwest State and Kudola Nailmon, personnel director for the Northwest State Library System, the program is scheduled for 1:30-3:30 p.m. at the Southern Northeast Community College Library Conference

Figure 7.2: Same Content, Simpler Design

Of course, you will probably prepare a few examples of ransom-note typography as you experiment with new typefaces and techniques. There's nothing wrong with that—as long as you don't regard those creations as serious publications.

Figure 7.2 shows the same material as in figure 7.1 with the typographic variety reduced to a minimum. You may regard figure 7.2 as dull by comparison—but a reader will focus on the content of the brief stories, not on the muddled mix of typography.

LaserCrud

Most Macintosh owners learned restraint and figured out that the fonts that looked best on screen weren't always the best fonts for printed output. Most desktop publishers learn early on that you should never use half a dozen typefaces on a single page. We've moved away from the low-resolution typefaces of the ImageWriter.

Ransom-note typography may be a thing of the past, but we may never wholly escape the more subtle problem of LaserCrud. Laser-Crud, as the name suggests, is cruddy-looking printed output generated on laser printers—and, more specifically, output that looks bad because it abuses the best ideas and tools.

Figure 7.3 suffers from LaserCrud. It uses a number of different techniques to add variety to a publication, each technique valid in its own right. Unfortunately, it uses them all, and it uses them too frequently. The result? Even though only two typefaces appear on the page, and there is no individual element that you can call bad, the page is disjointed, confused, and disruptive. In other words, LaserCrud.

It would be easy to generate dozens of different versions, each suffering from different forms of LaserCrud. Some of them might not bother you—and, indeed, many forms of LaserCrud are in the eye and taste of the reader or reviewer. My interesting document design may be your LaserCrud. To my eye, many of the designs offered up in magazines and books on desktop publishing are LaserCrud—including many of the illustrations intended to show the successful results of correcting design problems.

Not only will you probably produce LaserCrud while you're learning to use the tools at hand and experimenting with new designs, but it's also quite probable that you will produce real publi-

LaserCrud Newsletter

Format Integration: Implementation Plans

*A*n overflow crowd attended this meeting on implementation plans for the integrated USMARC formats. Mary Alice Ball of Loyola University introduced the program with a brief history of USMARC and introduced the proposals to integrate the formats.

Handling the Additions and Subtractions

*S*ally McCallum (Library of Congress) discussed the goal of creating a single format for all materials.

The Problems

*T*hree problems were identified:
- 1) meaningless fields,
- 2) multivalued fields, and
- 3) useless fields.

The Tasks

*T*hese problems led to three tasks:
- ☐ 1) weed out the useless fields,
- ☐ 2) resolve conflicts, and
- ☐ 3) extend elements.

The Changes

*T*hree types of change were identified: extensions, obsolete elements and deletions.

Extensions add subfields and values to formats *in which they were not previously valid.*

Obsolete elements are fields and subfields *that will continue to appear in USMARC documentation but which will no longer be used;* the elements will not be reassigned.

Deletions are fields, subfields and values *that will be removed from USMARC documentation and can be reassigned in the future.*

... *obsolete elements are fields and subfields that will continue to appear in US-MARC documentation but which will no longer be used; the elements will not be reassigned.*

McCallum gave examples of these changes, then discussed conflict resolution. One example of conflict is byte 6 of the 008 field, for which the meanings of values *c* and *d* differ in monographs and serials. In the integrated formats, serial values will remain as defined; monographs will change, with *t* replacing *c* for "actual date and copyright date" and *e* replacing *d* for "detailed date.

... *many of the items that will be affected by the new format are likely to be on a library's cataloging problem shelf at this time.*

McCallum noted that the impact on linking entry fields of extending values across all formats is not yet known.

Coordinating Implementation at the Utilities and LC

*K*athleen Bales (Research Libraries Group, Inc.) reported that the Library of Congress will be ready for implementation in 1993. She pointed out that, with the Linked Systems Project and other data-sharing projects, implementation cannot occur until all of the utilities are ready.

Some portions of integrated USMARC can be used immediately, such as cases where an existing field will be used for data currently in another field that will become obsolete. Changes involving new fields, subfields and values cannot be implemented without preparation by the utilities.

Bales then gave the status of each U.S. utility:

◊ *LC is currently planning to complete new automated systems by the end of 1993, and hopes to release more details of the schedule by the end of 1989.*

◊ *OCLC's implementation depends on their new system development. OCLC plans to do batch conversions, since they have multiple copies of their database. The OCLC 007 input patterns are very flexible.*

Figure 7.3: LaserCrud

cations that, to some people's eyes, are LaserCrud. Sometimes, it seems unavoidable: choices that you make in order to complete a publication make you wince when you look back at it months later.

That kind of reaction may be inevitable, and it may not be so bad. If you can look back at the page and spot what went wrong, it shows that your design sense is improving. Sometimes, going a bit too far in one direction is the only effective way to arrive at the middle ground.

These things happen. Deadlines and conflicting priorities will sometimes combine to ensure that LaserCrud develops. Fortunately, most readers, most of the time, won't be offended by—or even notice—any but the most egregious instances of LaserCrud. If the front page of a publication or article is inviting enough to get them started, some interior flaws probably won't stop them.

Design for Overall Clarity

A clear document makes sense textually, has a transparent organization, and looks good—or at least good enough so that the appearance does not interfere with the text.

How do you evaluate the look of a document? One traditional method is to look at a proof copy upside down; by turning the pages over, you can evaluate the appearance without thinking about the text itself. Another is to set out the printed page or pair of pages and step back far enough so that you can no longer read the body text.

Paragraph and heading design influence overall appearance as well as lucidity. Lists and special text also influence the overall look of a document and separate material for special attention. Textual widows and orphans affect appearance; stranded headings look awful and can reduce the coherence of a document.

Paragraphs

You need only consider four basic questions when designing standard paragraphs for a document:

- Should the first line of a paragraph be indented—and, if so, how far?
- Should there be white space above a paragraph—and, if so, how much?
- Should all regular paragraphs be treated the same?
- Are the paragraphs too short or too long?

The normal answer to the first and second question is that you should either indent the first line of a paragraph or leave white space above it, but not both.

The worst possible solution—but one that you will find in some publications—is to do neither. In that case, the only clue to a new paragraph is the short line at the end of the preceding paragraph and the capital letter that begins the new paragraph. That demands a lot of effort from the reader. It turns the page into a solid mass of gray, giving the eye no easy way to separate paragraphs. I can see no justification for ever using such a design, no matter how stylish it might be.

The two customary methods of separating paragraphs lend slightly different feels to the material. If your text is intended to be continuous, with paragraphs serving as logical breaks but not as discontinuities, you should probably indent the paragraphs. If paragraphs tend to be distinct subtopics with relatively little connection, you may be better off with white space. And, frankly, while it may be frowned on in some quarters, you may very well prefer to use both indents and white space in this case.

A typical paragraph indentation in typesetting is narrower than in typewriting. One good guideline is to indent 1 em for narrow columns (e.g., two-column layouts) and 2 ems for wide columns (single-column pages), possibly 3 ems for overly-wide lines. Remember that an em is always the point size; thus, for 11-point type, suitable indentations might be 11 and 22 points for narrow and wide columns.

One good rule for vertical spacing is that you should never leave the equivalent of a full line. Once you do that, the paragraphs become so separated that the visual flow of text is lost. If your software doesn't allow fractional-line spacing, don't use vertical spacing. If it does, roughly half a line—perhaps 6 or 7 points for 11 on 13 typography—is probably the most space you should use.

You will find that your publications generally look better if paragraphs immediately following headings and subheadings are not indented. There will usually be some vertical space below a heading, and the indentation isn't needed.

Full-page paragraphs, whether in training manuals or other publications, pose a barrier to readability, while extremely short paragraphs impose a choppiness on the page appearance and the flow of content. Writers may object to the idea that paragraph length is part of document design, but it is, just as much as the level of vocabulary is part of overall publication design. It may not matter that long paragraphs are aesthetically displeasing—but it does matter that they encourage the reader to give up on a publication.

Keeping It Together: Widows and Orphans

Text should flow, and headings should precede text in a logical way. You should always control breaks across pages or columns to prevent bad breaks; as almost all unsightly elements do, bad breaks disrupt the flow of a document.

A bad break can simply be incorrect hyphenation—and you should double-check the hyphenation in a document—but more frequently it is one of the following:

- A *widow*, the last line of a paragraph appearing at the top of the next column or page, isolated from the remainder of the text. While widows are mostly unsightly, they also cause a loss of context, since the column or page break inherently forces a slight break in reading.

- An *orphan*, the first line of a paragraph appearing isolated at the bottom of a column or page. Not only is an orphan more unsightly than a widow, but it also does more damage to continuity.

- A *stranded heading*, any heading or subheading appearing at the bottom of a column or page without some portion of the text that it heads. This bad break is the most disruptive; it destroys the logical relationship between heading and text.

- A table, figure, or otherwise self-contained entity that breaks across a page or column.

- A single word as the last line in a paragraph, called a widow by some typographers.

- A hyphenated word ending a column or page (and, thus, beginning the next column or page in mid-word).

Ideally, you should avoid all of these—although few desktop publishers (or readers) concern themselves much with the last two cases. Depending on the software you use, you will find some bad breaks very easy to control, while others may require more work than you're willing to take on.

Widows and Orphans

Some advanced word-processing and desktop-publishing programs provide direct control over widows and orphans, typically defaulting to prevent them but allowing you to change the option. In that case, simply make sure that the option is on. When either an orphan or a widow is impending, the line in question (the first line of a paragraph for an orphan, or the next-to-last line for a widow) will be moved to the next column or page automatically.

Unfortunately, some such programs do not control widows and orphans. In that case, your only options are to go through manually forcing new pages when needed (if you can do that without also starting new paragraphs) or to live with the orphans and widows.

If I had to do it manually, I would probably let widows be—but there's really no excuse for orphans, since you can always add blank lines before the paragraph or force a new page directly. Naturally, you should not be concerned with those details until the final stage of preparation.

Stranded Headings

A widow or orphan may look unprofessional, but a stranded heading looks stupid. Allowing a stranded heading to survive into a printed publication is a sign of complete carelessness. There is absolutely no excuse for stranded headings. If you must control them manually, do so as the final preproduction step; it is always a serious error to leave a stranded heading in place.

Fortunately, the same programs that automatically control widows and orphans will make sure that headings appear on the same page as the text below them—as long as you let the programs know what they should do. The controls will probably be part of a style sheet, tag, or similar device; the terminology might be "keep with next" or "keep follow" or something along those lines.

As you define headings, make sure to set these controls—and also controls to disallow breaking within the headings (since a two-line heading broken across pages is just as silly as a heading separated from its content). Once you've done that, you can relax.

Broken Tables

The solution for stranded headings is also typically the solution for broken tables—and, since a table should usually be captioned, both parts of the solution make sense.

That is, if you define a table as a special form of paragraph, you should specify that it must appear within a single page, and probably that it should appear with the next paragraph (the caption).

Any coherent program that provides for inserted figures will assure that those figures stay on a single page—either because they don't move as the text is revised, or because the movement is controlled.

Short Last Lines

Should you worry about short last lines? I don't, but you may have more exacting typographic standards. Yes, it makes sense to avoid a hyphenated word portion as the only contents of a last line, but even that is a nicety. You'll find short last lines in almost every book; there are two worst-case short last lines on page 1 of this book, for example. Did you notice them as you were reading?

If short last lines bother you, you're on your own. To the best of my knowledge, none of the popular word-processing or desktop-publishing programs will do anything to prevent such an occurrence. You can use one of three strategies to prevent short last lines manually:

- Force the previous word down to the next line. This will probably make the next-to-last line loose, and is probably the worst way to control a short last line.

- Rewrite the paragraph to either eliminate a word or add one or two words.

- Track the entire paragraph differently, if you have that ability—either slightly tighter, to pop the word up to the previous line, or slightly looser, to force another word down.

Your best bet? Ignore the situation. That's what professional publishers do; a book without single-word last lines is a rarity.

Words Broken across Page Boundaries

When you think about this, it sounds bad: a single hyphenated word broken across two pages. But in the real world...well, while writing this section, I opened up the *Chicago Manual of Style* and Tom Lichty's *Design Principles for Desktop Publishers*—opening to a random page in each case. In both cases, a word was broken across pages within two pages of the random opening. A little further checking says that this sort of break is like short last lines: the professionals don't worry about it. Most probably, neither should you.[1]

If you decide to tackle it, your weapons are the same as for short last lines, with one addition: you should be able to tell the program that this particular word can't be hyphenated, which will force the entire word to the next column or page.

Headings

Depending on your printer and software, and the disk space available, you may be able to generate type as large as 120-point, 256-point, or even 720-point—that last being roughly the printable height of a standard letter sheet. For most purposes, those limits are much larger than anything you will use.

Signs are an exception; if you produce signs with your desktop equipment—as you probably should—you will find a single 60-point font to be useful, probably accompanied by a compatible 30-point font and possibly one or two sizes in between. Type that large is *display type*, really useful only for signs and other special situations—including, for example, the banner of a newsletter or cover of a special

---

1   Examples in this book include pages 19–20 and 27–28.

publication. The only reasonable limit on the size of such type is what fits the situation. Inch-high (72-point) type is not at all unusual for banners or covers. Figure 7.4 shows some fairly typical headline sizes: 24, 30, 48, 60, and 72 points.

Figure 7.4: Headline Type Sizes

Headings tend to fall into a narrower range. One rule of thumb is that each level of heading should be 2 points smaller than the next higher level, with the smallest heading either being the same size as body type (but boldface or italic) or 2 points larger. Chapter titles (in a manual) or article titles (in a newsletter) become the highest level of heading.

Thus, a newsletter set in 11-point type might use 13-point subheads, 15-point major heads, and 17-point headlines. If you use pull quotes, they might be 2 or 4 points larger than body type.

The largest type in a typical publication might be big initial letters, if you use them. Such letters can be twice the size of body type or much larger. This book uses 24-point big initial letters. Some publications use initial letters that take up three, four, or even five lines; the type might be 72 points or larger in such cases.

Don't get carried away with big headings for normal materials. Anything much larger than twice normal body size requires special care in designing the page; letters effectively become bigger at a faster rate than the actual increase in type size. That's partially a matter of appearance and partially reality: remember that 22-point type occupies four times as much space as 11-point type, not twice as much.

If the watchword for very large headlines is caution, the word for very large subheadings is *don't*. The effect is to break the document apart into little individual pieces, since any type that is considerably larger than regular type effectively serves to end one logical document and begin another. Subheadings should serve to open up text and organize it; any type larger than, say, 150 percent of regular body size will disrupt the text.

One other general rule: don't use all-capital headlines except in special situations. Any all-capitalized text is hard to read (it has substantially less variety than lowercase text); if you want the added intensity that an all-caps heading will provide, try using a larger or bolder font instead.

Line Breaks and Hierarchy

You can establish a hierarchy of headings in any of several ways, already discussed in previous chapters. The general rules here are straightforward:

- Establish a clear hierarchy and use it consistently throughout a document;

- Don't use too many levels or too many headings; rarely does a document need more than four levels of heading.

Headings may take on special forms, particularly in newsletters and similar publications. You may add kickers (brief text lines just above a headline that add textual interest) or bylines; you may even add blurbs—short, lively summaries of articles that appear just below the heading, usually in a special font. You may also use rules or boxes to set off headings; rules and boxes are discussed later in this chapter.

Figure 7.5, part of a page scanned from *Information Standards Quarterly*, shows a kicker (*"CD-ROM? That's Publishing!"*) and a byline (*Paul Evan Peters*). You've seen blurbs in almost every magazine, either above or below article titles; in journals, blurbs become formalized as abstracts.

Figure 7.5: Kicker, Headline and Byline

Nearly every publication you prepare will use headings of some sort, even those that consist only of a title and body text. The general rule for headings is to treasure and exploit the variety they add to the page, but to use restraint. Don't have extremely long headlines (anything more than three lines is pushing it); don't have too many headlines on a page; don't use headlines that overpower the page.

Bulleted Lists

Bulleted paragraphs, used throughout this book, highlight individual points in a list while allowing room for textual expansion of each point. Some programs will allow you to define a bulleted paragraph as an entity, including the definition of the bullet itself. In some cases, you might use a pointing hand, an arrow, a check mark, or some other device to introduce each paragraph.

Figure 7.6, also scanned from *Information Standards Quarterly*, shows the use of a special character (in the Symbol typeface) to set off special list entries in a newsletter that also uses standard bullets. The page also shows simple tabular lists (the voting results) and the use of a special closing device, the small boxed *ISQ*.

⇒ *Z39.41-1979: Book Spine Formats.* Balloting period: September 6, 1988-December 9, 1988.

Results:

34	Yes
9	Yes with comments
5	No (LC; STC; AJL; MedLA; ALA)
3	Abstain

Comments have been sent to B. Tannehill for resolution.

⇒ *Z39.57-198x: Non-Serials Holdings.* Balloting period was December 1, 1988 to March 15, 1989. This standard was *approved* and will be forwarded for publication.

Results:

41	Yes
7	Yes with comments (NLM; MusLA; LC; RLG; ALA, NFAIS; AJL)
0	No
5	Abstain

ISQ

Figure 7.6: Special Bullets and Closing Device

Columnar Lists

When you need a columnar list, you'll probably know it. Tables, tabular lists, and columnar lists can serve many purposes and can take on many forms. There are no simple guidelines for such lists; you may find that experimentation produces the best results.

Good software will provide good support for tables—but the support for columnar text may be very different from the support for pure tables (where every entry is one line long). If you will frequently have more than one line's worth of information in one column of a tabular entry, you're dealing with side-by-side paragraphs, and that's how the software is likely to support such tables. If the need for a second line is an exception, regular tabular support—which is generally easier to key and maintain—may work out reasonably well.

Block Indents

Most paragraphs begin with an indent, then return to the left margin for other lines. There are occasions when you do the reverse—start the first line at the left, then indent each additional line. That form of paragraph can be called a hanging indent, a block indent, or even (rarely) an outdented paragraph. A block-indented paragraph may not have a first line flush-left.

Such paragraphs can serve to distinguish certain types of information. Common examples include glossary and bibliography entries, such as those in this book; hanging indents for such entries are fairly standard. Most software will support hanging indents; you should establish the occasions when they are used and use them consistently.

Block-indented paragraphs and those with hanging indents do benefit from some vertical spacing. While the flush-left first line does serve as a visual marker for the paragraph, it is a sufficiently unusual marker that it deserves the aid of some white space.

Quoted Material

What do you do with lengthy quotations, those longer than one or two sentences? Several options can be considered; as usual, the trick is to choose one option and use it consistently.

Perhaps the most common technique is to set the quoted material or excerpt in a slightly smaller font than the regular text, block indented on one or both sides. Note that you would not typically surround excerpts with quotation marks; these should be used only when the brief quotation appears within a paragraph of regular text.

Special Effects

Quite a few special effects can be included in documents; this section mentions just a few. When used carefully, special effects open up a page, improve the organization, and add interest. When used badly, special effects can ruin a publication. It's all a matter of taste and intelligence.

Big First Letters

Each chapter in this book begins with a big first letter. So does each article in the *LITA Newsletter*—and, in some cases, each section of a long report. Such letters can be wonderful typographic devices, particularly when done in handsome typefaces, but they can also be overused.

Note that big first letters can be dropped—that is, set so that the letter falls below the first line of text—or raised, as in this book. Either method can work; it depends on the rest of the layout and your own preferences.

Special First Letters

pecial first letters—like the one here, taken from a Geoffroy Tory alphabet created in Paris, 1522–1529—must be used carefully but can serve as remarkable devices in their place. Such letters are a form of illustration and should be treated accordingly; as discussed in chapter 14, Dover makes thousands of such letters available for legal scanning and use.

I would not use more than one decorative initial (the proper name for special letters) on a page, and I would probably not use such an initial in a manual or request for proposal—but as part of a newsletter for the friends of the library, or even as part of a special bibliography or booklist, decorative initials can be quite effective.

Closing Devices

Figure 7.6 shows the use of a closing device to end an article—in this case, the initials of the newsletter (*ISQ*) set in very small type, boxed, and set flush-right on the last line of the story.

If you publish newsletters, you might want to consider such a closing device—it could be a special graphic, a reduced library logo, or something as simple as a small black square. The function of a closing device is to establish a clear, unmistakable termination point for an article—and perhaps to add a small amount of graphic variety to a publication. If you use bylines at the ends of articles, you should probably not use closing devices, and for the many publications (most library publications) that don't consist of separate articles, there's no reason to consider them.

Pull Quotes

When you need variety in an all-text page, or when some text deserves more attention than it will normally receive, a pull quote may be the perfect device.

A pull quote is a portion of the text, pulled out and repeated as a special element, usually in larger type than the regular body and set off by rules of some sort. Figure 7.7, a scanned portion of a page from the *LITA Newsletter*, shows one variety of pull quote; they can be handled in various ways.

Pull quotes can be particularly effective for annual reports and other publications where you wish to give special emphasis to certain text. The rules for pull quotes are fairly straightforward:

- The text should be distinctly different than regular body text but not incompatible with it. Typically, a slightly larger font, possibly set bold or italic and probably set flush-left, will suffice.

- The text should be distinctly set off from surrounding text—typically by rules above and below, unless such rules are used for other purposes in the publication. (Thus, figure 7.7 uses a vertical rule for pull quotes because horizontal rules are used for signed columns and program reports.)

- Text in pull quotes must be chosen carefully, so that its lack of context and the prominence it receives will not distort the meaning of the document.

- Pull quotes should be used sparingly; one pull quote per page or column is generally enough.

- 1988: Barbara E. Markuson, INCOLSA
- 1989: Patricia Culkin and Ward Shaw, Colorado Alliance of Research Libraries (CARL)

... think about the giants in the field—particularly the ones not on the list above. If you're aware of an individual (or a small group of individuals) who has provided distinguished leadership, notable development or application, or superior research, education or contributions to the literature, perhaps you and your colleagues should prepare a nomination.

In 1986, no award was made. According to Charles Hildreth, chair of the 1989/90 LITA/Gaylord

---

Figure 7.7: Pull Quote

Reverse Type

Few typographic elements stand out more than reverse type—and few elements are so easy to abuse. As it happens, you may not need to worry about this; under normal circumstances, many laser printers such as the HP LaserJet simply don't support reverse type, unless it is done as graphic images.

The trouble with reverse type is that it is inherently hard to read and makes the page darker. If you do choose to use it, don't use very much of it, and make sure that the letters are big enough and simple enough so that they will stay clear through the reproduction process. Sans serif typefaces may prove useful here—but the best course may be to avoid reverse type entirely.

Rules and Borders

Most good word-processing and desktop-publishing programs provide rules as graphic elements: as lines above, below, or around headings; as frames (used for illustrations or special items); and as column dividers. Several illustrations in this and other chapters show such rules and borders; they are a standard part of document design, although many documents don't necessarily need them.

The key word, as usual, is restraint. A double-line box, with one line thicker than the other, can be very effective; but if every heading within a document has some different combination of one, two, or three lines, things can get confusing and even silly.

You may not be limited to straight lines of various thicknesses, although these will be the most suitable for most purposes. With clip art or a scanner (or access to someone with artistic abilities), you can also use an incredible variety of decorative lines and borders—but use them carefully, if at all.

I would see nothing wrong with a decorative border separating sections of a staff newsletter or other friendly, informal publication, and such borders and rules could be quite useful for special signs and occasions. They will, however, substantially influence the apparent mood and seriousness of a publication, and they should be used with that proviso in mind.

Shading

Some programs will provide a shaded background for a paragraph or article, with the shade running anywhere from 10 to 90 percent coverage. Should you use shaded text? Yes, possibly—but rarely and carefully.

The problem with shading is that it makes the text more difficult to read—and, given the limitations of laser printing, it can seriously muddy the look of a page. Colored shading is one thing, but that's in a different category of price and complexity. The shading that a laser printer will provide is a scattering of dots across the background; if there are too many such dots, the text becomes unreadable.

I've used shading occasionally, but never at more than 20 percent, only for very short items, and usually with slightly larger body type so that the text remains clear. Don't rule out shading as a possible attention-getter, but do test the results through your copying or reproduction process before you use it. What looks elegant and interesting in the original may be muddy and unreadable in the copies—or the shading may simply disappear in the copying process.

Putting It on Paper

The final steps in any desktop publication are printing it out and, typically, preparing multiple copies. Most aspects of those steps are either straightforward or so varied that this book cannot reasonably address them. A few points might be made, however.

Paper for Laser Printing

Modern laser printers (e.g., the LaserWriter IINT and LaserJet Series II) will work with most letterhead, most stationery, and any good paper for high-speed photocopying, such as Xerox 4024 paper. The only possible danger in feeding letterhead is if the letterhead was printed using thermal printing techniques for a raised look; it is possible in such cases that the printed letterhead will melt under the heat of laser printing.

A number of special papers have been produced specifically for preparing laser-printed originals that will be used as printing masters. These papers typically have very smooth surfaces, are likely to be a heavier weight than normal 20-pound paper, and may have special coatings. If you plan to use offset printing for the finished product and you want the best possible quality, you might consider special papers—but for most purposes, including anything to be reproduced on a photocopier, good-quality copier paper will work just fine.

I have tried several special laser papers. One was disastrous—a 25-percent-cotton bond that would not take a consistent image from the laser printer; consequently pieces of some letters wouldn't print.

Most other experiments have worked fairly well, including Hammer-mill Laser Print and Neenah NP (another 25-percent-cotton bond, but this one works very well). Both of these papers actually do produce a crisper, cleaner image than typical copier paper; I use them for newsletters and books. They are more expensive than copier paper, at $8 to $15 per ream, and for most projects the difference may not be worth the price and the nuisance.

There are many other special papers. Also, if you're producing single copies or small runs, laser printers will print onto some colored paper without any difficulty. There are indeed papers that won't work well—either because they are too thin (and jam while printing), or because the surface is too rough (and doesn't take a clear image), or, in some cases, because the surface takes such a precise image that you see stray particles of toner on the page and fringes on some letters. Try any special paper before you buy more than a ream.

While this has little to do with desktop publishing, you should be aware of the special requirements for labels and other special stock such as transparencies. Laser printers do use mechanisms similar to photocopiers, but the mechanisms are not identical. Don't assume that sheets of self-adhesive labels or regular transparencies will work well in the laser printer; they may gum up the works, melt, or even catch fire. The companies that produce such forms now produce versions specifically designed for laser printers; it is definitely worth the extra expense to use the right products.

Proof, Original, or Final?

You can use a laser printer one of three ways in desktop publishing. Most probably, you will use it to produce the originals, the pages from which printing plates are made (or which are used for photocopying). But if you read the magazines on desktop publishing, you may notice that they assume you "pull proofs" on the laser printer and prepare your final originals on a higher-resolution device.

If you plan to do that, you should also plan to use PostScript, at least for now (this situation may change in the early 1990s). Thousands of typesetting and copy shops now provide phototypesetting service for PostScript files—but at a stiff price, probably several dollars per page. Taking the document through this extra step will take extra time and negate much of the cost savings of desktop publishing, but you may find that for some documents the difference in print quality is worth it.

You can produce higher-resolution images on a desktop laser printer, if you're one of those rare people who really do find 300 dots per inch unacceptably coarse (in which case you must find this book painful to the eye.) If you already have a LaserJet Series II, the LaserMaster LX6 controller will double the horizontal density to 600 dots per inch and produce any size of Bitstream type on the fly; other devices also increase the resolution of the LaserJet and similar printers. There are also higher-resolution laser printers; at least one $6,000 device has been advertised as printing 1,000 by 400 dots per inch. That's probably just about the limit of laser printing, given the mechanical problems of toner-particle size and paper handling.

Some people say that you should use lighter settings when you prepare originals on a laser printer than when you prepare finals (that is, pages that will be used directly). Some photocopying processes and some processes related to printing do darken the image slightly; in other cases, however, the plate prepared from a laser-printed original will have precisely the same darkness. You might consider turning the print intensity down slightly if you're using a photocopier—but probably not if the final printing process will be offset lithography.

These details concern the way that a publication is handled after the original pages are produced—and that depends so heavily on your own environment (who does your printing, how copies are produced, etc.) that you should investigate it on your own.

Conclusion: The Power of Simplicity

Desktop publishing gives you all the power you need to prepare clear, open, readable, interesting publications. It also gives you the power to create dazzling publications that scream out, "This was prepared by a new Desktop Publisher!"

Do some of the latter; they are a good way to think through design problems, and they can be a particularly effective way to extend your range of knowledge, as you learn more features of the software by trying them out. But don't release them on an unsuspecting world: save those special effects for flashy signs and other special occasions.

The most effective book designs have always been relatively simple—and simplicity is the key word for effective desktop publishing. That doesn't mean blandness or dullness; it does mean that, like spice in food, special effects and design tricks should be used to enhance a publication, not to dominate it.

Tips and Reminders

- Make it easy for the reader to identify paragraphs: indent them or leave white space between them. Don't indent the first paragraph after a heading or subheading. Try to avoid groups of very short paragraphs or very long paragraphs.

- Avoid widows if you can, and never leave a heading or the first line of a paragraph stranded (orphaned) at the bottom of a column or page. For most publications, don't worry about single-word last lines of paragraphs or words broken across pages.

- You can use bulleted and numbered lists in the same document, but you should use them for different purposes.

- Quotations more than one or two sentences long should usually appear as block-indented paragraphs in a slightly smaller type size than the surrounding text.

- Pull quotes can add variety to heavily textual publications, but the text must be chosen carefully, and you should rarely use more than one pull quote per page.

- Reverse type stands out, but it should never be used for more than a word or two, because it is very hard to read.

- Good-quality copier paper will serve well for most laser printing, but special laser paper may be worth the extra expense for important publications.

8

Sources for Design

Finding good ideas for publication designs should be no harder than finding well-designed publications and paying attention to them. If you need more help than that, it is readily available—in the software you use, in add-on software you can buy, in books and magazines, and in an exchange of ideas with other desktop publishers.

This chapter discusses some specific sources for design ideas and adds some thoughts about moving from "canned" designs to original designs.

Avoiding the Blank Screen

If you are a graphic artist, a blank electronic pasteboard may be an exciting opportunity. If you're like most of us, however, a blank Ventura or PageMaker page has much the same terror as a blank sheet of paper does for many writers. How do you start to fill in that empty space?

The simple answer is that you don't start out empty. First, of course, you should have text prepared before you start to design the page—even if you plan to generate the design within your word-processing program. Second, you should have some concept of the final result that you want, although that concept may be quite rough. But most importantly, you never do need to start out with a completely clean slate—and most of us never do.

Virtually every program used to write or design pages comes with some sample files. One good way to get over the initial blank-screen shakes is to load such a file—and immediately change the name you'll save it under, so you don't destroy the original as you make changes. Then you can manipulate the document design until it suits your needs, get rid of the existing text, load in the text you want, and proceed.

You may find that technique useful even for word processing, possibly setting up a series of dummy files for various kinds of documents you need to generate. The files can show how the text should fit together and should carry enough settings so that you can get up to speed rapidly. You are building your own document templates—and those can be just as valuable in simple word processing as in advanced desktop publishing.

It may seem stupid to load in a document, then immediately get rid of all the text (or the linked files, as the case may be). Why waste the time? Mostly for two or three reasons, depending on the software involved.

- For many word-processing programs and desktop-publishing programs, loading the document or chapter will set up margins, tabs, styles, fonts, and other aspects of the document environment. When you clear out the text, the background information remains; as you key in new text or load new files, they fit into the existing framework—maintaining a consistent look for a type of document and saving you the trouble of reestablishing the settings.

- If the template is an indicative document, such as the sample letter in figure 8.1 (to be produced directly in Microsoft Word) or the sample chapter in figure 8.2 (to be produced in Ventura Publisher), the text already included will guide you or another user to enter the new text properly.

- Many people find the blank screen intimidating and will begin work on a new document more rapidly when something already appears on the screen.

```
—
DT                                                      Month·day,·year¶

TO    to·name↓
      to·institution↓
      to·address↓
      to·address↓
      to·city,·state,·zip:··USE·5·lines!¶


FP    Dear·salutation,¶
SP       This·is·the·body·of·the·letter.·Key·as·many·paragraphs·as·required.¶
SP       This·is·a·second·paragraph.¶
AD                              Sincerely,↓
                               ↓
                               ↓
                               ↓
                               ↓
                               your·name↓
                               anything·else¶

SP    ◆

Pg1 Li12.12 Co58  {}                ▉              F17P1.DOC
```

Figure 8.1: Model Letter

```
—

TI                   @CHAP·=·number↓

                 Chapter·Name¶


FP    @FP·=·First·paragraph·goes·here.·First·letter·will·
      be·enlarged.¶


H1                   @H1·=·Heading·Level·1¶


FP    @FP2·=·First·paragraph·after·heading·level·1¶
SP       Any·other·paragraphs.¶
H2    @H2·=·Heading·Level·2¶


FP    @FP2·=·First·paragraph·after·heading·level·2¶
SP       Note:·Word·styles·indicate·rough·spacing·only.▣
Pg1 Li41.62 Co50  {}                ▉              F17P2.DOC
```

Figure 8.2: Model Chapter for Ventura

Supplied Designs in Current Software

Chances are, most of the programs you use all came with samples of some sort. Every word-processing program I've ever heard of includes sample documents prepared with that program; every graphics program includes sample graphics; every desktop-publishing program includes sample publications, templates, or both. For that matter, spreadsheet programs usually come with sample spreadsheets and database managers come with sample databases.

That's only reasonable. The samples may or may not be used for tutorials, but in any case they give you something to start out with—a chance to see how the program works by examining the results.

Most advanced word-processing programs, and every desktop-publishing program I know of, go further. They provide not only sample documents, but reasonable design samples for various kinds of publications, ready to be used with your own text. A design sample may include full text (ready to be replaced with your own), or it may just include markers where your text should go. In either case, the design sample can be modified or used as is.

As competition in both word-processing and desktop-publishing fields increases, the number and quality of design samples or models supplied with programs will probably increase as well. For many people, the bulk of their early desktop-publishing output can be based entirely on those models or on modifications of the supplied models.

The kinds of models that are included may also say something about the kinds of documents for which the program's producers consider it well-suited. The extent to which you can use models directly will depend on the nature of the program, your own needs, and whether your installation includes all of the files and fonts that the models use.

The sections that follow show the range of templates and design models available in a few contemporary programs.

Styles and Templates in Microsoft Word

Microsoft Word 5 comes with a set of predefined style sheets and macro files for specific documents. A special document, "Sampler: An Idea Book," shows how the style sheets are used.

Style sheets include RESUME.STY, to prepare a standard résumé; OUTLINE.STY to make best use of Word's outline features; two styles for legal documents; a set of macros for script production; and a style for academic papers using Turabian conventions.

Word's formatting capabilities far outshine its supplied set of styles; that will typically be true of other advanced word-processing programs as well. The files used within tutorials may give some additional guidance.

Templates in pfs:First Publisher

The first sentence to chapter 8 in the First Publisher manual says it all: "It's often easier to copy and modify a page design than it is to start from scratch, especially if you're new to desktop publishing." First Publisher does not support separate style sheets, but it does provide seven templates to get users started and shows how to use them.

Templates include a fairly fancy one-page newsletter (combining two-column and three-column layout on the same page), a business form, a flier, a dealer list, a letterhead and business card on the same page, a restaurant menu, and a greeting card (designed to be folded twice after printing, to a final size of 4¼ by 5½ inches). A set of templates also provide various newsletter layouts using some combination of one, two, or three columns on the same page (that is, either one and two, one and three, or two and three).

These templates do suggest the general areas in which First Publisher shines: very brief publications involving graphics and straightforward design, particularly involving subjects for which the large set of First Publisher clip art can be useful.

Styles and Chapters in Ventura Publisher

Typical of advanced desktop-publishing programs, Ventura Publisher includes an extensive set of style sheets and chapters intended to be models for publications. The chapters show how the style sheets can be used, and they are illustrated and discussed in the Ventura *Reference Guide*.

Model styles and chapters include one- and two-column books, a two-column landscape brochure and a three-column portrait brochure, an invoice, a two-column product list, a standard business letter, a three-column magazine, two- and three-column newsletters, a two-column phone book or directory, a press release, one- and two-column proposals/reports, two styles of tables and technical documentation, and two styles of viewgraph (transparency).

All of the styles are professionally designed and provide useful starting points for other documents; the viewgraphs, in particular, include sample text that discusses how to create a successful viewgraph. This is not to say that all of the styles are the final word or even wholly successful; for example, the press release uses single-spaced body text, which is generally considered bad form for press releases.

Templates in Finesse

Logitech's Finesse, which supports master pages but not named styles or style sheets, includes seven master pages: a calendar; a three-column landscape brochure intended for Z-folding (that is, folding into thirds so that the sheet forms a Z); two different newsletter designs; a "business communication" design; a résumé; and a memorandum.

The designs are all suitable for direct use or modification and fairly represent the general range of applications for Finesse—which combines a moderately high degree of typographic sophistication with the clip-art orientation and limited page length of other low-end packages.

Templates in Aldus PageMaker

Aldus PageMaker includes a set of templates—that is, style sheets and master pages—roughly as complete and varied as those in Ventura, but with differences that show the companies' differences in primary orientation.

PageMaker includes templates for brochures, newsletters, business reports, distribution lists, overheads (two styles), speakers' notes, executive summaries, price lists, directories, product specification sheets, memos, slides, name tags, bulletins, calendars, invitations, and fliers.

Note that PageMaker ignores books and technical documentation, while Ventura Publisher does not include templates for invitations, name tags, calendars, or slides. That's reasonable. You can certainly use PageMaker to produce a book—but Ventura would be more typical. Likewise, you can use Ventura to produce brief, design-intensive items such as fliers—but that's really where PageMaker shines.

Problems with Supplied Designs

You can make good use of the designs, templates, and models supplied with your software, but you should be aware of their limitations.

First, you must have the proper fonts and files installed in order to use the models. That will probably be the case when you first install a program, but you may eliminate some of the supplied fonts to make room for those you actually expect to use. Depending on the nature of the template, it may make less sense without the proper fonts—or it may not work at all.

Second, the models generally represent "safe" and predictable designs—although some of the designs definitely show thoughtful professional design work. If you use these models without alteration, your documents will look the same as those produced by every other software user who uses the models. That may be fine, but it is something to consider.

Third and last, you won't really understand the principles of page design until you create your own designs. Going through the models and seeing how they work is definitely a good way to start—but if you simply use the models, you will not have gained the experience necessary to meet new challenges.

Use the supplied models, but make sure you understand how they work and revise them to meet your own needs. They represent good starting points for various types of documents; however, they should not be the only designs you use.

Packaged Designs

Depending on the program you use and the kind of document you need to prepare, you may be able to buy packaged designs on diskette. These may come in the back of a book on desktop-publishing designs, or they may be sold independently. More than one source sells sets of Ventura style sheets, and at least one sells Word-Perfect 5 style sheets; similar services may be available for other programs.

The examples I've seen have been reasonably priced (perhaps $40) and include a range of style sheets with annotation. The packages should show you how to fill in the supplied style with text, and they may also tell you enough so that you understand the design principles at work.

Think of packaged designs as extensions of the software itself, just as third-party books about software represent extra-cost extensions of the software. If you feel that you can use the extra help, understand what you are buying, and consider the price to be fair, packaged designs may serve you well. I haven't used them, and I can't imagine ever paying for machine-readable designs for my own use—even though I can certainly see paying for books on design techniques.

Any set of packaged style sheets suffers even more from the fact that you must have the appropriate fonts available if you are to use the style sheets fully. Vendors of such sheets have only three choices: limit their fonts to those normally installed with a program (which will result in somewhat limited styles); tell you what's needed and expect to acquire the fonts (which only works if the fonts used suit your needs); or include the fonts on the disks (likely to be impossible for high-quality fonts). None of those choices is particularly happy.

If you don't have the fonts needed for a packaged style sheet, you're not entirely out of luck—but it may take you a little while to relate the intended design to what you can actually achieve.

Many of the books and magazines devoted to desktop publishing include design examples, sometimes quite detailed. If they do not come with diskettes, or if the diskettes are for a different program than the one you use, you can still use the discussions as a basis for building your own designs.

One advantage of this route is that you can consider not only what you like in the designs but also where you disagree with the designer. Don't be surprised if you frequently do disagree. Some designers have little patience with text, seeing it as a necessary evil that should be minimized in favor of more striking designs.

New Designs from Old Documents

The most inexhaustible sources for new designs are publications—the ones you prepared before desktop publishing and the ones that others prepare. If the classic advice for would-be writers is *read, read, read,* the advice for new desktop publishers should be *observe, observe, observe.*

You will develop an eye for what works and what doesn't work by looking at the publications produced by libraries in your area, but also those produced by businesses, schools, associations, and others. While few library publications fit neatly into the mold of magazines or books, you will still gain design experience by studying these publications.

Studying a publication is different from reading it, and one can interfere with the other. If you see something that strikes you as being attractive and effective, set it aside after you finish reading it, then study it for design elements. Turn it upside down to look at the page balance; back up a few feet to look at the overall appearance. Don't try to study the design while you're reading—unless, of course, you find that you are bothered by the design while you are reading.

Look for the defects in publications as well as the successes. Very few publications represent total failures, but many publications—particularly those produced using desktop publishing or word processing—show a mix of good ideas and flawed ideas and techniques. Both can serve you in building your own designs.

Tools

You really only need two tools to study publication design effectively: a typographer's rule or set of rules and a notebook. The notebook—

which could be on a computer, if you are so inclined—lets you record what you've seen. (A photocopied page with notes attached will work even better.)

A transparent typographer's rule showing leading, picas, point-size examples, and the like will help you to understand just what it is you're seeing. Bitstream used to send a first-rate transparent typographer's rule to anyone who registered a purchased copy of a Bitstream font outline; that offer may still be available. Any store that sells artist's supplies and most stores that sell office supplies should also have such rules available.

There are several different types of typographer's measuring tools. Opaque rules with pica measures will prove useful for measuring the overall aspects of a page, but only the transparent rules will help you to determine the actual leading and point sizes used in a document.

Experimentation

One of the best ways to build your own skills as a publication designer is to recreate existing designs—a challenging process that will sharpen your skills—then experiment carefully with those designs in an effort to improve them.

You can do this for fun, with no intention of ever using the results; if you have the time, that can be a particularly stress-free and enjoyable way to build a set of skills. You can also do it with the clear intent of using the results—but don't try to improve on an existing design if you're under deadline pressure.

Keep track of your experiments, and consider the principles of good design as you carry them out. If the final design is one you will use extensively, you should be able to document where you started, what you changed, and why you changed it. That document, if you prepare it, will be particularly useful six months or a year later, when you look back at it and consider how far you've come (and whether you should rethink your design).

What could be more satisfying than improving an existing model? Each time you succeed—and each time you can validate that success with the favorable opinions of others—you sharpen your design sense and come that much closer to being a full-fledged desktop publisher.

Exchanging Ideas

Remember: you're not alone. Other librarians prepare publications on the microcomputer, using word processing and a variety of desktop-publishing packages—and you can be sure that, as software and hardware prices fall and the programs become more powerful and easier to use, thousands more will join the crowd. Since every library produces printed products and most libraries will use more microcomputers as time goes by, an ever-growing use of desktop publishing in libraries seems a near certainty.

If you have the opportunity, it makes sense to exchange ideas with others—learning from those who are more experienced, helping the newcomers, and generally swapping bright ideas and tales of horror. Naturally, you will find more desktop publishers outside of libraries than in them—but, in whatever circles you find that deal with personal computers, chances are you'll find a growing circle of desktop publishers.

Everybody has their own style of learning and growing; I can't tell you that you will definitely find users' groups and other information exchanges worthwhile. I have only participated to the extent of subscribing to a magazine published by a very large users' group (see below). But I know very well that others have found such groups extremely worthwhile, and, unless you are in a very remote area, chances are that there's a group nearby.

LITA Desktop Publishing Interest Group

If you are a member of the Library and Information Technology Association, and you care about desktop publishing, you should look into the activities of the recently formed LITA Desktop Publishing Interest Group. Like every other LITA interest group, it is an informal organization that gets together to discuss topics of interest and prepare formal programs for some ALA annual conferences. If you have a chance to attend group meetings, you should find quite a few librarians who share your interests. You can get more information on the interest group by contacting LITA at the American Library Association, 50 East Huron Street, Chicago, Illinois 60611. (If you're an ALA member and not a member of LITA, please consider joining the division.)

This group covers a range of programs—which is probably a good thing. Design problems cross program boundaries; even if you can't always use the advice that's offered, you will see how other librarians are tackling problems and making the most of their systems.

Local Groups

Almost every community large enough to have more than a hundred PCs has at least one PC users' group. Larger users' groups may have special-interest groups devoted to desktop publishing or advanced word processing and possibly to a particular program.

A large number of users' groups have sprung up specifically devoted to desktop publishing, typically to particular programs. One cluster of such groups, dedicated to Ventura Publisher, numbers fifty-two groups (including seven in Europe) as of January 1990; if you are near a major metropolitan area, there's a good chance that one of them is nearby. I would be surprised if such groups did not also exist for PageMaker and other programs.

Ventura Publisher Users Group

The primary cluster of users' groups devoted to Ventura Publisher operates under the umbrella of Ventura Publisher Users Group, Inc. (VPUG), which publishes a monthly magazine, *Ventura Professional!*

The idea of a national users' group serving as an umbrella for local chapters clearly works; it has been done before, and it will certainly be done in the future for other programs with large user communities. The virtues are considerable, and the groups can be worthwhile whether or not they are affiliated with (or sponsored by) the manufacturers. (VPUG appears to be in a halfway state. The organization has been independent, but Xerox has incorporated its own support publication for Xerox Ventura Publisher into *Ventura Professional!*, blurring the boundaries.)

This discussion is not to push this group specifically, but rather to note that you may find some users' groups useful even if you never attend a meeting. I found that to be true for one of my computers; the newsletters that the users' group published helped me to use the computer, even though I never found the time or motivation to attend a monthly meeting. You may also find that to be true.

Online bulletin boards or teleconferencing systems may also be good ways to exchange ideas and problems with other users. In any case, don't be isolated unless you want to be: there are a lot of other desktop publishers out there, and all of us are constantly learning.

Building New Designs

Whatever else you do, try your own hand at building new designs. Every other technique helps you to get going, but until you create your own designs, you will never really know the full satisfaction of desktop publishing.

First, you might want to develop designs for brief documents consisting entirely of text, such as invitations and special-hours signs. Then, you should try something that involves both text and graphics. For example, you might try your hand at a bookplate: it doesn't involve much text, it will help you explore scanned art (if that's what you use), and it's a good small canvas to start out on. Figure 8.3 shows a sample bookplate; that took me half an hour to prepare. You can certainly do better.

Simple signs also offer chances to try radical ideas with little overhead and little penalty for failure. You can do things in fliers and signs that you would not dare do in an annual report, and some of the ideas that spring up in preparing casual fliers may prove useful for more formal, finished products.

Fun

Desktop publishing should be fun, at least some of the time. That's one real advantage of low-end packages such as The Print Shop, pfs:First Publisher, and the like: although they aren't good at producing terribly refined designs, they are fun to work with.

Word-processing packages may not be as much fun, particularly since you usually can't see what the results will be until you print them or use a preview function, but trying out some different ideas can still be interesting.

Ex Libris

Edna Curmolly
Collection in
Contemporary
Journalism

Figure 8.3: Simple Bookplate

Even the most advanced and production-oriented software can be used to whip out something simple or to try some radical new variant on an existing document. So what if the results can only be passed around for amusement? Preparing an occasional publication just for the fun of it is liberating; it frees you from deadline pressures and the seriousness of it all, so that you can enjoy working with the page.

Document design is a craft and, to some extent, an art. Good software turns the page into a plastic medium, ready for you to shape as you see fit. Ninety percent of the time, you may simply be pouring text into a series of well-designed containers: that's what productive desktop publishing is all about. But save some time for sheer enjoyment. What about a really awful-looking page that catalogs all your frustrations with the software you're using? Give it a try; afterwards, you may find that you are a lot less frustrated!

The Trap of Perfection

You will produce documents that contain design flaws. Count on it—and don't worry too much about it, unless you find that your designs are getting worse as time passes.

Don't think that every single design must be perfect. For one thing, that's the easiest way to waste time in desktop publishing—spending hours, days, and weeks trying to refine that design just a little more before you send the pages out for reproduction.

If you are preparing a book of local history that will be printed and bound, yes, you should spend some extra time getting the design into very good shape. If you're doing a staff newsletter, it's ridiculous and self-defeating to spend a month sweating over every last possible detail before producing the first issue. Assume that the design will change over time; balance the desire for perfection with the realities of schedules and conflicting needs.

Don't be too surprised when you make a substantial leap forward in publication design, and the first examples of the new design are less than wholly satisfactory. If you are adding a major new technique, there's a natural tendency to overuse it the first time. Professionally published magazines with half a million circulation do that (almost universally, in fact); why should your friends newsletter or series of bibliographies be any exception?

If you are very lucky, one of your readers will suggest that you've gone too far—but, much more probably, you'll have to spot it for yourself. Most readers see right through most designs, at least at the conscious level, which is exactly as it should be. Remember that: while it doesn't mean that better designs are not worth striving for, it does mean that occasional lapses will neither ruin your reputation nor fatally damage ongoing publications.

Tips and Reminders

- The software you use probably includes templates, style sheets, or sample documents. Study them, use them, and modify them, but don't rely solely on them.

- Study existing publications for good ideas to use (and bad ideas to avoid) in your own designs. Recreating an existing design—and improving it—can sharpen your own skills.

- If you learn well by exchanging ideas with others, join the LITA Desktop Publishing Interest Group and look for interest groups in your own area.

- Try your own skills, and have fun doing it. Don't expect perfection the first time around. Good designs keep evolving over time, and the occasional lapse does not ruin that progress.

PART 3

Tools for Desktop Publishing

Desktop publishing uses several different computer-based tools and requires a number of different skills. Not everyone has all the skills in equal measure, and there's no need for one person to handle every aspect of every document. Well-chosen tools will give your library the flexibility to make the best use of individual talents.

Different Tools, Different Styles

My favorite word-processing program may not be yours, and each of us may have legitimate reasons for our favorite. The same goes for all tools in personal computing and for the ways those tools are used.

The next six chapters deal with the tools most likely to be used directly to support desktop publishing.

- Chapter 9 discusses the hardware you need to build an effective desktop-publishing system and some options worth considering.

- Chapter 10 considers the layout functions available in advanced word-processing programs as an alternative form of desktop publishing.

- Chapter 11 describes one of the most advanced desktop-publishing programs for MS-DOS computers, the one that I personally feel may be best suited to a typical library publication program;

- Chapter 12 describes two very different low-end alternatives in the diversified, crowded desktop-publishing field.

193

- Chapter 13 illustrates some typefaces and discusses sources of type-faces.

- Chapter 14 introduces and illustrates some aspects of graphics used to support desktop publishing.

Each chapter discusses aspects of the tool selection process, but does not attempt to review the entire field for any type of tool. Except as noted in chapters 11 and 13, none of the discussions should be considered to be endorsements of particular products as better than their competitors. Some of you will find competitive software or hardware better suited to your needs and styles, which is as it should be.

Creation and Production

These chapters proceed on the assumption that you will not attempt to use a single program for every aspect of document production. Currently, that seems to be the most sensible assumption, although some programs do claim to support the complete cycle. The most successful programs, however, have less modest goals; they do not attempt to provide full-fledged word processing or complete graphics processing together with comprehensive desktop publishing. To my mind, the separation of writing and editing from layout and the rest of production still makes sense.

Separating the Steps

In the past, writing, editing, and production have been separate steps, with writers and editors increasingly using the same tools. That separation still makes sense in many cases. Programs for word processing, database management, and graphics directly support those who create the content of a publication; desktop-publishing programs directly support the final steps in production.

Most probably, every professional in your library will contribute to publications produced by the library, as will paraprofessionals and other staff members. With current techniques, the person who cre-ates the content may also produce the finished product, except for those special products that require sophisticated design, layout, and typography.

When you implement desktop publishing, you should not expect that everyone who writes will see his or her documents through to completion. More likely, a few people will specialize in desktop-publishing design techniques, with others contributing the content. The reasons are both mechanical and philosophical. Mechanically speaking, you may not want to turn every personal computer into a desktop-publishing system. It makes better sense to install the software and hardware where it can be used heavily, repaying the investment more rapidly. Philosophically speaking, there is no reason why every person who creates bibliographies, collates special-events information, or writes articles for a newsletter should care about design issues. Some people simply aren't interested in design and typography, and that's fine; they should be allowed to do what they do best.

The Limits to Separation

I would mislead you if I said that writing, editing, and illustrating should always be kept entirely separate from desktop publishing itself. The real world doesn't work that neatly. While original creation probably should be kept separate, the various steps in producing publications interrelate to varying degrees.

The most obvious interrelationships arise because text and graphics won't magically fit the space available. Even if the length of a document is not preordained, fitting the copy to the space can be a problem. The problem is particularly significant in fliers, monthly schedules, newsletters, and the like, where a change in the number of pages can be important. You really don't want the monthly calendar to be one sheet plus one column-inch, and if a newsletter is printed on both sides of 11-by-17-inch sheets (with four pages to the sheet), you really don't want a planned twelve-page issue to run over by half a page.

You can estimate length reasonably well as copy comes in, but the final length won't be apparent until you lay out the pages. At that point, you may find that there's just a little too much copy, or that the amount is right but the break points are wrong. The traditional solution, and one that still makes sense for desktop publishing, is to do additional copyediting so that the copy fits.

Even though desktop publishing makes review cycles much faster and simpler, it is not always practical to go back to the editorial staff (or the librarian who put together the copy) to ask for a two-word cut in an article. For effective operation, the desktop publisher must have some editorial leeway—at the very least, to cut words and show the results to those responsible for editing. Under deadline, such trial cuts become straight editing.

Spreadsheets and Databases

The chapters that follow mostly ignore other tools that may play a part in desktop publishing. That selectiveness is partly a recognition of the speed with which personal computing can develop and partly a deliberate effort to avoid the giantism that afflicts so many books on personal computing. Neither I nor G.K. Hall wanted a 700-page book!

It may suffice to say that the work you do with spreadsheets and, in most cases, with database programs can feed into your desktop-publishing operation without too much trouble. If your spreadsheet can save graphs in either the Lotus 1-2-3 ".PIC" format or one of a large number of standard graphics formats, typical advanced desktop publishing programs (and advanced word-processing programs) will be able to read and recreate the graphs. (Chapter 14 does include examples of such graphs, but it certainly does not offer an adequate discussion.) You can also import portions of a spreadsheet itself, either as printed or (in some cases) directly.

Any database with flexible report-generation capabilities can produce output that will feed directly into desktop publishing, with all the keystrokes in place to make the database output look the way you want it. That process takes some thinking and a little work, but the results can be well worth it. For both of these areas, software-specific books should provide additional information and suggestions on how to proceed.

Maintaining Flexibility

Just as no single set of tools is best for all users, no single method for producing publications will work equally well for all libraries or even for all groups within a given library. Desktop publishing will almost certainly change the way that publications are produced. Try to accept and welcome such changes. It does not pay to establish a production method in concrete, with no allowance for flexibility or new developments.

Assume that your production style will change as you become more familiar with desktop publishing. The changes need not be disruptive, but they will inevitably happen.

9

Hardware

Hardware requirements for desktop publishing can exceed those for word processing, spreadsheets, or simple database management, but they need not be as onerous as you might assume. Even so, you should consider the equipment needed with some care. Without adequate equipment, desktop publishing becomes slow, tedious, and difficult. If you can't afford good equipment, you probably can't afford advanced desktop publishing.

The discussion in this chapter deals primarily with advanced desktop publishing as typified by Xerox Ventura Publisher or Aldus PageMaker. There are other, somewhat less sophisticated options available that may require lesser investments in hardware; chapters 10 and 12 discuss some alternatives.

You need to deal with the following questions in order to establish the hardware basis for desktop publishing.

- Can you add desktop publishing to an existing system? If so, should you?

- If you need one or more new computers, should they be compatible with or identical to your existing computers?

- Should you dedicate computers exclusively to desktop publishing, should you add desktop publishing to other functions on shared computers, or should you install desktop publishing on personal computers used by specific staff members?

- How much money can you spend—and where do you prefer to spend it?

The sections that follow should help you answer some of these questions. The last question becomes particularly significant when you go beyond the basics of desktop publishing, since different uses for extra money bring different benefits. One significant cost aspect of desktop publishing—scanners and other devices for importing graphics—is discussed later, in the chapter on graphics.

Using What You Have

By all means look at your existing computer as the first possible hardware platform. That choice offers several advantages:

- Hardware costs will be minimized;

- You (your staff) already understand the hardware and operating system, eliminating part of the learning process;

- File interchange should be simplified, since you will be using the same computer used for writing (and graphics, if any).

But using what you have only works if your existing computer will handle desktop publishing well and if that computer is the most appropriate place for desktop publishing. If you attempt to add desktop publishing to an underpowered or obsolescent computer, you may restrict your flexibility or wind up with a system that runs so slowly that it is difficult to use. If the desktop-publishing software is on the wrong computer from the standpoint of those needing to use it, a different set of problems will arise.

Inadequate Power and Older Computers

At this writing, the only advanced PC desktop-publishing systems with wide user bases and many choices for supporting programs run on two hardware platforms: PC-DOS/MS-DOS computers and the Apple Macintosh. If your existing equipment is an Amiga or Atari ST, good software is also available—but with fewer choices and probably less support than the two major platforms. If you're still using Apple IIs or Radio Shack TRS-80s, this may be a good time to consider new computers. Just as with CP/M computers, no serious desktop-publishing software is likely to be available.

If your computer qualifies in all other respects, but you only have five megabytes of spare disk space or your hard disk is relatively slow, it may make sense to upgrade your hard disk or add another one, if that is feasible. Upgrading will probably mean backing up all your existing information and restoring it to a new disk, but it is still a reasonable option. The $500 to $600 you will spend for a modern high-capacity disk subsystem is much less than the cost of a new computer.

Other computer upgrades can be almost as expensive as a new computer. Before taking them on, make sure that it really makes sense to add desktop publishing to your existing system. You might be better off with a separate system.

"The Wrong Computer"

As a rule of thumb, the director's computer should not be the first one with desktop publishing, particularly if the computer is in the director's office. That's not to say that the library director should never use desktop publishing—but he or she is unlikely to be the person most directly involved with it.

The computer should be located where those who need to do desktop publishing can use it most readily. Deciding where the system should live is like any other aspect of library space planning. A desktop-publishing system is a tool; like any other tool, it should be kept in the location where it will be most needed.

A Balanced System

Good desktop-publishing hardware should be balanced. That is to say, the computer, memory, hard disk, input systems, and display should be at reasonably comparable levels. If your computer is an original IBM PC/XT, adding a large high-speed hard disk may make the computer itself a bottleneck—just as putting the XT's hard disk into a contemporary high-speed computer would make the hard disk a bottleneck. Desktop computing can place heavy demands on the computer, the hard disk, and the display; the performance of the full system will be no better than its weakest, slowest link.

Balance means building strong fundamentals before spending money on fancy accessories. Don't bother with a full-page monitor if you don't have high-speed disk storage. Don't spend so much on a state-of-the-art computer that you are forced to use a dot-matrix printer or to do without a sufficiently good hard disk and controller.

Don't assume that a complete computer system will be well balanced as it is shipped. Many manufacturers and dealers skimp on one aspect of a computer, then advertise the aspect that happens to be strong. The most common hardware failings in contemporary PC-DOS/MS-DOS computers are:

- Computers shipped with only 512 kilobytes of memory—which is not enough to run the best desktop-publishing programs—or priced without any memory;

- High-speed AT-compatible computers shipped with no hard disk at all;

- High-speed computers shipped with small or slow hard disks;

- Computers shipped without any display or, worse, shipped with poor-quality displays.

Those computer manufacturers and dealers who do deliver complete, well-balanced systems now make a point of it in their advertising. For example, Northgate and Dell go into considerable detail on exactly what is included in their systems; CompuAdd, which in mid-1989 was shipping both unbalanced and well-balanced systems, at least gives you enough information to make the distinction.

Elements of a System

Macintosh users may want to skip most of this section. What the Mac owner needs to know is whether the computer is fast enough, has enough hard-disk capacity, and has a good enough display to run PageMaker (or a competitor) effectively and not run out of document and font storage space too quickly. Every Macintosh is fundamentally designed for graphics and includes a mouse, so that Macintosh owners don't need to think about those features. A Macintosh SE with at least 10 megabytes of available disk space should be adequate.

Naturally, the Mac II will be even better. The native Mac screen is small for comfortable desktop publishing, but it has certainly been used for that purpose. A full-page or two-page monitor makes a good upgrade, but first be sure you have a good large high-speed disk.

MS-DOS/PC-DOS users need to consider each aspect of the computer system. The good news is that you will almost always find the total purchase price to be less than that of a Mac with comparable speed and capacity. The bad news is that there are so many more decisions to make.

Computer Power and Memory

How much computer power you need depends on the program you expect to use, but also on what you can afford. At least one advanced program (Xerox Ventura Publisher) will run acceptably well on an original XT-compatible computer, as will the most popular advanced word-processing programs. On the other hand, Aldus PageMaker requires a much faster computer—and Ventura Publisher will certainly be more pleasant to use on a faster system.

In any case, XT-compatibles and even high-speed PCs based on the same chip as the XT (the Intel 8088) are not good purchases in 1990 for any but the lightest use, particularly since such computers don't mesh well with high-speed hard disks. You should plan to use computers based on one of the newer IBM-compatible central processing units (CPUs): the Intel 80286, which was used in the IBM AT; the Intel 80386, used in the most powerful IBM PS/2 models (70 and 80) and in many other computers introduced since 1987; and the Intel 80486, the heart of the most powerful PCs in the early 1990s.

When you buy an MS-DOS (IBM-compatible) computer, you will probably become embroiled in chip numbers, operating speeds—expressed in megaHertz (MHz)—and disk sizes and speeds. The numbers can get overwhelming, and a good explanation of what it all means would take many pages.

A good starting point for comparison is the original IBM AT, which used an 80286 CPU running at 6 MHz, later upgraded to 8 MHz. For 1990, the basic model you might consider is now a 12 MHz 80286-based system, from any of more than a hundred suppliers. That system is 50 percent faster than the fastest original IBM AT; it represents the least powerful computer that makes sense to purchase for serious uses such as desktop publishing. Such a computer, with a sufficiently fast hard disk, will run Ventura Publisher and similar software nicely: it changes the program from being leisurely or slow (as on an XT) to being quite responsive. (This book was prepared using such a system.)

All else being equal, more powerful is always better. A 20 MHz 80386-based computer with appropriate display and hard disk makes Ventura as responsive as a good word-processing system. But all else is never quite equal. Within a given budget, you may find more benefit by adding a very-high-speed hard disk, some expanded memory, or a full-page display to a fast AT-compatible than by moving up to a 386-based computer.

If you expect to use PageMaker on a PC, you must have at least a fast 80286-based computer, and you would cherish a 386. Neither PageMaker nor its graphic user interface (Microsoft Windows) is as efficient as Ventura and its GEM user interface; they really need higher-speed computers.

Memory

You must have a "fully loaded" PC to use advanced desktop publishing; that means a minimum of 640K of RAM (random-access memory), and it may mean more. Advanced desktop-publishing software is much more complex than most other PC software. Not surprisingly, the programs are large.

If you are in the habit of using memory-resident programs such as SideKick, you may need to rethink your habits when you move to desktop publishing. Advanced programs need as much of the memory as they can get—and the chunk required for memory-resident programs may be too much.

Expanded memory may make your software run far more efficiently. If you already have expanded memory—or the ability to enable expanded memory—make sure you know how it works. If you don't, you may or may not want to add it later on. However, don't run out and buy more memory before you decide on the software you will use. Most lower-end desktop-publishing programs and advanced word-processing programs will work just fine in 640K, and for most purposes so will some advanced desktop-publishing programs.

Math Coprocessors

Math coprocessors (additional chips such as the Intel 80287 that handle floating-point calculations many times faster than the regular microcomputer) can cost several hundred dollars but can speed up some computer operations. You can expect faster work in spreadsheets and some graphics programs (for example, drawing programs or Computer-Aided Design [CAD] programs). That does not necessarily mean that your desktop-publishing program will run any faster; it may ignore the coprocessor altogether.

You may save some time in generating new fonts, and you may save considerable amounts of time if you work extensively with graphics. Don't rule out a coprocessor, but don't expect any direct improvement in desktop publishing. Try to make sure that some of your software will be able to use the coprocessor before you buy it; in many cases, the software won't have the capability.

Mass Storage

Allow plenty of high-speed hard-disk storage for desktop publishing—especially if you plan to use extensive graphics. If you have never learned how to organize a hard disk, you will need to do so in order to use desktop publishing effectively. The program and its accompanying files may use three to five million characters of memory and total more than 100 files—before you produce any documents.

Files proliferate in desktop publishing, particularly when you add new fonts, incorporate graphics, and prepare slightly different publication styles for different publications. If you don't organize subdirectories and understand how to use a hard disk effectively, you will have chaos after a few months' use.

If you buy a new machine it should probably have at least a 40 megabyte hard disk—and preferably a contemporary one, which for 1990 means no more than 28-millisecond average access. *Average access* is just that—the average time required to access any information on the hard disk, no matter where it is. If you are uncomfortable with specifying "28 millisecond average access" you can always specify by equivalence. In this case, the proper term would be "Seagate 251-1 or better," since the Seagate 251-1 is by far the best-selling 40-megabyte, 28-millisecond hard disk.

For AT-class computers, anything smaller than 40 megabytes doesn't make much sense: the savings on smaller disks are minimal, except for very slow hard disks that manufacturers are trying to get rid of. You may find that much larger and significantly faster hard disks are practical purchases.$IComputers;Mass storage

With 40 megabytes, you will have room for all of your applications and desktop-published documents, at least for a reasonable period of time. You will still want to move outdated documents to backup media (or delete them, if you're sure you'll never reuse them) from time to time, but you won't need to do so just to keep going.

Utility Software

Large hard disks require good backup software and benefit from disk-maintenance software. Backup software doesn't help if you don't use it. Consider a good set of disk utilities for any computer with a large high-speed hard disk—particularly when you're using software that works with many files the way desktop publishing does. You need fast, reliable disk backup (so you'll actually back things up now and then); you want to keep your disk unfragmented; you may well want to optimize its performance and refresh the low-level formatting periodically; and you probably want the ability to restore accidentally deleted files.

You may also want to move from directory to directory and file to file using a "DOS shell" that shows you the directory structure. If you have more expanded memory than your program will use directly, you can also benefit by using a software disk cache. For example, my current system uses 512K of expanded memory as a disk cache; in a typical desktop-publishing and word-processing session, the cache may eliminate as much as 95 percent of all disk reads, speeding up operations and reducing mechanical wear on the hard disk. Good utilities, singly or in combination, can provide all these functions and more. I use Central Point's PC Tools Deluxe and Gibson Research's SpinRite and like them very much. You may find other combinations better for your needs.

If you're like most PC users, you may have fallen out of the habit of making regular backups of your changing hard-disk files. The

DOS BACKUP program is slow at best; it does not encourage use. Any of the good utility-software backup programs work much faster, are generally more informative, and should encourage you to safeguard your data more frequently. With good preventive maintenance, it is possible that you will never have trouble with your hard disk—but failing to maintain it and failing to do backups simply invite trouble.

Minimal Displays

Desktop publishing works with graphics, even when you only use text: that's how you see what you're going to get. Technically, you can use the lowest-level graphics, called Color Graphics Adapter (CGA). Don't. You will be working with such a small portion of the page that you will be frustrated by desktop publishing.

Hercules or Hercules-compatible monochrome displays should be considered minimal for desktop publishing, and they're good enough for most uses. You can't use a "pure" monochrome display such as the display systems IBM sold with its PC, XT, and AT, because that can only display text. But a Hercules-compatible display adapter costs $50 or less, a trivial expense in the overall move to desktop publishing. If you actually have an original IBM monochrome monitor, do your eyes a favor and get a new flat-screen monitor, 12 or 14 inches and amber, paper-white, or green (whichever you prefer). With built-in tilt-and-swivel stands, high-quality 14-inch flat-screen monitors cost as little as $90 to $120. For that modest sum, you will lose glare and reflection problems, gain clarity, gain ease of use (through the tilt-and-swivel stand), and generally be happier with your computer.

Most desktop publishing reverses the monochrome screen: thus, an amber-on-black display becomes black letters on an amber background. That works very well, as long as you remember to turn down the brightness! If you're moving from green to amber, that should be your first change in any case. Eyes are much more sensitive to amber than to green; you can see the characters just as well while turning down the brightness considerably. That makes the screen easier on your eyes. But the choice of screen color is very personal. Some people really can't abide amber and many people much prefer paper-white displays.

Good monochrome displays are too cheap for you to tolerate bad ones. Since desktop publishing means working closely with the display, the minimal display should be one that you find pleasing.

Up from Hercules?

You can certainly use Enhanced Graphics Adapters (EGA) or Video Graphics Array (VGA) adapters as well as Hercules-compatible adapters. The monitors will be somewhat more expensive, but not out of reach (at least for monochrome). The better desktop-publishing programs support color quite well—but do you really plan to produce color publications? If so, get a good-quality color monitor (preferably VGA or Super VGA). If not, remember that a monochrome monitor is always sharper than a color monitor with the same resolution. That's inherent in the way color monitors work. Unless you need the color display for other reasons, it is inherently inferior. The most realistic display combination for the early 1990s may be a VGA or Super VGA display adapter and a monochrome monitor capable of handling the 800-by-600 pixel Super VGA mode: that combination should not be very expensive, and it will make your desktop-publishing system work significantly faster and easier than Hercules will.

There are many advanced displays specifically designed for tasks such as desktop publishing. You don't need one to make desktop publishing work well, but you may want to consider one as an option. That option will add anywhere from $600 to $3,500 to the cost of your system—but it may also make layout and final production much faster and more pleasant.

A good full-page display has at least one million picture elements (pixels), or about four times as many as a Hercules-compatible display. That means that it can show four times as much information—if arranged properly, as a full page with all of the letters legible. At least one MS-DOS display has two million pixels and can show two pages with extremely good legibility.

The advantages of full-page displays are fairly clear:

- You can gain a much better idea of how a complex page will look, since you can see the full page with all its details

- Editing and quick review tend to be much faster, since you will never need to move the image itself.

The disadvantages depend on the particular display, but can include the following:

- All full-page displays are expensive, and many are very expensive, some costing more than a laser printer,

- Full-page displays with large screens are heavy, bulky, and sometimes awkward to use.

- Full-page displays usually require their own display adapters, which can run much hotter than typical display adapters.[1]

- Some full-page displays do not work well with regular software.

- Full-page displays frequently take longer to redisplay than do regular displays.

- Less-expensive full-page displays may have visible flicker or may display characters at an uncomfortably small size.

Most MS-DOS full-page displays are at least "megapixel" displays; the lower-priced full-page displays for the Mac, however, are lower resolution (for example, the $900 CornerStone SinglePage is 640 by 870, or roughly half a million, pixels).

If you do have the extra money and places where you can try out some of the options, you should investigate full-page displays as an option. You don't need them immediately; a good monochrome display is so cheap that you won't waste much money by starting out that way.

Ask hard questions before buying a full-page monitor and make sure you like the results under your own working conditions. Do you notice a green afterimage when images change—and if you do, does it drive you crazy? Do you notice visible flicker (or anything semi-

---

1   And, if your computer has display circuitry built into the main circuit board, these adapters use up an extra slot.

visible that seems a little less than rock-steady)? In either case, avoid the display: the extra speed isn't worth the headaches and eyestrain. Does it work well under normal lighting conditions—and how sensitive is it to glare and reflections? Do the Ventura or PageMaker drivers (which should be supplied with any contemporary full-page monitor) work properly?

Will it work with your other software? Some full-page monitors only emulate CGA; others emulate either Hercules, EGA, or VGA, giving you much better support for other applications. Do you like using it with other applications—or are the letters so big that they become hard to read?

Finally, what do you know about the company and the reliability? Will the monitor last long enough to justify the purchase price— or will the image start fading after a few months? Is the company a known quantity?

I have no good personal advice to offer on full-page monitors. When I started using Ventura, it was with a regular rock-bottom (but high-quality) Samsung amber Hercules-compatible monitor. Some time later, I gained use of an Amdek 1280 high-resolution monitor: not precisely full-page (too wide and not quite high enough) but very close. After some months, I removed the Amdek and went back to the Samsung.

Mouse

You almost certainly need a mouse for desktop publishing. Find a mouse that feels right, and find some extra space on your desk. There are two big names in PC mice: Logitech and Microsoft. There are some smaller names as well—some reselling Logitech mice, some manufacturing their own. The range of choices in mice is surprising, particularly for what appears to be (and is) such a simple device:

- Some mice use a mechanical movement-and-sensing system; some use an optomechanical system (mechanical movement with optical sensing); some use an entirely optical system. The optical ones require a special mouse pad but don't have any moving parts—however, some of the ones with moving parts now carry lifetime warranties. Logitech mice, usually regarded as the best-performing, are optomechanical.

- Some mice are squared off; some are low-slung and boxy; some, increasingly popular these days, have curved shapes something like teardrops. Most people seem to find the new curved "ergonomic" shapes better, and both Logitech and Microsoft have moved to such shapes.

- Some mice connect to a spare serial port; some come with their own little circuit card (they are called "bus mice" because they connect to the electrical bus of the computer). If you have a spare serial port, a "serial mouse" saves a slot. If you have a PS/2, there are special PS/2 mice, because IBM builds a special "mouse port" into the computer.

- Some mice operate at a fixed resolution of 200 dots per inch—that is, for each inch you move the mouse on a surface, the mouse pointer moves 200 pixels on the screen. That's fine for most uses, but it's a real pain when you use a full-page monitor for desktop publishing (there may be 1,000 or more pixels in either direction). Some operate at higher resolution (300 to 350 dots per inch); some newer models have variable resolution, possibly even "ballistic" resolution (if you move the mouse faster, its resolution goes up—thus, quick strokes move farther than slow strokes).

- Some mice come bundled with menu software for popular programs; some come bundled with paint programs or low-end CAD programs. Some bundles even include low-end desktop-publishing software. At one point, for example, you could buy the Logitech mouse bundled with pfs:First Publisher at a very good price.

- Some mice have two buttons, some have three. Two are sufficient; three may occasionally be slightly faster.

- Some aren't even mice. You can buy other pointing devices such as trackballs or digitizing pads.

Yes, it is possible to use an advanced desktop-publishing program without a mouse—but it is slow and annoying. Given that a good mouse costs somewhere between $50 and $100, you should consider a mouse as a basic purchase on the road to desktop publishing.

Printer

It's only desktop publishing when you produce paper. That requires a printer. The major desktop-publishing programs support a wide range of printers including inexpensive dot-matrix units and very expensive phototypesetting systems (normally used on a per-page basis).

If you are at all serious about desktop publishing, you need a laser printer. And, unless you're extremely serious about it, there is only one obvious choice in the marketplace: the Hewlett-Packard LaserJet Series II in any of its models.

You can get started in desktop publishing with a lesser printer—but, with the HP LaserJet IIP selling for less than $1,000 in late 1989, you may not want to. Most good software will drive Epson or Epson-compatible dot-matrix printers; increasingly, most software will also drive the Hewlett-Packard DeskJet, offering near-laser quality for less than $600 (early-1990 prices). The DeskJet may be a reasonable short-term solution; dot-matrix impact printers are generally not good choices for desktop publishing. They are slow, noisy, and simply incapable of producing the quality of a laser printer.

That is even true when you see potential print resolutions higher than those of laser printers. Some 24-pin dot-matrix printers can print at a resolution of 360 by 360 dots per inch; that's 20 percent higher than standard laser resolution. But the dots are larger; while they can achieve that very high resolution, the characters will still not be as well defined. In any case, you will quickly tire of the lengthy, loud process of high-resolution dot-matrix printing.

PostScript or Not PostScript?

Some writers will tell you that you need PostScript in order to do serious desktop publishing. That's not true; it is almost certainly the case that most desktop publishers use non–PostScript printers. (Hewlett-Packard alone sells something like 75 percent of all desktop laser printers; while HP printers can be modified to run PostScript, very few are.)

The big advantage of PostScript for most desktop publishing is that you can use any available font in any size; the printer generates specific character sizes on the fly. A much smaller advantage is that phototypesetting options are more readily available—but for most library desktop publishing, you don't need phototypesetting. Post-Script also offers some additional flexibility for graphics, but this is rarely an issue.

The big disadvantages, for now, are slow printing and high price. A smaller disadvantage, and one that can cause endless argument among type fans, is that Bitstream typefaces on a LaserJet frequently produce better-quality output than PostScript typefaces on an Apple LaserWriter IINT. (Note, however, that many PostScript-compatible printers, as opposed to true PostScript, use Bitstream typefaces and offer the superb quality of those typefaces.)

Fortunately, with an HP LaserJet Series II you can hedge your bets. You can begin with an inexpensive printer that produces high-quality output and has no known disadvantages other than lack of PostScript. Later, if you decide you need the extra flexibility, you can add a circuit-board combination such as the QMS PC Publisher Kit or Princeton Publishing PS-388 Accelerator. In the first case, the total cost will still be a little cheaper than a LaserWriter IINT, you'll have both HP and PostScript capabilities, and the printer will produce PostScript graphics faster than a LaserWriter IINT. In the second case, the total cost will be a little more but graphics printing will be many times as fast. (In 1990, this possibility may look even better: circuit boards have a way of coming down in price.) For that matter, you may later decide to upgrade your output by adding a circuit card like the LaserMaster that both generates Bitstream fonts on the fly and doubles the resolution of the HP Series II—for a fairly steep price.

There are many other laser printers. Very few are less expensive than the HP, and none have the marketplace presence of the LaserJet and LaserWriter. These two printers also have an advantage in terms of supply availability (and, in many cases, discount pricing), shared with a number of other printers: both LaserWriter II and HP Series II are based on the Canon SX print engine. In other words, mechanically they are essentially the same printer—and they take the same replaceable parts. The HP LaserJet IIP is based on a different Canon engine that is of similarly high quality, and it is assured of wide marketplace success.

Scanner

Scanners are discussed further in chapter 14—but, based on current prices and power, you may want to consider a scanner as part of any complete desktop-publishing system. A scanner allows you to bring in artwork that isn't prepared directly on the computer. It isn't essential by any means, since much of desktop publishing never requires any illustrations, but it can be quite helpful.

Hand scanners—handheld devices that typically accept a 4-inch image—have become quite inexpensive and reliable. A good hand scanner from a very reputable company, the Logitech ScanMan Plus, costs less than $200 in early 1990 and includes a useful graphics program.

A full-page scanner will cost significantly more (e.g., roughly $1,000 for the Hewlett-Packard ScanJet). If you need full-page scanning, that expenditure will be worthwhile. If all you need is the occasional logo or clip art, a $200 hand scanner may be just the thing.

How Much?

You can set up a good MS-DOS desktop-publishing system for roughly $3,200 to $5,000 in hardware—less, if you wait to buy a laser printer. You can set up a Macintosh desktop-publishing system for $7,000 to $8,000. You can also very easily spend more than $15,000 on a PC-DOS or Macintosh desktop publishing system. If you are comfortable with having a less popular system, you can also assemble a complete Atari desktop-publishing system, including PostScript-compatible laser printer, hard disk, and software, for just under $4,000.

Consider some plausible systems, including all well-established brand names, at early-1990 prices (certain to go down):

- You could purchase a CompuAdd 286/12 monochrome PC with 40-megabyte hard disk($1,500); an HP LaserJet Series IIP ($995); a Logitech Mouse and Logitech ScanMan Plus ($270 total); and Ventura Publisher ($485), for a grand total of $3,250, giving you a complete advanced desktop-publishing system. If that's too much, you could substitute Publish-It!, pfs:First Publisher, or Finesse ($110) for Ventura and an HP DeskJet ($575) for the LaserJet IIP, and you could postpone the ScanMan Plus; while these changes will restrict your capabilities, you will still have good-quality desktop publishing for a total of less than $2,300.

- A very fast, quite powerful system might include the Northgate 386/20SM computer, which includes a 14-inch monochrome monitor and 66-megabyte high-speed hard disk (around $2,600); an HP Laser-Jet Series II with one megabyte of extra memory ($1,985 total); the Logitech Mouse and ScanMan Plus; and Ventura Publisher. Total price: around $5,500.

There are many price points in between, and many ways to move to more power for more money. For $500–$2,000 more, you can either add PostScript-compatible capabilities to the LaserJet or purchase an Apple LaserWriter IINT. Roughly $400 more will buy a Super VGA adapter and suitable monochrome monitor. For $600–$3,500 more, you can buy varying levels of full-page monitors. Roughly $800 more will buy a full-page scanner instead of the ScanMan Plus.

Beyond that, the sky really is the limit. Start out with an IBM PS/2 Model 70-A21 or other top 80386-based computer; add a big, fast hard disk (150-megabyte, 16-milliseconds access speed to balance the computer); add several megabytes of memory, a full-page display, and one of the new very-high-resolution laser printers; and you come up to roughly $20,000.

Choose your hardware carefully, making sure you have a balanced system with plenty of disk space. You don't need the fastest and the biggest, but you need a system that those using desktop publishing will find comfortable.

Tips and Reminders

- You can use your current computer for desktop publishing if it is fast enough, has enough disk space, and has a good monitor—but you may want a separate computer.

- Desktop-publishing software requires all of a computer: make sure you're not using unnecessary memory-resident programs.

- Desktop publishing requires balanced power: good CPU speed; a large, high-speed hard disk; a high-quality display; and an appropriate printer.

- You do need a mouse—and you may want a scanner.

- You don't need to spend a fortune on desktop publishing; a first-rate system can cost as little as $3,000 to $4,000 including the computer.

10

Advanced Word Processing

Not too many years ago, a word-processing program was considered advanced if it offered any support at all for proportional fonts and multiple fonts within a single document. At least one of the best-selling word-processing programs produced truly horrendous spacing and justification when used with proportional fonts; others could not support proportional fonts at all.

Even then, however, it was possible to do fairly sophisticated text-only page preparation using MS-DOS word-processing tools. The FinalWord II offered moderately sophisticated typographic options—if you could learn to manipulate its built-in language and deal with the lack of automatic hyphenation, WYSIWYG, and other niceties. (WYSIWYG stands for *what you see is what you get*—being able to see the document on the screen roughly as it will appear on the page.) Microsoft Word offered more accessible typographic controls, including full control over leading and interparagraph spacing and style sheets to provide consistency among documents. But the program was slow to operate and somewhat difficult to learn.

Times change. The burgeoning laser-printer market, the success of desktop publishing, and users' increasing typographic sophistication have all encouraged word-processing producers to add more and more layout and font-handling capabilities to their programs. Recent releases of Microsoft Word, WordPerfect, and WordStar all offer moderately advanced typographic and layout control combined with page-preview modes that attempt to show realistic versions of the printed page; competitors are also adding such features. Recent versions of such programs can also integrate graphics to various degrees.

These programs blur the line between word processing and desktop publishing; for some libraries, and for some publications in almost any library, advanced word processing may offer all the desktop-publishing power you want or need. This chapter considers some aspects of advanced word-processing programs, things you should consider when deciding whether to go to full desktop publishing.

Note that the remainder of this chapter uses the term *advanced word processing* as a synonym for word-processing programs that offer some of the advantages of desktop publishing. That's not really the right term, but it will have to do; since most word-processing programs are either moving in the direction of desktop publishing capabilities or moving toward simpler operation with fewer capabilities (sometimes called *executive word processing*), the term may be reasonably accurate in a year or two.

Preferences and Possibilities

You should be aware in advance that I regard full desktop publishing as a preferable solution for most libraries, at least for those documents that will benefit from complete control over layout and typography. The additional costs of full desktop publishing represent a relatively modest portion of the full system cost—about $500, the cost of the program itself—and, in my opinion, the benefits justify that cost. If you currently use simpler word-processing programs, ones that lack sophisticated layout functions, the cost differential is substantially smaller—$250 to $300, the difference in typical selling price between an advanced word-processing program and a desktop-publishing program.

On the other hand, layout within word processing will serve libraries well in at least two situations:

- When the budget, the available training time, or both factors will extend to a laser printer and advanced word processing, but not all the way to advanced desktop publishing. In this case, library staff can develop publications and publication designs, then move up to full desktop publishing when they can afford the time and money.

- When the library is producing publications that may not benefit substantially from full-scale desktop publishing, and when circumstances argue for using simpler tools in such cases.

It is certainly the case that many library publications can be done just as well with advanced word processing as with full desktop publishing. Which technique will be faster or more effective depends on the people and the publication.

Integrating Editing and Layout

Advanced word processing combines editing and layout in a single program. Depending on the program, that combination may take different forms. Amí (a word-processing program running under Microsoft Windows) combines the two in real time; as with some Macintosh programs, you work with text in the context of a page, with all fonts shown as you work. That's one extreme, feasible only if you have a computer that's fast enough.

More typically, at least as of this writing, you enter codes or select menu options to establish aspects of layout and text formatting, but you only see the actual page layout in a page-preview mode. During normal editing, you work with plain text—but you're still thinking about layout and text simultaneously. That may not be a good thing. It is easy to shift your concentration from the words to the layout, spending more time making the pages look good than being sure that the content is in good shape.

Combined word-processing and desktop-publishing programs have not generally been very successful, partly because they combine too many functions in a single process and partly, I suspect, because people recognize the useful distinction between writing and graphic design. That distinction also argues that, even if you use word processing as your publication tool, you should not give substantial extra weight to programs that show you the finished product as you write. That may not be what you want to see—at least not while you're writing.

Minimal Capabilities

Some capabilities must be present for any word-processing program to be considered a candidate to substitute for desktop publishing. If a program doesn't offer nearly all of these capabilities, it does not offer a plausible alternative to desktop publishing for the needs of most libraries.

Complete Word-Processing Capabilities

The best argument against advanced word processing, from a purely practical standpoint, may be that providing all of the functions of two complex tasks puts too much into a single program. Although frequently denigrated as an "easy" task for a PC, good word processing actually demands quite a bit from the program and the computer. You should not be willing to compromise on the power of word processing simply to achieve integrated layout capabilities.

- Every feature mentioned in the section "Editing Functions" in the introduction to Part II of this book should be available.

- Spell-checking should be available and should work effectively.

- The program should work swiftly, so that you can concentrate on writing and editing. Every time you must wait for the program, your concentration is damaged.

- Editing functions—particularly such basic functions as block marking, deleting, moving and copying, search and replace—must make sense to you and be available in a way that becomes habitual without too much effort.

Document Design and Production

You must be able to build long documents and work with them. That typically requires two capabilities:

- The ability to edit long files effectively. If you generate bibliographies, information and referral directories, and new-title lists, you should be able to edit them in one piece—and you should be able to edit the longest chapter in any major publication as a single unit. The latter capability can probably be satisfied by a 60,000-character limit; the former may require significantly longer documents, perhaps up to 600,000 characters or more.

- The ability to treat more than one text file as part of a single publication. That means, at a minimum, being able to specify explicitly that the starting page number for a file be something other than page 1; ideally, it means being able to chain files together in some manner for certain purposes.

In order to organize long documents, an advanced word-processing program should offer facilities to produce a table of contents and, ideally, an index. The program should also enable you to produce lists of figures and tables. If the table of contents, index, and other lists can be produced across linked files, so much the better.

You need some equivalent of style sheets in order to establish and maintain stylistic consistency for various types of documents. Named style sheets represent one approach, but that is not the only workable approach. Skeleton or model documents, sets of custom macros, stored "ruler lines," and other techniques may provide workable ways to build and maintain your document styles.

Page Design and Preview

Advanced word processing requires full, precise control over all margins on the page. You must be able to define multiple columns and should be able to specify the space between columns. You must be able to specify headers and footers, incorporating page numbers where you want them. You must also be able to see how the page will look when it is printed, at least in terms of overall design. The fonts may not be accurate, but the spacing and layout should be realistic.

Ideally, you should be able to specify optional vertical rules between columns and horizontal rules as design elements. You must be able to establish placeholders for figures and attach captions to those placeholders; you should be able to define ruled boxes in which figures can later be placed. Even if a program supports graphics directly, you must be able to add separately prepared graphics later in a sensible manner.

Effective advanced word processing also requires footnote capabilities, with options as to the way footnotes are identified and formatted.

Text Design and Font Selection

If you can't use multiple typefaces, styles, and sizes in a single page, your program can't substitute for desktop publishing. If you can't use soft fonts (for HP LaserJet printers and some others) and PostScript fonts effectively, you don't have advanced word processing. It's that simple. You must also be able to mix different typestyles (bold, italic) on a single line; the ability to mix different typefaces or sizes on a single line is nice, but it's not nearly so critical.

Just being able to use multiple fonts is not enough. You must also be able to deal with them effectively. You should be able to specify fonts in a natural manner, preferably from a callable menu that shows actual font names; the same is true for sizes.

In addition to fonts, you must also have control over the other basic aspects of textual design.

- You must be able to prevent widows and orphans, preferably automatically.

- Headings and subheadings must stay with the following paragraphs; that design stipulation should also be automatically supported but under your control.

- You must be able to specify tab stops and, at the least, left-aligned and right-aligned tabs (and also, preferably, decimal-aligned and centered tabs).

- Full control over leading (interline spacing) and special space requirements for given textual elements is essential, including space above, space below, indents and hanging indents, and special left and right margins.

You should be able to specify page and text design elements in either inches or picas and points, or in a combination of the two. If a program only deals with vertical spacing in terms of lines, it will not substitute for desktop publishing—and neither will any program that deals with horizontal spacing only in terms of characters.

Typographic Quality

Advanced word processing requires competent support for proportional fonts and should include more support for good typographic quality. Even if you never produce a justified document, you should pay some attention to proper typography. If a program assumes some average number of characters per inch, it will inevitably yield lines that are too short and too varied, with cases in which the first word on the next line could obviously fit on the line above.

Realistically, you should be able to produce attractive justified publications. That requires support for soft hyphens (line-breaking hyphens). At the very least, a program should show you when hyphenation might be needed; and it really should offer a plausible hyphenation point.

Extended Capabilities

Advanced word processing may add even more capabilities—but at some point you may be better off using a real desktop-publishing system. You might expect to see some combination of the following features in an advanced word-processing program, together with others not considered here:

- The ability to import text from a variety of other programs including other word-processing and database-management programs;
- The ability to mix single-column and multicolumn layouts on the same page;
- Soft-font downloading capabilities, with intelligence so that only the necessary fonts are downloaded to the printer;
- Support for typographic fractions (e.g., 13/17), bullets, big initial letters, and other typographic devices;
- Outline support coupled to heading levels and autonumbering capability;
- Complete tab facilities including leaders;

- Kerning—preferably automatic, but also manual when needed;
- Letterspacing and explicit control over the width of an interword space.

Graphics

Graphics represent a crucial aspect of desktop publishing but may be irrelevant for many (perhaps most) of your publications. Most contemporary advanced word-processing programs include some level of support for graphics, although the level is usually fairly limited.

Typically, you might be able to import spreadsheet graphs and two or three different graphic formats. You should always be able to interrupt text in order to place a box to hold an illustration and be assured that the box will stay on a single page. In some cases, the program may be able to flow text around the box.

You can anticipate that programs attempting to show a graphic on screen will run slower than those that simply leave an empty space for the graphic—or show a textual placeholder except in page preview mode. You can also anticipate that an advanced word-processing program will offer fewer graphic options than a good desktop-publishing program—but the word-processing program may provide more graphic support than you will ever use.

Typical Problems and Deficiencies

Seeing what you're doing while you're doing it—that's the real advantage of WYSIWYG systems, since what you see on the screen is almost never precisely what you'll get on paper. When you put together a page and document style in desktop publishing, you can immediately see what it looks like and how changes will affect the document.

Working with the numbers—specifying layout controls through style sheets and other mechanisms—may be precise, but it is less likely to be intuitive than working directly with an editable on-screen page display. As a result, you're more likely to make mistakes or less-than-ideal judgments when using advanced word-processing programs than when using desktop-publishing programs. Some of those will simply require changes and more trial listings, wasting paper and time. Others won't be corrected: you're less likely to achieve a completely satisfactory result when you can't deal with the layout interactively.

If you read that 120 percent leading works in most cases, you'll probably set all leading at 120 percent of font size—or accept automatic leading, which typically means 120 percent leading. If you've heard that white space increases legibility, you might set a 4-pica gutter between two columns; you might also combine indentation for paragraphs with 1-pica spaces between paragraphs. And if you produce documents with those settings, you might even be satisfied with the results.

You shouldn't be—and, with good desktop publishing, you probably wouldn't be. In the first case, that leading percentage is fine for most body text, but it's too high for some sizes of some typefaces when used as multiline headings. A 36-point typeface set on 43-point lines looks awkward. The second example is just bad advice: the gutter is far too wide, eating up white space that would work better as part of the left and right margins. The third example is controversial: some designers say that you should not use both forms of paragraph identification, while others consider the technique useful. An interactive page display would show the flaws in these decisions or at least allow you to experiment with other decisions without wasting paper each time through.

Justified text, a design decision which is well suited to many library publications (although not all), requires a kind of support that few advanced word-processing programs can offer effectively. The best desktop-publishing programs combine effective hyphenation algorithms with exception dictionaries, or provide full dictionary-based hyphenation. Beyond that, such programs will show you which lines contain "trouble spots" so that you can decide what action to take.

Some other deficiencies in typical advanced word-processing programs:

- Kerning may not be supported, and interactive kerning is particularly unlikely;

- You may not be able to track text looser or tighter—or, if you can, it will be an indirect and laborious process;

- You probably won't get a very precise on-screen rendition of the fonts you'll actually use; you may just get different sizes of a generic font. Since leading and other spacing decisions depend partly on the character of a particular typeface, this lack makes page previews considerably less useful.

Advantages of Advanced Word Processing

There are several good reasons to consider advanced word processing, either as an adjunct to desktop publishing or in place of the more sophisticated layout programs. Some of the reasons have already been mentioned or are obvious:

- Doing it all in one program means less training, at least for those who need to worry about layout as well as writing;

- Advanced word processing is a little cheaper and may save a significant amount of disk space;

- Depending on the publication and the people working on it, advanced word processing may yield the desired product faster and more conveniently than desktop publishing.

One other advantage may disappear over the next few months or years, and is irrelevant if you use PostScript printing or Microsoft Windows. That advantage is that you need only store one set of soft fonts, rather than two. At the moment, Bitstream and other soft fonts for laser printers must be stored in a format that is unique to each program that supports them: the fonts used by Word can't also be used by Ventura, for example. Thus, if you expect to use both advanced word processing with soft fonts and desktop publishing, you may wind up with two sets of soft fonts—which tend to hog disk space in any case.

Glyphix Typefaces

One rather surprising advantage of the two most popular advanced word-processing programs over desktop publishing—and, again, it is certainly a temporary advantage—comes in the form of Glyphix typefaces from Swfte International (discussed and illustrated in chapter 13).

Glyphix typefaces only work with HP LaserJets and compatibles, but they will work just fine in desktop-publishing programs—however, for those programs they are generated and stored like any other soft fonts (i.e., each different size takes up additional disk space). For Microsoft Word and WordPerfect, however, Glyphix fonts can be generated on the fly—which means you can use any point size up to 120 points, choosing it as you need it, without taking up extra disk space.

Since Glyphix typefaces are also much less expensive than most other reasonably high quality typefaces, this offers a very attractive solution for flexible use of multiple typefaces—and one that won't work in desktop publishing, because of the tricks that Swfte uses to provide the function. Again, it's only a temporary advantage, but it can certainly be useful.

Is Advanced Word Processing All You Need?

Doing all your text work in one program has real appeal, and you can be assured that revisions will go smoothly when you're revising right within the layout system. If you use a system running under Microsoft Windows or OS/2 Presentation Manager (or on the Macintosh), you may find that you have all the import facilities you need and that on-screen font support is quite satisfactory.

With cartridge fonts, Glyphix typefaces, or other suitable fonts, you should find that advanced word processing makes a useful alternative for many library publications where sophisticated layout is not an issue. You can certainly use both advanced word processing and full desktop publishing within the same library; indeed, it would be quite unusual to find a library using desktop publishing for all publications!

Which program will be appropriate for each publication? That really depends on your own situation. Typically, newsletters, annual reports, brochures, and other similar publications can benefit from full desktop publishing; so can directories and similar publications. Typically, letters and memos don't need the advantages of desktop publishing. In between these categories are new-title lists, subject bibliographies and many other publications; they can be done effectively using advanced word processing, but you may find that you can produce them even better (and, in some cases, more rapidly) using the tools of desktop publishing.

The design issues discussed in the first half of this book are the same for advanced word processing, desktop publishing, and traditional methods. If you feel that you are in a position to begin designing publications, but you find advanced desktop-publishing programs too formidable, you might consider advanced word processing as an interim step. When you do move on—and you probably will—you will have the second set of tools to serve your library well for its less sophisticated publications.

Tips and Reminders

- Don't be dazzled by fancy layout tricks if the word-processing program doesn't work superbly for editing text.

- Make sure you can handle long documents effectively for both editing and layout.

- Substituting word processing for true desktop publishing means some loss of interactive layout; make sure that loss is acceptable.

11

Xerox Ventura Publisher

Desktop publishing began in 1985 with Aldus PageMaker on the Macintosh. Indeed, Paul Brainerd of Aldus coined the term to describe his new program. PageMaker has dominated sales of desktop-publishing programs for the Macintosh ever since its introduction.

A small software company named Ventura developed the first major desktop-publishing software for MS-DOS: Ventura Publisher, marketed by Xerox. Ventura Publisher, introduced in 1986, ran under Digital Research's user interface GEM, offering graphics interaction similar to that found on the Macintosh. Since its introduction, Ventura Publisher has been the best-selling advanced desktop-publishing program for MS-DOS computers.

Aldus PageMaker became available in 1987 in a slightly different version designed to run on MS-DOS computers, supported by the Microsoft Windows user interface. It rapidly became the second best-selling MS-DOS advanced desktop-publishing program and has retained that position.

Early versions of Ventura and PageMaker offered distinctly different strengths and weaknesses and approached desktop publishing from different perspectives. The competition has improved both programs, giving each many of the strengths of its competitor. Ventura and PageMaker seem likely to be ahead of the pack for some time, if only because both programs now have a base of support materials not available for other programs. You can buy several books and other learning devices to help you learn either program; classes and seminars are frequently available for both systems; software add-ons are readily available; and other software vendors strive to assure that their output can be used by Ventura and PageMaker. Both programs are so widely used that user groups have formed, and hence it is relatively easy to find users to discuss problems with. Both programs show the results of inspired original programming and design efforts and strong ongoing development work.

It would be foolish to suggest that no new desktop-publishing program will ever arise to replace either or both programs as market leaders. It is reasonable to assume, however, that both Xerox Ventura Publisher and Aldus PageMaker will be widely used and well supported for several years to come.

This chapter does not show you how to use either Ventura Publisher or Aldus PageMaker. There are any number of very good books to help you learn these programs and to provide guidance and tricks for advanced users. Ventura, the one I am familiar with, includes a very long and fairly good reference manual, an excellent 200-page training guide that you use with real Ventura examples, and a 200-page workbook to help you plan and create your publications.

Most of this chapter deals with Xerox Ventura Publisher 2.0, noting some of its features. The last section of the chapter notes some of the differences in the approach used by Aldus PageMaker 3.0, including the key differences in its basic approach. The names Ventura and Ventura Publisher are used throughout this section; unless otherwise qualified, all refer to Xerox Ventura Publisher Version 2.0 without the Professional Extension.

Document-Oriented Publishing: Why I Prefer Ventura Publisher

Aldus PageMaker, as the name implies, works best on a page-by-page basis. It is ideally suited to designers creating short publications where each page requires special attention and where each publication is unique. While newer versions of PageMaker provide the support necessary to produce longer documents effectively, it is still the case that short, design-intensive publications are PageMaker's forte.

Ventura Publisher, on the other hand, has always had a document-production orientation, easing production of long, repetitive, and periodic documents. While the program provides powerful tools for manipulating portions of individual pages, the basis of Ventura is the chapter or document. Ventura's document orientation runs through its tutorials and other documentation: in fact, the first tutorial uses the beginning of a book as an example. By automating the repetitive aspects of document production, Ventura minimizes the amount of interactive work required to prepare a professional-quality finished document.

There are several good desktop-publishing programs, and a library could profitably use any one of them. I believe that Ventura Publisher represents a particularly appropriate choice for most library publishing programs, at least for libraries that currently use MS-DOS computers. Ventura is my choice here because it specifically supports revision and repetition. For example:

- Once you design a new-book list (or a bibliography) that looks the way you want, producing additional new-book lists or bibliographies will require little or no work within Ventura Publisher, quite possibly only a dozen keystrokes and mouse clicks.

- You need not worry about widows, orphans, and stranded headings once you establish your document patterns; Ventura assures appropriate column and page breaks far more automatically than most desktop-publishing programs.

- By providing optional automatic section numbering, indexes, tables of contents, lists of figures, footnotes, and page headings that can vary automatically with content, Ventura provides strong support for complex manuals, directories, and other structured documents.

One additional factor is that Ventura Publisher does not require as much computer power as other advanced desktop-publishing systems. People can and do use Ventura productively on original IBM PC/XTs and compatibles.

User Interface

Ventura Publisher runs under the GEM user interface, a product of Digital Research. GEM is a graphic user interface (GUI), a system to provide consistent interactive graphic controls for programs on a computer. Graphic user interfaces (largely developed at the Xerox Palo Alto Research Center) have become increasingly popular since 1984. The best-known Graphic User Interface forms the basis for Macintosh software; the most widely used GUI for MS-DOS computers is probably Microsoft Windows.

Every GUI is slightly different, but the elements of GEM as used by Ventura include the following key aspects:

- The top line of the screen always includes a set of basic menu options;

- The window for the application has a title at the top and scroll bars—bars showing the location of the current visible screen within some larger "virtual" page or screen, which can be controlled directly to move the visible screen—on at least two sides;

- Applications work in graphics mode rather than strictly through characters, thus making it possible to show different typefaces on the screen and mix graphics with text;

- The user interface usually displays dark text on a light background;

- A mouse may be used to pull down menus from the top line, make selections, control the scroll bars, point at items on the screen to work on them, select them, move them, etc., and (in some cases) draw lines, curves, or pictures on the screen;

- Applications use *icons* (small visual representations of some simple idea or choice) and work through choices from lists, pop-up windows, dialogue boxes, and other interactive features.

Figure 11.1 shows the GEM interface in action, with Ventura Publisher running and one of its pull-down menus in use. If you're a mouse-hater and yet plan to use a productive desktop-publishing system, you'll have to learn to adjust. It would be nearly impossible to achieve the richness and flexibility of Ventura Publisher without the mouse and graphic user interface. I'm a keyboard man myself, but I absolutely believe that the mouse-driven graphic user interface is essential for workable interactive desktop publishing. I can't imagine making things work as well in a purely command-driven, keyboard-driven environment. There are simply too many options and controls to do everything effectively through the keyboard.

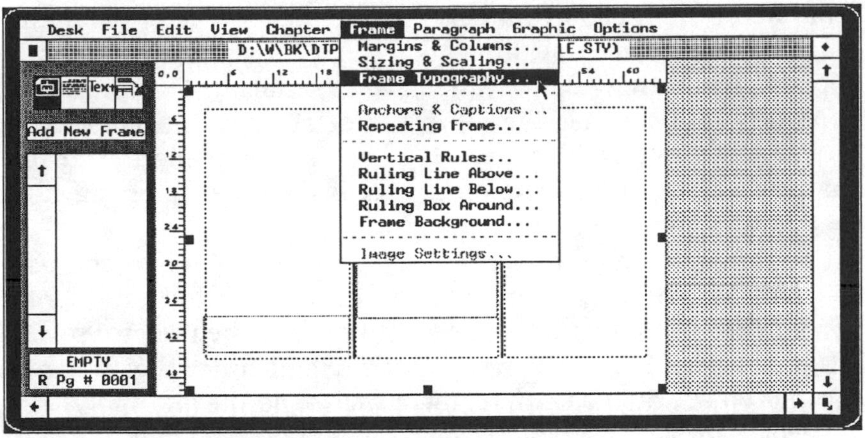

Figure 11.1: GEM User Interface (Ventura)

Style Sheets, Tags, Chapters, and Frames

Perhaps the most important element in Ventura's automated document facilities is the *style sheet*. A style sheet is a file that contains fundamental information about a document and its contents.

- For the document as a whole, it specifies page layout, margins, columns, and general typographic rules.

- For each specific paragraph (including headings, etc.), it specifies: all typographic and spacing rules; typeface, size, and style; kerning, letterspacing, and tracking; breaks; and special effects (bullets and big first letters).

A desktop publisher normally uses the same style sheet for all documents that are similar or identical in appearance—all the chapters in a book, all the books that follow the same rules, and so on. Thus, for example, a library might build style sheets named FRIENDS.STY, CALENDAR.STY, BIB.STY, PR.STY, LARGE.STY, and MANUAL.STY for the friends newsletter, monthly calendar, bibliographies, press releases, large-print lists, and internal manuals, respectively.

Tags

Style sheets include *tags*—named paragraphs. When you select tags thoughtfully and use them consistently, you establish a smooth publication production routine. A tag defines a type of paragraph that differs in some way from "body text," a standard tag that is applied to everything that doesn't have a special tag. The user names most tags and controls the attributes of all tags, including those provided by Ventura. Each new tag begins by copying the current characteristics of body text or, if specified, some other tag, thus speeding the definition process.

Good tag-naming conventions, planned beforehand and used consistently, form the foundation of effective production-oriented Ventura use. Note that the same tag names may be used for several different types of publications to label the same functional elements; the tags will be defined differently in each style sheet.

For example, every style sheet I use has tags "FP" and "Bullet"— the first for "first paragraph," the second for a bulleted point. Typically, the sheets also have "H1," "H2," and "H3" for three heading levels and a number of other tags, some of them specific to certain style sheets. But "FP" works differently for different style sheets:

- In this book, it creates a 28-point big first letter raised from the first text line and specifies 11/13 Zapf Calligraphic text;

- In the *LITA Newsletter* it creates a 30-point big first letter dropped down to take up two text lines and specifies 11/12 Zapf Calligraphic;

- In *Information Standards Quarterly* and styles for Research Libraries Group documents, it creates a paragraph of 11/12 Zapf Calligraphic with no indentation but also no big first letter.

Similarly, the tag "Bullet" always means "a block-indented paragraph with some form of leading symbol," but the symbol used, actual indentation and other spacing details differ from style sheet to style sheet. By using consistent tag names for equivalent elements, you can assign tags while editing text without trying to remember particular tag names for particular publications.

Chapters

A style sheet establishes the consistent overall look of a single document or category of documents. A *chapter* defines a specific document, containing some elements of the document and pointing to other elements. A Ventura chapter is also an MS-DOS file. It identifies a style sheet (which may be shared with many other chapters). But it also carries the information specific to a particular document, such as:

- The text and graphics files used in the document;
- The first page number and how page numbers should appear;
- Running headers and footers, either as actual text or references to tags (e.g., "use the most recently encountered ChapTitle as part of this running header", if "ChapTitle" is a tag used for chapter titles);
- Specific frames—special areas to receive graphics or to hold text that doesn't flow through pages and columns normally;
- Widow and orphan control and any other special aspects of the document.

Frames

Frames are simply rectangular areas on specific pages. Every document has a base frame—the text area used throughout the document—but you may also need special frames for special purposes. For example, in order to add a predefined illustration to a page of text, you define a location for the frame and its dimensions and special characteristics, then load the graphic file into it.

Special frame characteristics can include: shading; lines above, below, or around; multiple columns within a frame; padding, to ensure that text doesn't touch the edges of the frame; different typographic controls; scaling and cropping for pictures; captions that are attached directly to frames and may be automatically numbered; and anchoring to text—that is, ensuring that a given frame always appears on the same page as a particular portion of text outside the frame.

This book uses special frames only for illustrations and some examples. Some special-purpose publications will include many frames, and some newsletter editors place each story in a separate frame (rather than combining all the stories into a single text file).

Incidentally, a publication can be more than one chapter—and something that you think of as a chapter may, for special reasons, actually contain more than one Ventura chapter. By using the multi-chapter options, you can build a document of up to 128 chapters—

and you can create a single table of contents, list of figures, or index for the full document.

Automatic Page Production

One key aspect of the underlying page frames and chapters is that, when text is loaded into the underlying page, Ventura will automatically create as many pages as are needed to hold the text. If, after revision, the text requires fewer pages, Ventura will eliminate trailing pages automatically—unless those pages include special frames. So, for example, I did not determine the number of pages in each chapter of this book ahead of time; I simply copied an empty chapter with the book's style sheet and characteristics, loaded the text file, and let Ventura determine the number of pages.

Style sheets and automatic page production may mean that you never need to inspect individual pages for bibliographies, new-title lists and other standard publications. When you build a suitable style sheet, establish easy-to-remember tags and use those tags in your word processing or in producing a database report-to-disk, you may give Ventura enough information that you don't need to do anything more. Indeed, it is quite possible to prepare a monthly title list using a total of three actions within Ventura (once the first list has been prepared). Assuming that the title list is saved under a standing name, you need only start Ventura, specify the file, turn on the printer, and make a single menu selection; the list will be fully formatted in your predefined style. You may need a day or more to build the document style for the first list—but after that, the operation is virtually automatic. This sort of capability typifies Ventura's production orientation: even though you can do almost everything interactively, you frequently don't need to bother.

Stepping through A Document

Let's go through a few of the steps in creating a more complex Ventura publication—to show you some of the features (and how they look on-screen) and to show you how Ventura works with word-processing programs to support revision. This quick tour includes quite a bit of material; Ventura is not as overwhelming as it may seem from this set of figures.

```
 1                         Children's·Events¶

 2     The·Children's·Hour▯
-3     Every·Saturday.·1-2·p.m.↓
       Children's·Room↓
       Main·Library¶

 2     Summer·Reading·Club¶
 3     August·1¶
SP        The·public·is·invited·to·the·Halfway·Awards·for·the·Summer·Reading·
       Club.·Awards·and·certificates·will·be·presented·to·Reading·Club·members·
       who·have·completed·the·halfway·requirements.·¶

 2     The·Story·Project¶
 3     August·8¶
SP        Make·sure·to·bring·your·stories·for·discussion·and·review!·¶

 2     Patricia·Driver↓                                                         ▮
       reads·from↓
       The·Rail's·Tale¶
 3     August·15¶
SP        Parents·and·children·are·invited·to·hear·noted·children's·author·
       Patricia·Driver·read·from·the·latest·in·her·"stories·for·the·birds."¶

Pg1 L131.37 CoZ0  {·}              7                              CALEN.DOC
```

Figure 11.2: Word File for Calendar

Figure 11.2 shows part of a document as created in Microsoft Word, with Microsoft Word paragraph styles applied to keep track of the document elements. This is probably how you would build the text for the first example of a new type of publication, although probably not how you would build later examples. (Later on, you would omit the Word styles.)

Defining the Page

The screen in Figure 11.3 shows part of the process of defining the overall page layout for this document. This menu, which could be used either for the underlying frame or for a special frame to hold special text or graphics, specifies the number of columns, margins for the page, gutter margins, and any special instructions. Column widths are normally assigned by Ventura based on specified margins and gutter widths, but they can also be explicitly stated—and can be uneven. The option "copy to facing page" will create a mirrored set of margins for left-hand pages—exchanging left- and right-margin specifications.

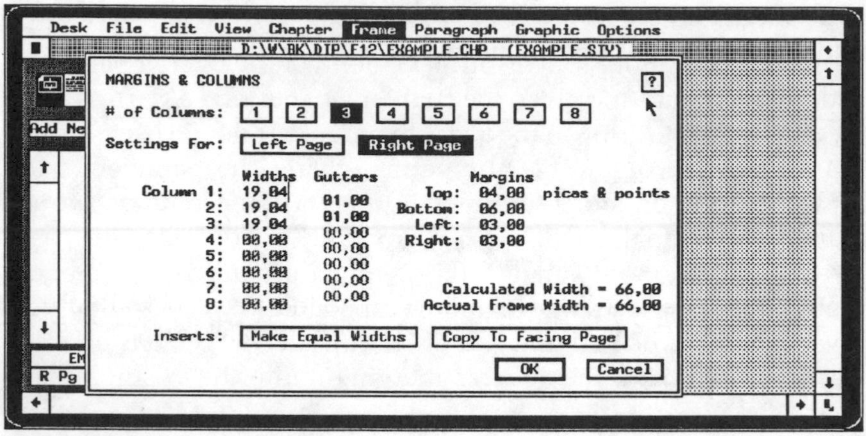

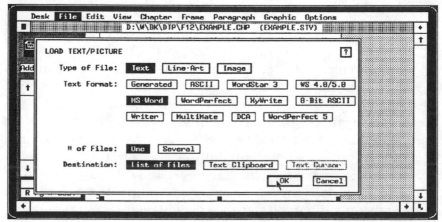

Figure 11.3: Margins and Columns

Other frame and chapter-related menus determine the overall page size and orientation, overall widow and orphan control, whether multicolumn pages should have balanced columns, the content of headers and footers, and how footnotes are handled. Menus can be used to specify precise measurements for the frame, captions for special frames, whether a special frame should repeat on every page, the existence and placement of vertical rules, lines above, below or around the frame, and the presence of a shaded background.

Figure 11.4: Load Text

Importing Text

For most publications, once you have defined the overall page (the underlying frame) and given the chapter a name (and a starting style sheet), it is time to bring in the text—or part of the text, at least. Figure 11.4 shows one of the file submenus, giving the parameters for importing one or more text files. Other top-line options would change the middle set of boxes, providing options for "line art" (vector graphics) and "image" (bit-mapped graphics) files, respectively. Note the wide range of import capabilities. Note also that you have the choice of bringing the file in for later placement or, once there is some text in the chapter, merging it into the existing document at any point.

In Figure 11.5, the file (identified in another submenu) has been imported and dropped into the chapter. At this point, however, everything is body text—unlike PageMaker, Ventura does not recognize Microsoft Word styles. (It does, however, recognize italics and some other text characteristics, as you can see in the figure.)

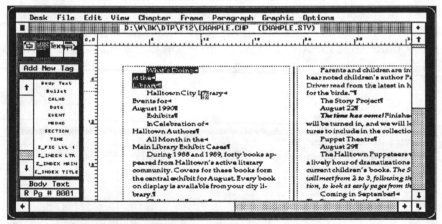

Figure 11.5: Calendar before Tagging

Specifying and Modifying Tags

Note the window toward the left edge of Figure 11.5, with the lines "Body Text," "Bullet," "CALHD," and so on. Since Ventura is currently in "paragraph mode" (as indicated by the reverse-video icon, second from left above "Add New Tag"), this is a list of the available tag names for paragraphs.

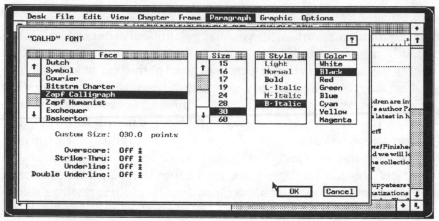

Figure 11.6: Font Selection

Paragraphs, as defined by tags, represent the most powerful aspect of Ventura Publisher's automated processing. After highlighting the first paragraph and selecting CALHD as its proper tag, you pull down the paragraph menu and font submenu. Figure 11.6 shows the font selection box for CALHD, with the current settings. (For a PostScript printer, "Custom Size" would be active; note that it is grayed out and inactive at this point.) You can see at a glance that this paragraph is 30-point Zapf Calligraphic Bold Italic printed in Black.

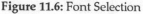

Figure 11.7: Spacing Options

Figure 11.7 shows the spacing menu for a different tag, the "Section" tag (the arrow points to a section name). This menu provides special margins for a given paragraph; it also controls leading. (A separate menu, not shown, controls justification, first-line indentation, and hyphenation.)

The "Breaks" menu (illustrated in Figure 11.8) automates the process of keeping things together and, when necessary, forcing new pages. In practice, you would change "Keep With Next" to "Yes" on this screen, so that the section heading is always in the same column as the first event beneath it. The "Line Break" and "Next Y Position" options support some special capabilities such as side-by-side paragraphs.

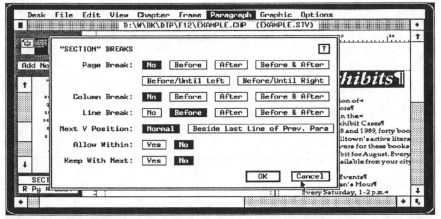

Figure 11.8: Breaks

Figure 11.9 shows one of three "Ruling Lines" menus that allow you to specify up to three ruling lines to go over, under, or around a paragraph or heading. This specification, for the "Event" tag, uses one of the special controls: rather than having a line going the full width of the column, "Width: Text" indicates that the line should only be as wide as the text—as shown in Figure 11.10.

Figure 11.10 shows the results of this tagging activity; it also shows the extent to which Ventura actually allows you to judge how the printed material will look. This is only a portion of the page, showing a section ("Children's Events"), several events ("The Children's Hour"), and some other items; it represents the text in Figure 11.2.

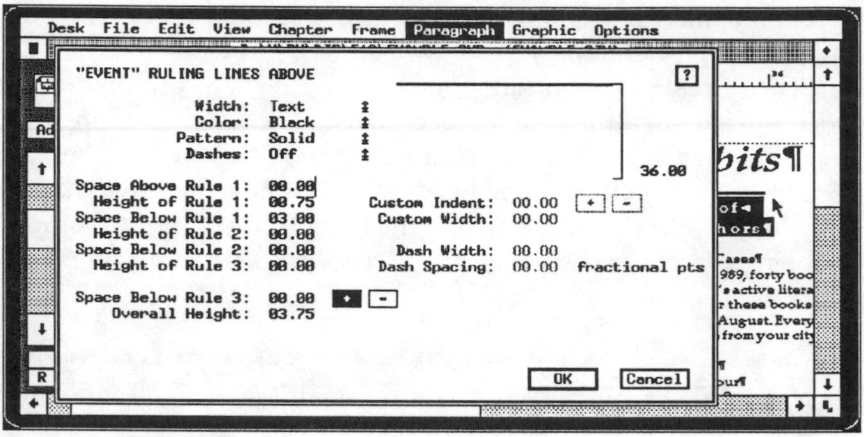

Figure 11.9: Ruling Lines

Other paragraph controls include: a full range of tab settings (up to sixteen) including leaders; special effects, specifically big first characters and bullets; and overrides for typography (letterspacing, tracking, and others). Without the wide range of tag-level controls in Ventura, it would not have been feasible to produce chapter 6 of this book as a single chapter; each example in chapter 6 involved at least one special tag with special characteristics.

Figure 11.10: Calendar Portion after Tagging

Adding Graphics

The document isn't ready quite yet—although, if it were a book list, it probably would be. We have a special image used for "The Children's Hour," and we want to include it in the calendar. In Figure 11.11, Ventura has been placed in Frame Mode, and a new frame has been drawn (the empty rectangle with eight black boxes around the sides).

Figure 11.11: Adding Frame for Graphics Import

At this point, you could add background shading, put lines around the box, add a caption, specify the precise size or otherwise modify the frame. We don't need to do any of these things, but we do need to bring in a graphic file. After doing so, we get to Figure 11.12.

Ventura has relatively few internal tools for dealing with graphics, but it can import a very wide variety of graphics and scale them to fit. You can directly draw straight lines, rectangles, and ovals; you can add arrow points to lines; and you can add textual annotations anywhere on the page. You can also crop a figure, cutting off some portion of the imported file. That's about it; any real manipulation of graphics must be done in other programs. (You can "erase" a rectangular portion of a graphic, but only by superimposing an empty frame over part of it.)

Figure 11.12: Calendar Ready to Print (Partial)

The Final Result

After importing one more graphic—the Halltown City Library logo—and checking the overall appearance of the calendar by reducing the view (to look at a full page, with most of the text appearing as little dots), you would print it out—and quite possibly get it just the way you wanted on the first try. Figure 4.3 shows the finished product (photoreduced to fit on the page).

Interoperability

There's one final phenomenon that you must be aware of. It represents one of Ventura's greatest strengths, but it can also be a trap if you are not aware it is happening. That phenomenon is *interoperability*. What this means is that Ventura not only imports files from many different word-processing formats; it also replaces those files in their original format—or, if you prefer, in some other word-processing format. The modified file includes all the markup work that Ventura uses to know what to do.

What this means is that, if you use your word-processing program to edit a file that was in any way modified by Ventura, the file may look very different than when you previously worked on it. For example, if you use Microsoft Word and assign Word styles to paragraphs, all of those assignments will be gone—and headings and other special paragraphs will begin with text that you didn't enter. Figure 11.13 shows the same Microsoft Word file as in Figure 11.2, after working with it in Ventura Publisher. As you can see, it has changed substantially:

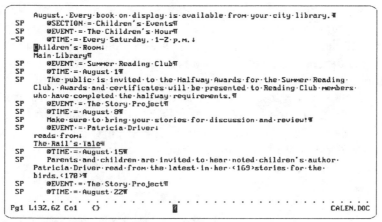

Figure 11.13: Word File, Modified by Ventura

- All of the Word tags have disappeared; as far as Word is concerned, every paragraph is a standard paragraph.

- Most paragraphs now begin with special text: for example, "@SECTION = " or "@TIME = ."

- The quotation marks around "stories for the birds" have been replaced with very odd strings—<169> and <170>. If there had been any double hyphens, each pair would be replaced by <197>.

The first change can be an annoyance—but, of course, the Word tags don't really matter if you're using Ventura for formatting. The second change shows you how to automate later calendar production. If you key in "@SECTION = " (and so on) when preparing the text in Word or WordPerfect, Ventura will apply the right spacing, fonts, breaks, etc. as soon as it loads the file. Apart from placing graphics and touching up problems, your layout work within Ventura will be done almost before you begin.

The third change, which is optional, is a matter of typographic nicety. Ventura has converted the quotation marks to true typographic quotation marks (with different opening and closing marks); the strings <169> and <170> represent the numeric equivalents of the open and close quotes, respectively. (<197> is the "em dash", the wide dash.)

Note that Ventura does not save the text internally, in the chapter or anywhere else. If you modify the text and restart Ventura for the same chapter, all of your changes will automatically appear in the publication. That feature saves disk space and ensures that editing changes won't be lost inadvertently—but it can mean that, should you go to produce a new set of pages for an existing publication, the pages won't look the way they did last time. You must be sure that the text and graphics files referred to in the Ventura chapter are in the same state as they were in the original; the Ventura chapter itself does not include either the files or any notation as to their version, date, or size.[1]

Some Other Features

This view of document production shows many of Ventura's most important features, particularly those that provide automated document production. A few other features should also be mentioned.

- Ventura provides full control for tracking—either at the tag level or interactively on selected text (you can highlight text and use cursor keys to tighten or loosen it). Interactive tracking allows you to make a headline stretch the full width of a column or fit a long headline into a short space.

- While Ventura is not a word-processing program, you can key in text and modify existing text. You can delete, copy, and move sections of text (or graphics). You can also insert special items—box characters that

---

1   Ventura does provide a special function to copy all of the files involved in a given chapter to a diskette or different disk drive, so that you can be assured of a consistent version.

don't exist in the character set, for example □; true typographic fractions such as 128⁄256 or even *abc/def*—which can also be entered as part of word processing; and footnotes and index entries (which can be entered in word processing).

- All measurements and rulers can be stated as inches, points and picas, fractional points, or centimeters.

Starting Points

This discussion and demonstration certainly does not cover all aspects of Ventura Publisher. If it all seems a little overwhelming—well, it is at first, but not for very long. You build most publications with one set of frames; you define text one tag at a time. Ventura handles most of the hard work and assigns most elements automatically. You really don't need to use most of these specific capabilities; frequently, Ventura's default assumptions work quite well.

There's no question that you need some time to learn Xerox Ventura Publisher or any other desktop-publishing program. You can choose from several ways to learn or combine different ways that make you most comfortable. Don't assume that you must learn everything at the beginning; you will add more subtleties as you become more familiar with the program.

Quite a few books have been published on Ventura Publisher. Some of them essentially rearrange Ventura's own documentation; some provide different treatments specifically designed for instruction; some provide additional information or ways of looking at Ventura facilities. Some video and audio training courses are also available, as are any number of classes and seminars. Finally, Xerox provides several aids to learning as part of the package:

- Chapter 6 in the *Reference Guide*, "Putting It Together," provides a useful fast overview of how Ventura's elements combine to produce documents.

- The *Training Guide* includes seven carefully prepared self-paced learning exercises, accompanied by sample files that come with Ventura so that you can try out the techniques introduced.

- The sample documents and style-sheet templates provided with Ventura offer good ways to learn; they may also offer good starting points for your own style sheets.

- The *Workbook* offers a structured approach to planning and creating publications. It may involve more paperwork and overhead than you would normally use, but it does show a way to set up your first real publication without being overwhelmed by the intermingled options of Ventura.

- When you send in your software registration card, Xerox sends you *A User's Guide to Basic Design*. This brief book deals with design issues in a clear, interesting and useful manner. While some of the design suggestions differ from those of many other designers, they are all reasonable and clearly identified as suggestions rather than rules. The book, which is only sixty pages long (in the version I received), is well worth reading when starting out and rereading for new ideas and reconsideration after you've used Ventura for a few months.

One warning: *Do not attempt to learn Ventura while you're on deadline for a publication.* The results will usually be disastrous for your morale, your schedule, and your attitude toward Ventura.

Professional Extension

If you have the money, the equipment, and the special needs, the Xerox Ventura Professional Extension adds six significant features to Ventura[2]. Two of these will be useful for many library uses but require expanded memory in your computer—in one case, at least 1½ megabytes of expanded memory. The features include:

---

2   Ventura Publisher 3.0, to be released in 1990, will apparently offer these features as options within the regular program.

- Ability to place the document in expanded memory, making it possible to create larger and more complex documents and work more rapidly with large documents;

- A hyphenation dictionary including 130,000 words, resulting in almost perfect hyphenation in all but the rarest cases (this dictionary requires 1½ megabytes of expanded memory);

- Equation-building facilities that expand Version 2.0's typographic fractions to support typographically correct mathematical equations;

- Fast facilities for building complex tables and importing spreadsheet information;

- More complex and sophisticated cross-reference capabilities;

- Vertical justification, so that columns on a page and pages in a publication always end at the same points.

If you think you may need the Professional Extension, talk to people in your chapter of Ventura Publisher Users Group (if you join one) or to Xerox. Those applications that really need the extension will justify it quite rapidly; most users may have little or no need for it.

Alternative Approaches

Ventura may be the most popular advanced MS-DOS desktop-publishing program but it is by no means the only one or the only approach to professional-quality output. The next chapter considers two lower-cost, less sophisticated approaches to desktop publishing. There are several such approaches, from the simplicity and limited power of The Print Shop to moderately powerful packages such as Publish-It! (which uses a control scheme similar to Ventura).

There are also other approaches to high-end desktop publishing, including Interleaf (originally designed for specialized computers, but now available on the Macintosh and IBM PC/RT) and Aldus PageMaker.

Aldus PageMaker

As already noted, PageMaker was the original—and it is still the favorite program of most graphic designers, probably because its operating philosophy is familiar and because it runs on the Macintosh. If you want to do extensive page-by-page design work, if you are familiar with the Macintosh, or if you prefer the pasteboard approach to document layout, you will probably prefer Aldus Page-Maker to Ventura Publisher.

PageMaker looks like most Macintosh programs, with a menu bar, scroll bars, rulers, title line, mouse pointers, and icons. It shows one or two pages and offers a toolbox and "palletes" as needed. However, the PageMaker screen also includes a *pasteboard*, the area around the page or pages. Galleys of text or graphics sit on the pasteboard, waiting to be used on a page. To graphic designers, the pasteboard approach of PageMaker is a key advantage over Ventura.

Typically, PageMaker work involves building pages, one by one; the pages already created pile up as little icons at the bottom of the screen—up to the 128-page limit of PageMaker. You can in some cases pour text into a PageMaker document such that new pages are created automatically, but you cannot automatically load multiple new files into multiple frames within an existing matrix, as you can with Ventura.[3]

PageMaker can import text and graphic files with much the same flexibility as Ventura—but once PageMaker imports a file, it stays imported. If you change the original file, that has no effect on Page-Maker's copy—and changes in PageMaker aren't reflected in the original files. That means three things:

- PageMaker uses more disk space because it stores its own text file;

- Revisions require significantly more work than in Ventura;

- You can't automate the production of repetitive documents such as bibliographies or new-title lists (i.e., each document must be prepared manually each time you need it).

While PageMaker excels at creating frames, you can't specify the precise size of frames or columns; you can only move them with the

---

3   For example, the *LITA Newsletter* includes the slogan, issue date, table of contents, masthead, and mailing strip—all of which go in the same position each issue. These are all automatically imported and placed in the Ventura chapter for the current issue of the newsletter.

mouse and rely on the ruler for sizing. On the other hand, PageMaker will flow text around an irregularly shaped graphic; that's quite difficult to do in Ventura.

PageMaker imports Microsoft Word style sheets and uses them; that option is not available in Ventura, but Ventura style sheets offer far more options. For example, you can't associate ruling lines or boxes with tags (called "styles") in PageMaker and you can't specify letterspacing or tracking for specific styles. PageMaker also does not build indexes or tables of content and, in general, does not provide the document-organizing tools present in Ventura Publisher.

PageMaker lacks most of the support for revision that is present in Ventura and most of the automated textual control. On the other hand, PageMaker offers a single-action Undo function (for some, but not all, changes); it will print thumbnail sketches of up to sixty-four pages per sheet on a PostScript printer, to check overall document design; and its graphics operations are generally considered more powerful and convenient than those in Ventura.

The competition between Aldus PageMaker and Xerox Ventura Publisher has resulted in PageMaker gaining document-oriented facilities such as style sheets, and the ability to add pages automatically for long text files. That competition has also speeded up the development of better graphics facilities in Ventura Publisher. Both programs have, to some extent, worked toward comparable features—even though the two companies don't necessarily consider themselves to be direct competitors. At this point, Aldus PageMaker continues to provide better facilities for design-intensive page-by-page layout. For the type of text-oriented documents that libraries are more likely to produce, Ventura's approach is more convenient.

Code-Based Typography

Computer-based page layout need not be interactive and visual. The most interesting example of code-based typography, where everything is done by inserting codes into text, is probably TEX. TEX is a language for typography designed by Donald Knuth of Stanford University. It provides incredible power and precise results and has been used for many scientific articles and books. But it is a pure coding system, and there are quite a few other such systems. Notably, recent advertisements for TEX assert that desktop publishing represents "distractions" and "extraneous, unnecessary design frivolities!" That last exclamation point (in the original) hints at the desperation behind these ads.

Code-based typography can work very well if you understand the codes, but it offers no feedback until the pages are printed out. If you are one of those for whom code-based typography makes sense, you probably know it. If not, you will almost certainly find either PageMaker or Ventura Publisher to be more useful and less frustrating.

Tips and Reminders

- Ventura Publisher will be most powerful if you plan style sheets for recurring publications, automating most of the production step.

- Tags should usually name logical elements of a publication (e.g., Head, Title, Bullet), not specifically how those elements will be formatted.

- Ventura has an enormous range of capabilities; you don't need to learn them all at once.

- Ventura will usually change the text files that it uses; it does not make its own copies of text files.

- You can use Ventura to convert a text file from one word-processing format to another.

12

Simpler Desktop Publishing

Xerox Ventura Publisher lists for $895 and sells for about $500. Another product, pfs:First Publisher lists for $129 and sells for about $80. Logitech's Finesse lists for $179 and sells for about $120. All three programs have a few things in common:

- Each is called a desktop-publishing program, each runs in a reverse-video graphic environment, each shows text and graphics as they will appear on the printed page, and each will run on less powerful computers such as the original IBM XT;

- Each will drive a variety of printers including some dot-matrix printers, the Hewlett-Packard LaserJet, and PostScript printers such as the Apple LaserWriter;

- Each will import text from the major word-processing programs and graphics from a variety of sources;

- Each supports Bitstream typefaces and includes a selection of Bitstream fonts as part of the package;

- Each can serve some libraries well for some purposes, and each represents a reasonably good bargain for its capabilities.

That's roughly where the similarities end. While all three programs do desktop publishing, it's not clear that they compete directly with one another.

Xerox Ventura Publisher represents the high end of microcomputer-based desktop publishing. It can form the basis of a sophisticated library publishing program and performs particularly well with long, complex, and repetitious documents. But you probably wouldn't turn Ventura over to the grade-school reading club to make their posters, and you probably wouldn't ask a library volunteer to produce a book-sale flier using Ventura. Ventura requires a significant amount of training, although it is straightforward to use once learned.

Don't even think about producing complex, text-intensive documents with pfs:First Publisher—and you'll probably be frustrated if you try to use it for long bibliographies, the library annual report, or any other formal document. The grade-school reading club might be delighted with pfs:First Publisher, however, particularly if some of the members have used MacPaint. For that matter, that retired library volunteer might get a kick out of it! The pfs:First Publisher program offers entry-level desktop publishing and entices you to add clip art to your publications. It has much in common with MacPaint; those who are familiar with the Macintosh will probably find pfs:First Publisher clunky but approachable.

Logitech's Finesse falls somewhere in the middle. As with First Publisher, it is designed for relatively short publications, requires relatively little training, and includes a (much smaller) collection of clip art—but, unlike First Publisher, it will directly support the Logitech ScanMan handheld scanner, so that you can scan and edit images directly into documents. As with Ventura Publisher, Finesse runs under GEM, provides mathematically precise control over frame sizes, produces all text at full printer resolution, and controls styles at the paragraph level—but in a very different way.

The first section of this chapter shows some of First Publisher's screens and methods, going through the creation of a partial one-page document, shows some completed First Publisher pages, explains how they were created, and discusses the fonts provided with the package.

The second section is a far less complete discussion of Finesse, including a few screen images from the program and examples of some fonts.

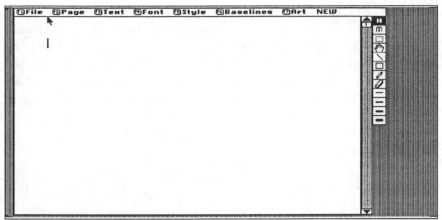

Figure 12.1: First Publisher, Opening Screen

First Publisher: Building a Document

Figure 12.1 shows the empty opening screen for pfs:First Publisher. The column of icons on the right edge show something of the program's orientation: with one exception, these are all "art" tools.

Figure 12.2: Page of First Publisher Art

Most First Publisher documents will include illustrations—and you usually begin by selecting the illustrations to be used. Typically, such illustrations will come from collections of *clip art*—ready-made images supplied in machine-readable form. First Publisher works with *pages* of clip art—that is, files that each contain as many related images as will fit on a letter-size page. Five such pages, including more than 100 images in all, are included with the program. Inexpensive "art packages" (available individually or as a complete $100 collection) include more than 100 pages and considerably more than 1,000 images in all. Most of the clip art was originally produced using MacPaint, from all appearances (and from the ".MAC" extension on the files). First Publisher can also import some other clip-art formats and some scanned images.

Selecting Art

Figure 12.2 shows one such page of images loaded into First Publisher, so that a particular image can be selected. The actual image desired is on the lower portion of the page. Figure 12.3 shows the image as selected, just before writing it out as a separate file. You would repeat this process for each image to be used. Naturally, images that are used frequently can be retained as separate image files.

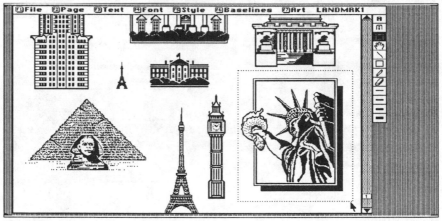

Figure 12.3: Selected Image (Statue of Liberty)

Defining the Page

After selecting and saving all images to be used in a document, you define the page itself, as shown in Figure 12.4. First Publisher doesn't have definable frames as such; it has a base page, with two "layers" for graphics and text. There aren't many options available—only number of columns, margins, overall justification, and the basic linespacing for text. First Publisher only creates letter-size, portrait pages; all measurements except leading are in inches. Note that all definitions are for the entire document.

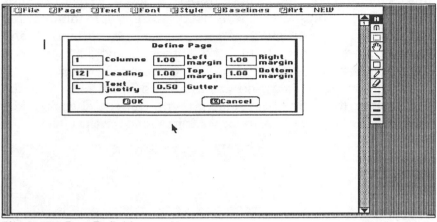

Figure 12.4: Page Definition

The leading measurement is important because it establishes a set of *baselines*—sometimes-visible lines that define where text will go. Almost all textual layout—centering or other modified justification, changing the number of columns for part of the text, leaving space above or below a headline, and so on—is done by adjusting the baselines.

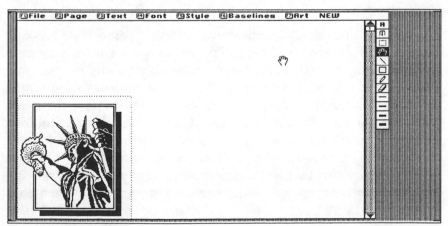

Figure 12.5: Reimported Illustration

Importing

At this point, you can either import illustrations, import text, or begin to key text directly. Figure 12.5 shows the illustration to be used, imported and placed in position (using the mouse to place the box surrounding the illustration). It would be possible to manipulate the image at this point or later: changing its size, inverting black and white, rotating it, making duplicate copies (turning a tree into a forest, for example)—and even editing it, adding lines, erasing portions, or adding and removing individual dots. Figure 12.6 shows the screen set up to modify the statue's crown: you would work on the large image while checking the smaller image to see the effects.

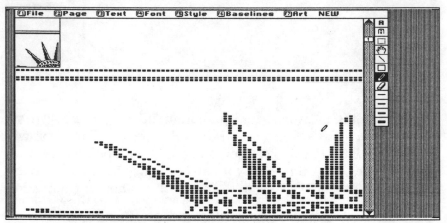

Figure 12.6: Magnified Figure for Editing

Unlike Ventura, which has very rich text-modification tools but quite limited graphics tools, pfs:First Publisher includes a modest paint program so that you can build and modify graphic images. You can draw boxes and straight lines in several thicknesses and add characters that are actually part of the graphic image (and, thus, can be resized or edited)—and you can also touch up an illustration, which is not possible in Ventura Publisher.

On the other hand, the illustrations have limited resolution: always 1/72 inch. In other words, the smallest unit you can work with is a full point; a dot on the screen is actually a square of sixteen dots (four by four) on a laser printer. That makes for limited quality in the illustrations—but it does make touch-up more plausible, since you can work on a significant part of the image at once.

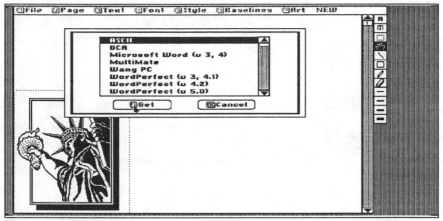

Figure 12.7: First Publisher Text-Import Menu

Now we import some text—using the menu shown in Figure 12.7. Text importing is problematic in three ways:

- The selection box will not traverse directories; you must know exactly where files are in advance, and key in the proper path.

- First Publisher tends to be a little behind on word-processing versions. I was totally unable to import files prepared with Word 5.0 using the "Word" option, and I was forced to save them as plain ASCII text—losing, as a result, any formatting information.

- While it is possible to specify font changes within word-processing text, that's about it—and, since First Publisher doesn't provide paragraph-level formatting, there are no automatic indents.

Figure 12.8 shows the results. The four separate paragraphs in Microsoft Word, exported as ASCII, become one collapsed paragraph. It would be necessary to add a blank line after each paragraph in order to have First Publisher start new lines. Text is not hyphenated as it is imported—and, indeed, there seems to be no way to hyphenate text in First Publisher except with "hard" hyphens. That makes fully justified text rather awkward and difficult to use.

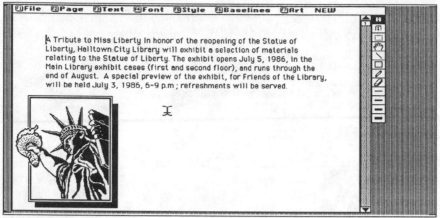

Figure 12.8: Imported Text File

Cleaning Up

To make the document look the way you want, you must modify baselines and assign new text characteristics. Figure 12.9 shows the screen in the midst of a baseline modification. First Publisher does a good job of indicating what material can be worked with—for example, in any graphics mode the text turns gray. Most baseline changes result in all text disappearing, however, until the changes are completed. This can make changes slow and difficult. Note, also, that if you've messed up the overall margins and leading, but have also set baselines for headings and the like, it's too late to make changes in the page definition! If you do, all the baseline changes disappear—but at least the manual warns you about that.

Finally, we have the partial page as it should be printed in Figure 12.10. This is a realistic view of how it will finally look, except for some problems in using Bitstream fonts (discussed later). Figures 12.11 through 12.14 show four different documents that I prepared using First Publisher—all without ever drawing anything or otherwise revealing my total graphic incompetence.

As should be obvious from these figures, First Publisher has one considerable advantage that offsets its many drawbacks for some short projects: it can be fun to use, and it can give gratifying results rather quickly. That advantage, and ease of learning, may explain why pfs:First Publisher outsells Ventura Publisher; indeed, it is the best-selling desktop-publishing program for MS-DOS computers.

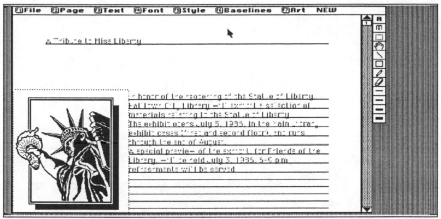

Figure 12.9: Baseline Adjustment

Notes on the Figures

Figure 12.11 includes three clip-art images and three different fonts. The truck (stretched horizontally), the plane (compressed), and the billboard were selected from various clip-art pages and put in place. Text was added to the billboard; in First Publisher, this requires no extra steps. Perhaps the most interesting parts of this figure are the footsteps and the train. These are not clip art; rather, they are characters from the Cairo typeface. (See Figure 12.18, later in this chapter.) The coarseness of the images may be apparent in the airplane and the lamps over the billboard; still, these images would be fine for this particular use.

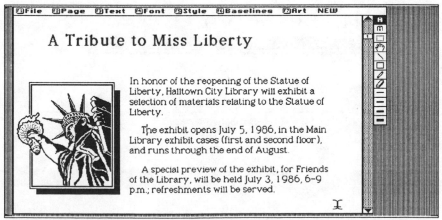

Figure 12.10: Adjusted Text and Graphic

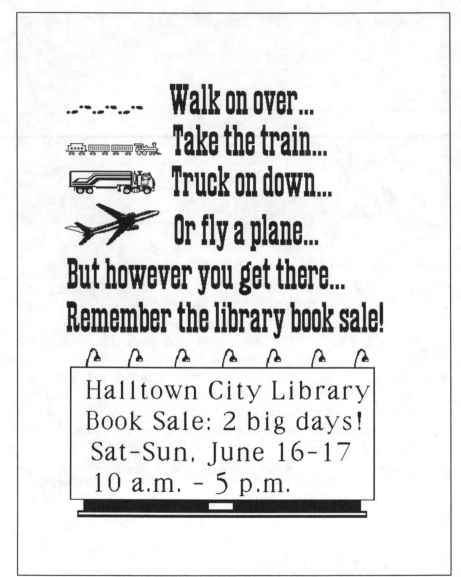

Figure 12.11: Book-Sale Sign (First Publisher)

Figure 12.12 shows the only case where I actually modified a clip-art image. The wonderful sketch of Mark Twain came on a dark background; I didn't eliminate all of it, but managed to erase most of it (using the eraser at normal screen size and, in some cases, at magnified size). Note that the citations on this page are crisp; they are Amerigo 12, a Bitstream font defined at 300 dots per inch (the other fonts are defined at 72 dots per inch). Note also that there are some spacing problems; this version of First Publisher apparently doesn't handle Bitstream width tables correctly, sometimes leaving no space at all between words. The Halltown City Library logo was created by taking a symbol from a clip-art collection, adding a horizontal line in First Publisher, and keying in the library name below the line.

Figure 12.13 uses another font available for First Publisher, called Inverness. Both presidential cameos come from clip-art collections; no retouching was done. Finally, Figure 12.14 uses a Bitstream font that has rather specialized uses—an invitation being one of them. I drew the rectangle (3 by 5 inches in the original, of course) with the box-drawing tool, and I added the shadows using a 3-point line-drawing tool, as suggested in the manual.

The Macintosh Connection

Macintosh users may be reading the font names and saying, "But those are Macintosh names!" Indeed, the Macintosh "accent" of pfs:First Publisher is so pronounced that the clip-art collection, for an MS-DOS program, has half a dozen well-drawn Macintosh images, with only one little computer that looks vaguely like a PC—and all of the dozens of disk images are 3½-inch microdiskettes, the Macintosh standard!

A Mark Twain Summer

The Jumping Frog in English, Then in French, Then Clawed Back into a Civilized Language Once More by Patient, UnremuneratedToil. Chronicle Books, 1985. 40 p. [Fiction]

Life on the Mississippi. Harper & Row, 1917. [917.7 C591]

Mark Twain's San Francisco, edited by Bernard Taper. McGraw-Hill, 1963. 263 p. [917.9461 C591]

The Prince and the Pauper: A Tale for Young People of All Ages. Harper & Row, 1906. 296 p. [Fiction]

The Adventures of HuckleberryFinn (Tom Sawyer's Comrade). The Zodiac Press, 1980. 335 p. [Fiction]

The Adventures of Tom Sawyer. Grosset & Dunlap, 1946. 317 p. [Fiction]

The Celebrated Jumping Frog of Calaveras County. Centennial ed. Filter Press, 1965. 32 p. [Fiction]

A Connecticut Yankee in King Arthur's Court. William Morrow, 1988. 374 p. [Fiction]

The Innocents Abroad, or, The New Pilgrim's Progress: Being Some Accounts of the Steamship "Quaker City's" Pleasure Excursion to Europe and the Holy Land. Harper & Row, 1905. [817 T969 1905]

Pudd'nhead Wilson and Those Extraordinary Twins. Norton, 1980. 384 p. [Fiction]

Roughing It. Buccaneer Books, 1960. 270 p. [817 C59r]

Tom Sawyer Abroad: Tom Sawyer, Detective, and Other Stories, etc. Harper & Brothers, 1905. 410 p. [Fiction]

The Book-A-WeekClub
1990 Reading List

Halltown City Library

Figure 12.12: A Mark Twain Summer

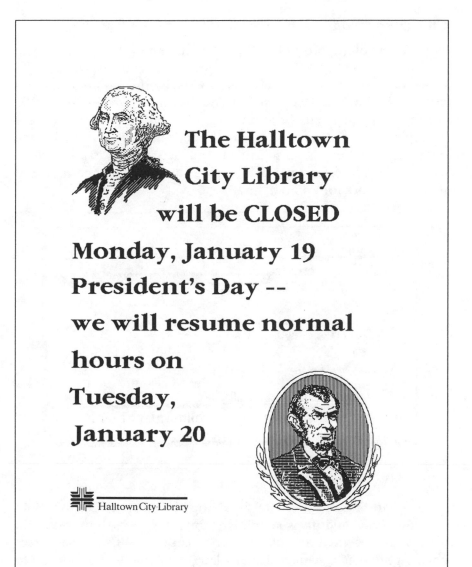

The Halltown
City Library
will be CLOSED
Monday, January 19
President's Day --
we will resume normal
hours on
Tuesday,
January 20

Halltown City Library

Figure 12.13: Presidents' Day Sign

Clip Art and Art Collections

There's no getting around it: clip art is fun, and it's one reasonable way to add illustrations other than graphs, if you're as artistically untalented as I am. Clip art also tends to be corny and predictable— but, as the book-sale sign suggests, there are times when a little corniness is just what the library needs. I don't think any of these examples would embarrass a typical public library—even with the obvious jagged edges on most of them. Figure 12.14 is an extreme case; the typeface, Coronet Bold, is almost too cute for words, but it just might work for an invitation.

You are cordially invited to a celebration of Halltown City Library's new Online Catalog, HALLCAT, and the ceremonial closing of the library's Card Catalog. Wine and cheese will be served.

Saturday, August 18, 7-9 p.m., Halltown City Library Reading Room
RSVP: (215) 555-LIBR

Sponsored by the Friends of the Library

Halltown City Library

Figure 12.14: Invitation

"Spicing up" a newsletter by doing one story in Coronet Bold would be cruel and unusual punishment for readers, however: that font is not designed for extended body copy, and it becomes a real challenge to read when used at any length. Bitstream didn't mean to suggest that Coronet would be good for body type—they specifically recommend using it for invitations and some fliers. They merely wanted to show the range of Bitstream fonts without giving away too many useful ones, and they succeeded.

Fonts in First Publisher

Figures 12.15–12.18 show 10 of some 110 fonts that are included with First Publisher or available in two low-cost add-ons. Of the 10 fonts illustrated here, 5 are Bitstream fonts produced at full laser resolution: 10- and 12-point Amerigo, 14-point Dutch and Coronet Bold, and 18-point Cooper Black. Clearly, neither Cooper Black nor Coronet Bold should be used for normal text; that's not their purpose. Amerigo is one of Bitstream's original designs and works well in text; Dutch is Bitstream's version of Times.

The other fonts—New York, Geneva, London, and Cairo—are much lower in resolution but are smoothed for laser output. If you compare 12-point New York and 14-point Dutch Roman, you can see how relatively crude the New York is—but it works reasonably well on its own.

Some of the fonts are rather specialized—including London, of course, but also several script fonts, a different black-letter font (Canterbury, which is simpler than London), and a traditional Germanic font (Heidelberg), as well as some typical advertising fonts that would never see use in normal copy. Additionally, you can purchase Bitstream fonts to use with First Publisher—but that may seem odd, since a typical typeface family for Bitstream will cost almost twice as much as First Publisher!

Except for the Bitstream fonts, all fonts are low-resolution, 72 dots per inch; these are PC equivalents of Macintosh QuickDraw fonts, with the on-screen advantages and printing liabilities common to those fonts. First Publisher's smoothing for laser printers does help, but these are coarse typefaces by any standards. Note, incidentally, that the count of 100+ fonts is exactly that—fonts, not typefaces. A *font* is a single typeface, in a single typestyle, in a single size; by using *italic* and **bold** here, this paragraph alone includes three fonts. (Note also that none of the "italic" fonts for First Publisher is a true italic. As with Finesse in this chapter and Glyphix in the next chapter, they are all oblique rather than italic; that distinction is explained in chapter 13.)

Bitstream Amerigo 10-point Roman:
Fonts vary widely in design and quality. Tests for legibility require
not only "character-set runs," e.g. [ABCDE FGHIJ KLMNO PQRST
UVWXYZ abcde fghij klmno pqrst uvwxyz 12345 67890 :;?{} !@#$%
^ &*()], but also difficult words such as LITA, Two and Wave or
WAVE. Add a Proper Name such as Johannes Gutenberg and a
sentence such as The quick brown fox jumps over the lazy dog.

Bitstream Amerigo 12-point Roman:
Fonts vary widely in design and quality. Tests for
legibility require not only "character-set runs," e.g. [ABCDE
FGHIJ KLMNO PQRST UVWXYZ abcde fghij klmno pqrst
uvwxyz 12345 67890 :;?{} !@#$% ^ &*()], but also
difficult words such as LITA, Two and Wave or WAVE.
Add a Proper Name such as Johannes Gutenberg and a
sentence such as The quick brown fox jumps over the
lazy dog.

New York 12-point Roman (Normal):
Fonts vary widely in design and quality. Tests
for legibility require not only "character-set
runs," e.g. [ABCDE FGHIJ KLMNO PQRST
UV WXYZ abcde fghij klmno pqrst uvwxyz
12345 67890 :;?{} !@#$% ^&*()], but also
difficult words such as LITA, Two and Wave
or WAVE. Add a Proper Name such as
Johannes Gutenberg and a sentence such as
The quick brown fox jumps over the lazy dog.

Figure 12.15: First Publisher Fonts (1)

New York "Italic" 10 point:
Fonts vary widely in design and quality. Tests for
legibility require not only "character-set runs," e.g.
[ABCDE FGHIJ KLMNO PQRST UVWXYZ abcde fghij
klmno pqrst uvwxyz 12345 67890 :;?{} !@#$% ^&()]*
but also difficult words such as LITA, Two and Wave
or WAVE. Add a Proper Name such as Johannes
Gutenberg and a sentence such as The quick brown
fox jumps over the lazy dog.

Bitstream Dutch Roman 14 point:
Fonts vary widely in design and quality. Tests
for legibility require not only "character-set
runs," e.g. [ABCDEFGHIJ KLMNO PQRST
UVWXYZ abcde fghij klmno pqrst uvwxyz
12345 67890 :;?{} !@#$% ^ & *()], but also
difficult words such as LITA, Two and Wave
or WAVE. Add a Proper Name such as
Johannes Gutenberg and a sentence such as
The quick brown fox jumps over the lazy dog.

Bitstream Coronet Bold 14 point:
Fonts vary widely in design and quality. Tests for legibility require
not only "character-set runs," e.g. [ABCDEFGHIJ
KLMNOPQRSTUVWXYZ abcde fghij klmno pqrst
*uvwxyz 12345 67890 :;?{} !@#$% ^ & *()], but also*
difficult words such as LITA, Two and Wave or WAVE.
Add a Proper Name such as Johannes Gutenberg and a sentence such
as The quick brown fox jumps over the lazy dog.

Figure 12.16: First Publisher Fonts (2)

Geneva 12-point Normal:
Fonts vary widely in design and quality. Tests for legibility require not only "character-set runs," e.g. [ABCDE FGHIJ KLMNO PQRST UVWXYZ abcde fghij klmno pqrst uvwxyz 12345 67890 :;?{} !@#$% ^&*()], but also difficult words such as LITA, Two and Wave or WAVE. Add a Proper Name such as Johannes Gutenberg and a sentence such as The quick brown fox jumps over the lazy dog.

London 18 point:
Fonts vary widely in design and quality. Tests for legibility require not only "character-set runs," e.g. [ABCDE FGHIJ KLMNO PQRST UVWXYZ abcde fghij klmno pqrst uvwxyz 12345 67890 :;?{} !@#$% &*()], but also difficult words such as LITA, Two and Wave...

Figure 12.17: First Publisher Fonts (3)

Figure 12.18: First Publisher Fonts (4)

The Missing Pieces

What do you lose with First Publisher? You lose tags, running heads and feet, built-in page numbering, widow and orphan control, and any built-in control of paragraphs. You lose tabs (completely), hyphenation, importation of typographic aspects from word-processing programs and such niceties as footnotes, table of contents, and index generation.

Ventura offers bullets and big first characters; you can achieve big first characters manually in First Publisher, but you can't do a good job with bullets. Typographic fractions aren't available; neither are expanded editable views, automatic or manual kerning, letterspacing and any automatic control of line breaks, paragraph indentation, and the like. Text will flow forward to additional pages automatically (on import only)—but it won't flow back automatically if you delete earlier text.

First Publisher is a convenient, relatively simple program for producing quick posters; it is also a good program for children and for volunteers who have neither the time nor the inclination to learn a full-fledged desktop-publishing system. Simplicity has its place; pfs:First Publisher can work in cases where Ventura would simply be overwhelming.

Finesse: Brief Comments

Logitech makes wonderful mice and very nice handheld scanners, as well as some software. In 1989, they introduced their own low-end desktop-publishing program, Finesse, with a heavy advertising campaign targeting it at people who don't have time for manuals or for learning heavyweight programs.

Figure 12.19 shows the opening screen for Finesse—which may seem mildly familiar. Like Ventura Publisher, Finesse runs under GEM; in my experiments, unfortunately, it runs substantially slower than Ventura, to the point that adding text is an aggravating experience on a medium-speed AT-compatible.

Everything in Finesse is based on master pages, but also on frames. You build master pages to define margins and columns—but you can't put anything directly on the master page. Instead, you define text frames for text, graphics frames for graphics.

Figure 12.20 shows some frames being defined. Like Ventura, Finesse offers the choice of establishing frames using the mouse or fine-tuning them with a menu; unlike Ventura, Finesse gives all

Finesse menu choices either in fractional inches or fractional centimeters (except for linespacing and spacing above and below paragraphs, expressed in points).

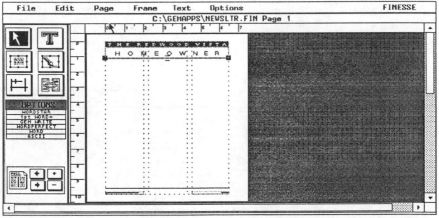

Figure 12.19: Finesse, Opening Screen

Finesse provides some support for running headers and footers. You must draw the frames, but special icons will provide incrementing page numbers and the date, if desired—and the concept of repeating frames is inherent in Finesse.

Figure 12.20: Finesse, Frames Added

In Figure 12.21, a clip-art file has been imported. Finesse's import capabilities are quite similar to Ventura's, and the selection routine is essentially identical; you can move through directories at will. Unlike Ventura, Finesse will control a scanner (the Logitech ScanMan) directly, making it easy to import clip art from any legitimate printed source directly into a document.

Figure 12.21: Imported Art

Finesse will never generate new pages automatically—because text never goes directly on the page. You must draw multiple frames (if needed) and define them as an explicit chain of frames. Once that's done, Finesse will maintain the flow of text between frames, even as you delete or modify text.

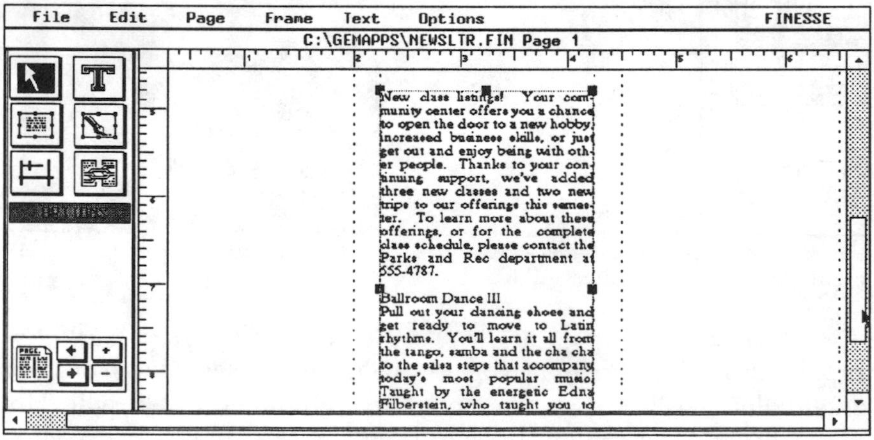

Figure 12.22: Imported-Text File

Note that this does mean you could do "continued on" stories, which would be extremely difficult in First Publisher—but it's also the only way you can handle such continuous text in this program. Finesse imposes an absolute sixteen-page limit; that's only reasonable, given the way text handling works. (But the starting page number need not be 1, so you can make a large document from several small ones.) Figure 12.22 shows imported text.

Finesse does, indeed, do paragraph-level definitions. It does not, however, give them names. To use the same style (justification and spacing) for several paragraphs, you can paste the paragraph style into multiple locations. That's better than nothing, although nowhere near as powerful as named styles. (Unfortunately, paragraph styles don't include font selection or style, so those choices would have to be made each time.)

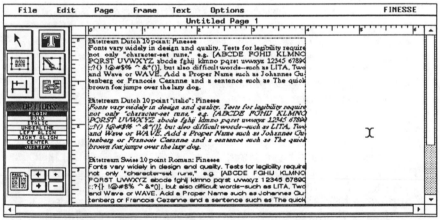

Figure 12.23: Text Ready for Printing

Figure 12.23 shows part of the text frame that appears in Figure 12.24, an example of Finesse fonts. As you can see, the on-screen representation is very good—and the fonts are all true laser-quality. In fact, the only fonts that Finesse can use are Bitstream fonts. The package includes several prebuilt sizes, but it also includes a Bitstream Fontware kit and Swiss, Dutch, Courier, and Symbol typefaces. Since the Fontware kit is included, you can generate almost any size of type with the software as supplied, and all sizes will be sharp and accurate.

There is a problem with the supplied fonts, however, which Finesse shares with First Publisher. As you can see in Figure 12.24, the italic version of Dutch is not really italic. As should be obvious from the lower-case *a*, it is oblique (that is, slanted roman). For as nice a typeface as Dutch, that's rather a shame.

Bitstream Dutch 10 point: Finesse
Fonts vary widely in design and quality. Tests for legibility require not only "character-set runs," e.g. [ABCDE FGHIJ KLMNO PQRST UVWXYZ abcde fghij klmno pqrst uvwxyz 12345 67890 :;?{} !@#$% ^ &*()], but also difficult words--such as LITA, Two and Wave or WAVE. Add a Proper Name such as Johannes Gutenberg or Francois Cezanne and a sentence such as The quick brown fox jumps over the lazy dog.

Bitstream Dutch 10 point "italic": Finesse
Fonts vary widely in design and quality. Tests for legibility require not only "character-set runs," e.g. [ABCDE FGHIJ KLMNO PQRST UVWXYZ abcde fghij klmno pqrst uvwxyz 12345 67890 :;?{} !@#$% ^ &()], but also difficult words--such as LITA, Two and Wave or WAVE. Add a Proper Name such as Johannes Gutenberg or Francois Cezanne and a sentence such as The quick brown fox jumps over the lazy dog.*

Bitstream Swiss 10 point Roman: Finesse
Fonts vary widely in design and quality. Tests for legibility require not only "character-set runs," e.g. [ABCDE FGHIJ KLMNO PQRST UVWXYZ abcde fghij klmno pqrst uvwxyz 12345 67890 :;?{} !@#$% ^ &*()], but also difficult words--such as LITA, Two and Wave or WAVE. Add a Proper Name such as Johannes Gutenberg or Francois Cezanne and a sentence such as The quick brown fox jumps over the lazy dog.

Figure 12.24: Some Fonts Used in Finesse

What's Missing, What's There

Finesse does hyphenate; it does provide easy one-step control over type fonts; and it will move text back and forth between frames as you modify the text, once an explicit chain is defined. It differentiates between right and left pages, handles Bitstream fonts properly, and does a good job with text and graphic imports. Within the main

Finesse program, graphics tools are limited to a line-drawing function, but Finesse also includes a Scan function, which controls the Logitech ScanMan and includes built-in facilities for editing a scanned image. The facilities include rotation, sizing, two sizes of magnification for erasure or additional lines, and the ability to take a pattern (shading, etc.) from one portion of an image and paint it into other portions of the image. An Undo function eliminates any single sequence of actions. In total, the Scan function (which the manual correctly labels as an essentially separate program) provides fairly robust image-editing capabilities.

Finesse does support manual kerning—changing the space between a particular pair of letters—but apparently not automatic kerning. On the other hand, Finesse provides a word-processing function that is unusual for desktop publishing: Search and Replace, with a "Find Next" option. Pages can be viewed full-size (for editing), as an entire page, or as a two-page view; there is no double-size view.

As compared to First Publisher, Finesse offers weaker graphics capabilities (except within the Scan function) but much stronger text handling. The clip-art collection is much smaller (seventy images), but the Scan function opens a world of inexpensive, copyright-free images: for $15 spent on three Dover books, I already have a clip-art library much larger than the entire First Publisher library. (Of course, the scanner does cost more than the First Publisher clip-art library.) I find Finesse somewhat clumsier to use for quick-and-dirty sign production, but it would clearly be faster and more precise for extensive text manipulation.

When would you use Finesse? Typically, in two different situations:

- When you are starting out on a very limited budget, insufficient to afford Ventura Publisher, but you need precise text handling and good layout capabilities for brief documents;

- When you will be using desktop publishing so infrequently that no staff member is willing to learn Ventura Publisher and maintain familiarity with that fairly complex program.

Finesse—and, according to reports, other programs such as Publish-It!—offers a middle ground for producing modest publications. It is cheaper and easier to use than Ventura, and it provides a reasonable portion of the typographical control and finesse offered by that program, with a considerably shorter learning period. You could probably also move from Finesse to Ventura fairly smoothly, with some gratitude for the substantially increased power and speed of Ventura.

Conclusion

If your idea of desktop publishing is First Publisher, Ventura may seem overwhelming, but it will also offer remarkable new capabilities for handling text. If your idea is Ventura, both of these other programs will seem rather lacking—but they both offer better graphics control, and the two manuals put together are much shorter than Ventura's tome.

If you want footnotes, indexes, tables of contents, automatic generation and text flow across many pages, and sophisticated styles that can be controlled from within word processing, you need an advanced desktop-publishing program such as Ventura Publisher. If you expect to do lengthy, complex newsletters, directories, manuals, or other publications, you too need advanced desktop publishing. But if you need something that beginners can use effectively, something to produce posters and simple documents, either Finesse or First Publisher may serve you well—and under some circumstances, much better than Ventura Publisher.

First Publisher offers easy integration of clip art and typefaces, but most of the typography and all of the art are relatively coarse. Finesse offers high-quality typography and reasonable facilities for document-building, but only within the context of short publications. Its scanning support and flexible graphics import provide very good overall graphics capabilities, but without the built-in variety of clip art that comes with First Publisher.

The Ventura Publisher documentation was produced using Ventura Publisher—just as most books on either Ventura Publisher or Aldus PageMaker are produced using the software being discussed. I see no claim in the Finesse or First Publisher manuals that they were produced using that software—and, in each case, it seems highly unlikely that the software actually could have been used to produce the manual.

I enjoyed using First Publisher. Finesse came in late (when Logitech loaned me a ScanMan, discussed in chapter 14, they tossed in Finesse as well)—but, if I had been less thoroughly familiar with Ventura, I'm sure I would have enjoyed it also. Both products are well designed; both have fairly stringent (but different) limitations.

There are a number of other competitors in the low end of the market, including Publish-It! and GEM Publisher, both of which have been reasonably well reviewed. For most library textual publications, Microsoft Word or WordPerfect may be a better package than any low-end desktop-publishing program, if you don't want the extended capabilities of Ventura or PageMaker.

Tips and Reminders

- pfs:First Publisher will not serve you well for long or complex publications, but it is fun and easy to use: young users and volunteers may find it preferable to Ventura or PageMaker.

- Finesse offers high-quality typography at an attractive price, and it is also easy to learn, but it lacks the total control and automated formatting of Ventura Publisher.

- Different low-end desktop-publishing programs offer different capabilities; they may be useful as starting points or for special purposes.

13

Typefaces

You should recognize by now that one key to effective publication design is paying attention to the things most readers ignore—partly so that readers will continue to ignore them and pay attention to your message. That message, in almost all cases, will be conveyed primarily by text. As a result, typeface selection is one of the most critical aspects of desktop publishing.

Typographers can identify at least 5,000 different typefaces. Hundreds of these can be used in desktop publishing, and the variety of such typefaces grows steadily. You probably don't need to concern yourself with hundreds of choices—and you most certainly won't need to make that many choices each time you design a document. Most probably, you will have between two and perhaps a dozen typefaces to choose from on an everyday basis—which can be more than enough.

This chapter will discuss some basic aspects of typefaces and some of the sources and choices for desktop publishing. Much of the chapter consists of illustrations of some typefaces available for the LaserJet II. Because of those illustrations, this chapter violates one cardinal rule of good design, one that you should always remember: with rare exceptions, a publication should use only two typefaces— and many good publication designs use only one.

Remember that, in the advice above and throughout this chapter, *typeface* is used as a synonym for *type family*: all styles and sizes of a type design. Thus, even though this paragraph includes *italic*, **bold**, and ***bold italic*** styles, the entire paragraph is in a single typeface, Zapf Calligraphic. Note, however, that when you're buying typefaces—or when you're being sold on the advantages of Post-Script, for example—typeface will be used in the narrower sense. In that sense, this paragraph contains four typefaces, all in the same family.

Notes about Typefaces

What distinguishes one typeface from another—and what distinguishes a superb typeface from a mediocre one, or one that doesn't work in the context in which it is used? Obviously, those are questions that can't be answered here; many books and articles discuss the fine points of type design, and designers disagree as to which typefaces work best in which situations.

The most basic distinctions between typefaces have been mentioned in earlier chapters: serif and sans serif, body type and display type. Beyond those basic distinctions, type can be described in terms of a number of characteristics, including the following:

- Compactness and *x height*. Typefaces vary substantially in terms of the number of characters that will fit in a given space for a given size: some 10-point type fonts require as much as 50 percent more space to set a text passage than others do. The *x height* is the height of the lowercase *x* (and all other lowercase characters without ascenders or descenders), relative to the type size; some typefaces have much larger x heights than others.

- Thick and thin strokes, and the extent of contrast between them. Some modern typefaces have only one thickness used for all strokes within letters (Courier is a prime example). Others, including some of those designed to work well with laser printers, have only small differences between the thinnest strokes (usually the horizontal strokes, e.g., the crossbar in a lowercase *e* or a capital *B*) and the thickest strokes (typically vertical strokes). Some of the best-known serif typefaces have substantial, sometimes even extreme, differences in thickness.

- Shape and size of serifs, and where serifs are used. For example, Zapf Calligraphic and Palatino omit serifs in some letters such as the capital *Y*, and serifs can vary widely in size and shape (consider the capital *T* in the typefaces shown in figures 13.8–13.18). Bowls and rounds (such as those in the letters *b, g, o,* and *p*) can also vary in size and shape, and they may be based on circles or ovals.

- "Families" within which the typeface fits, including such terms as Transitional, Old Style, Egptian, and many more.

- The designer or redesigner of the typeface, and the extent to which this typeface relates to others designed by the same person. Hermann Zapf, Ed Benguiat, and Matthew Carter are some of this century's important type designers; there are many others, now as in the past.

The Name Game

When you start to explore the world of typefaces for desktop publishing—and even when you read the rest of this chapter—you will encounter typefaces with different names that appear to be very nearly identical. You will also encounter typefaces from different suppliers, where the typefaces have the same name but don't look quite the same as finished products.

The first case occurs because it is not possible to copyright the design of a typeface—but it is possible to establish the name of the typeface as a trademark. Thus, any type foundry can produce a typeface that looks exactly like Palatino—but they can't legally call it Palatino without a license from the owners of that trademark.

The second case occurs because most of the best typefaces for desktop publishing are, in fact, licensed from traditional type foundries, and most such licenses are nonexclusive. Thus, when ITC licenses ITC Korinna to both Adobe and Bitstream digital-type foundries, it is licensing the name and a set of letter designs. Adobe and Bitstream use different methods to turn those designs into digital outlines, and they establish different sets of kerning and width tables. As a result, the two typefaces with the same name will be slightly different on output: both recognizably Korinna, but subtly different.

Is it ethical to use an unlicensed version of a typeface? That's a difficult question to answer, particularly since the history of typography consists (at least to a great extent) of designers making subtle variations on typefaces prepared by other designers. It's also important to note that the use of a different name for a similar typeface does not necessarily mean that the typeface is a copy. It may indeed be a complete reinterpretation, possibly even using the services of the original designer. The clearest examples of this are Zapf Calligraphic and Zapf Humanist; these Bitstream typefaces were designed by the same man who created the originals (Palatino and Optima, respectively), Hermann Zapf.

This chapter illustrates quite a few typefaces, but they represent only a tiny fraction of what's actually available for desktop publishing. I don't provide detailed descriptive notes on any of the typefaces; you should study them yourself.

Body Text and Display Text

Most typographers and designers speak of two categories of text: body text and display text. What you're reading now is *body text*: it is part of the body of the chapter. The word *Typefaces* at the top of the previous page is *display text*—any text used for headlines, large initial letters, or other purposes outside of normal body text.

You can certainly use the same typeface for both body text and display text—this book does. But the two categories serve different purposes and make different requirements on typefaces.

Body Type

Body type stays in the background, at least for most publications. The point of body text is the text itself. The typeface should provide good legibility and readability, and it should be pleasant to the eye, but the reader should not be paying attention to the typeface as such. The typeface, and various aspects of textual design discussed in the next two chapters, should serve to turn letters into words, words into sentences, and sentences into paragraphs; the reader should not be staring at the individual letters.

That's one reason that you should use the same typeface for all body text in a publication—or at least in a given article. Changing to a different typeface will cause the reader's attention to shift from the text itself to the design of the text, thus reducing coherent understanding of the text. That shift may not be conscious, but there will be some awareness on the part of the reader that something has changed—and some expectation that the change is significant.

It is also the reason that the best typefaces for body text show certain similarities, lacking the extreme range of shapes found in display type. Body types do differ, with each typeface lending a slightly different "feel" to the text, but those differences are generally subtle.

Every rule has exceptions. Consider the typefaces illustrated in chapter 12. Bitstream Amerigo and Dutch are both good typefaces for body text; except for the low resolution, New York would also be effective in this role and Geneva might be workable. But consider figure 12.14. While Coronet is distinctly not suitable for normal body text—virtually defying the reader to ignore the typeface—it is quite suitable for this special situation. Indeed, it falls into the category of "special" typefaces: well suited to specific publications and absolutely not suitable for most others.

Bitstream Dutch 10 on 12

While typefaces used for body text should not call attention to themselves, this is not to say that the subtle differences among such typefaces are meaningless. Even among the best typefaces for body type – which are, generally, clear serif faces with open, readable designs – the differences will influence the overall look of text.

Bitstream Zapf Calligraphic 10 on 12

While typefaces used for body text should not call attention to themselves, this is not to say that the subtle differences among such typefaces are meaningless. Even among the best typefaces for body type—which are, generally, clear serif faces with open, readable designs—the differences will influence the overall look of text.

Bitstream Charter 10 on 12

While typefaces used for body text should not call attention to themselves, this is not to say that the subtle differences among such typefaces are meaningless. Even among the best typefaces for body type—which are, generally, clear serif faces with open, readable designs—the differences will influence the overall look of text.

Figure 13.1: Body Text 1

Figures 13.1 and 13.2 show six different typefaces well suited for body text. As these figures show, there are real (albeit subtle) differences among the best serif body types, differences that influence the "feel" or "tone" of the text. Note that all six typefaces are set identically: 10-point type set 10/12, fully justified.

The first paragraph in figure 13.1 is set in Dutch, Bitstream's version of Times Roman. This typeface is extremely readable and quite compact—note that the paragraph requires less space than the other five versions. It is also so familiar as to be essentially invisible. You can't really go wrong with Times Roman and its equivalents, but that's about the best you can say for it.

The second paragraph is Zapf Calligraphic. I regard Zapf Calligraphic as my own "signature typeface" and use it almost exclusively for body text. It is more distinctive than most first-rate body typefaces; at larger sizes and when many capital letters are used, some people find it too "personal" for effective use in business situations.

Bitstream Charter finishes out figure 13.1. Matthew Carter, one of America's premier type designers and vice president of Bitstream, designed Charter as a digital typeface, specifically designed to work well at laser-printer resolution and be legible and readable under all conditions. Charter is a simpler, subtler typeface than more classic designs.

The typefaces in figure 13.2 come from a different digital type foundry, Swfte (which uses the name Glyphix for its font system), and they are all unlicensed versions of major typefaces. The first, Baskerton, is Swfte's interpretation of Baskerville. The second is Rockland, Swfte's interpretation of Rockwell—a slab-serif font that is marginal as a body type, at the outer reaches of acceptability and probably not useful for lengthy texts. Finally, Garamand is Swfte's interpretation of Garamond, one of the greatest older typefaces (dating back three centuries).

Note that none of the typefaces in figure 13.2 uses space as efficiently as Times Roman; only Rockland is as compact as Zapf Calligraphic and Charter. Still, all six typefaces fall within a narrow range of space efficiency; by most standards, all six would be considered very efficient—and all six have tight letterspacing, with the Glyphix fonts possibly erring on the side of being too tight.

These examples do not exhaust the range of body type, but they do show a fair sampling of those typefaces most acceptable for lengthy text (although I personally would not use Rockland for such work).

Glyphix Baskerton 10 on 12

While typefaces used for body text should not call attention to themselves, this is not to say that the subtle differences among such typefaces are meaningless. Even among the best typefaces for body type—which are, generally, clear serif faces with open, readable designs—the differences will influence the overall look of text.

Glyphix Rockland 10 on 12

While typefaces used for body text should not call attention to themselves, this is not to say that the subtle differences among such typefaces are meaningless. Even among the best typefaces for body type—which are, generally, clear serif faces with open, readable designs—the differences will influence the overall look of text.

Glyphix Garamand 10 on 12

While typefaces used for body text should not call attention to themselves, this is not to say that the subtle differences among such typefaces are meaningless. Even among the best typefaces for body type—which are, generally, clear serif faces with open, readable designs—the differences will influence the overall look of text.

Figure 13.2: Body Text 2

Display Type

Display type calls attention to itself—sometimes to the text but, more frequently, to the type as a series of shapes. Indeed, display type may be the most important graphic element in most desktop publications, and individual letterforms do make a difference.

In practice, there are many more display typefaces than body typefaces, covering a far broader range of design. Some display typefaces can be intermixed with body typefaces—that is, used for subheads as well as headlines—while other display typefaces really stand alone and would clash with normal text. Most good body typefaces also make good display typefaces, but many useful display typefaces would be ludicrous for normal text.

Figures 13.3, 13.4, and 13.5 show six typefaces that should typically be used exclusively for display type and for certain special documents. In this case, in addition to the same paragraph as in figures 13.1 and 13.2, each typeface appears as a 24-point headline. (These figures were created using Microsoft Word and are all Glyphix fonts.)

University_Ornate

While typefaces used for body text should not call attention to themselves, this is not to say that the subtle differences among such typefaces are meaningless. Even among the best typefaces for body type—which are, generally, clear serif faces with open, readable designs—the differences will influence the overall look of text.

Buckingham

While typefaces used for body text should not call attention to themselves, this is not to say that the subtle differences among such typefaces are meaningless. Even among the best typefaces for body type—which are, generally, clear serif faces with open, readable designs—the differences will influence the overall look of text.

Figure 13.3: Display Text 1

The upper portion of figure 13.3 is University Ornate, Swfte's version of University Roman. Beautifully suited to certificates of appreciation and similar special uses, the typeface is far too ornate to make sense for regular reading, as the paragraph should show. The lower portion of the figure is Buckingham, a dark typeface that provides very bold headings. Note the range of space usage, much wider than for typical body types: Buckingham takes half again as much space as University Ornate for the same material in the same point size, while most body types would fall squarely in the middle.

That range grows even wider with figure 13.4. The top half is New York Deco, a version of Broadway; the text takes almost twice as much space as University Ornate! The lower half is Exchequer Script, a relatively simple script typeface that could be used for invitations and similar uses; it is more compact than Dutch but more spacious than University Ornate.

New York Deco

While typefaces used for body text should not call attention to themselves, this is not to say that the subtle differences among such typefaces are meaningless. Even among the best typefaces for body type—which are, generally, clear serif faces with open, readable designs—the differences will influence the overall look of text.

Exchequer Script

While typefaces used for body text should not call attention to themselves, this is not to say that the subtle differences among such typefaces are meaningless. Even among the best typefaces for body type—which are, generally, clear serif faces with open, readable designs—the differences will influence the overall look of text.

Figure 13.4: Display Text 2

Finally, figure 13.5 shows Copperfield, a version of Cooper Black that is virtually unreadable as body text and not wonderful even for headlines, and Manuscript, a rather good black-letter or Old English typeface. Surprisingly, the latter is extremely efficient in terms of space—but you really would not use it for many purposes.

The range of display type is enormous and sometimes incredible in its diversity, but most display types are really intended for a strict definition of "display," not for headings and subheadings within textual publications. If you're doing lots of signs, one or two of the more unusual display typefaces may prove to be worthwhile; and, as noted, some of these typefaces do have a few uses in text.

But for most publications and most desktop publishers, display typefaces serve more as a distraction than anything else. Remember that most typefaces suitable for body text also work quite well for headlines. Indeed, several of them—for example, Times Roman and Palatino (or Dutch and Zapf Calligraphic)—take on very strong sculptural characteristics in large sizes that are only hinted at in body type.

Copperfield

While typefaces used for body text should not call attention to themselves, this is not to say that the subtle differences among such typefaces are meaningless. Even among the best typefaces for body type—which are, generally, clear serif faces with open, readable designs—the differences will influence the overall look of text.

Manuscript

While typefaces used for body text should not call attention to themselves, this is not to say that the subtle differences among such typefaces are meaningless. Even among the best typefaces for body type—which are, generally, clear serif faces with open, readable designs—the differences will influence the overall look of text.

Figure 13.5: Display Text 3

Sans Serif as Body Type

All six of the body types illustrated in figures 13.1 and 13.2 have serifs. When you're choosing typefaces to use for body text, I recommend that you stick with serifs. The extra strokes tie the letters together into words and provide faster identification of letters, thus making the text more readable.

Most American publishing does use serif typefaces for body text, with notable exceptions in advertising and some special applications such as parts lists—where, partly due to misapprehension about relative legibility at small sizes, sans serif faces tend to prevail. (If you wonder about the legibility of serif faces at small size, look at any Merriam-Webster dictionary.)

European publishing shows much greater use of sans serif for normal text. A surprising number of graphic designers argue for sans serif type as being more modern and open, and they assert that the readability studies aren't really convincing.

Bitstream Swiss 10 on 12

While typefaces used for body text should not call attention to themselves, this is not to say that the subtle differences among such typefaces are meaningless. Even among the best typefaces for body type—which are, generally, clear serif faces with open, readable designs—the differences will influence the overall look of text.

Bitstream Zapf Humanist 10 on 12

While typefaces used for body text should not call attention to themselves, this is not to say that the subtle differences among such typefaces are meaningless. Even among the best typefaces for body type—which are, generally, clear serif faces with open, readable designs—the differences will influence the overall look of text.

Figure 13.6: Sans Serif Typefaces

Figure 13.6 shows the same paragraphs as in 13.1 and 13.2, set in the same manner and using what may be the two most likely candidates for sans serif body type: a variant on Helvetica and Zapf Humanist, Hermann Zapf's rethinking of his classic Optima. Humanist is a classy, interesting typeface; still, it lacks the sheer readability of a good serif body type.

You can form your own opinion. To my eye, while either typeface works very well for headlines and short advertising copy, I don't find either one to be as pleasant to read as the better serif body faces.

Monospaced Typefaces

All of the typefaces discussed and illustrated so far are *proportional*—some letters are wider than others. That's true of virtually all traditional typography, as it is of handwriting and inscriptions. One hallmark of modern word processors is effective use of proportional type, and almost all desktop publishing uses exclusively proportional type.

But sometimes, for some reason, you may want a typeface in which all the letters are the same width. Such typefaces are always available; every laser printer that I know of includes at least one monospaced font (usually Courier) built into the printer itself. (The LaserJet's built-in typefaces are both monospaced: Courier and Line Printer.)

You've seen Courier, in computer printouts and typed letters. Developed by IBM, it is extremely legible and has the interesting characteristic of being nearly "indestructible"—no matter how poor the printing medium, Courier will survive. That's largely because, although it has very bold serifs, it has no thick and thin lines: every stroke in a proper Courier font is exactly the same thickness.

I suspect that most of us now think of Courier as a typical typewriter typeface—but that was not true until fairly recently. Typical typewriter typefaces such as Prestige or Pica commonly had thick and thin strokes and were frequently more complex than Courier. The common element is monospacing.

Figure 13.7 (prepared with Word) shows three "typewriter" typefaces, one of which is not really typical of typewritten copy. The first paragraph is a version of Courier, as legible (and boring) as Courier always is. The second, a Letter Gothic somewhat similar to HP's LinePrinter font, is typical of sans serif at its worst: if you find this to be a suitable body text, you may not be cut out for desktop publishing.

The third paragraph, set in a typeface called *Classic Typewriter* by Swfte (the supplier of all three typefaces), is tricky. It has the spirit of good traditional typewriter typefaces—but it is not monospaced. While character widths show less variation than is typical for proportional fonts, the typeface is indeed proportional.

When would you use monospaced typefaces? When you're illustrating a computer display but not actually capturing a computer display, as in a user's guide for an online catalog. Possibly for spreadsheets or other heavily tabular forms, where having everything line up perfectly is more important than readability of continuous text. Possibly for letters that, for some reason, should look typewritten—in which case Classic Typewriter might be an interesting alternative to the typical Courier. For most text, however, including most tabular forms, monospaced and "typewriter" typefaces should be left to typewriters.

SWFTE Courier

While typefaces used for body text should not call attention to themselves, this is not to say that the subtle differences among such typefaces are meaningless. Even among the best typefaces for body type—which are, generally, clear serif faces with open, readable designs—the differences will influence the overall look of text.

Letter Gothic

While typefaces used for body text should not call attention to themselves, this is not to say that the subtle differences among such typefaces are meaningless. Even among the best typefaces for body type—which are, generally, clear serif faces with open, readable designs—the differences will influence the overall look of text.

Classic Typewriter

While typefaces used for body text should not call attention to themselves, this is not to say that the subtle differences among such typefaces are meaningless. Even among the best typefaces for body type—which are, generally, clear serif faces with open, readable designs—the differences will influence the overall look of text.

Figure 13.7: Typewriter-like Typefaces

Moving On

It would be easy to spend the rest of this book illustrating typefaces and discussing their characteristics; indeed, there are books that do nothing but that. You have seen examples of seventeen different typefaces used to present the same paragraph; that's probably at least ten more typefaces than you will really need for all the desktop publishing you do over several years. For now, we must move on to consider some of the sources for desktop-publishing typefaces, including another series of examples that show the complete alphabet for each typeface.

Figures 13.8 through 13.18, scattered throughout the following discussion, each show a pair of typefaces including the full alphabet for each face—and with the typeface name appearing at the end of each example. These examples, including eleven of the typefaces already illustrated and eleven others, represent a mix of Bitstream and Swfte (Glyphix) fonts, discussed later in this chapter. Some notes on the fonts appear at the end of the chapter—but, by seeing the examples in the absence of direct commentary, you should be encouraged to draw your own conclusions. How good do the typefaces look? How would you use them—and would you want to? As before, each example is set 10 on 12.

Bitstream Dutch

Fonts vary widely in design and quality. Tests for legibility require not only "character-set runs," e.g. [ABCDE FGHIJ KLMNO PQRST UVWXYZ abcde fghij klmno pqrst uvwxyz 12345 67890 :;?{} !@#$% ^ &*()], but also difficult words – such as LITA, Two and Wave or WAVE. Add a Proper Name such as Johannes Gutenberg or François Cézanne and a sentence such as The quick brown fox jumps over the lazy dog.

Glyphix Tymes Roman

Fonts vary widely in design and quality. Tests for legibility require not only "character-set runs," e.g. [ABCDE FGHIJ KLMNO PQRST UVWXYZ abcde fghij klmno pqrst uvwxyz 12345 67890 :;?{} !@#$% ^ &*()], but also difficult words – such as LITA, Two and Wave or WAVE. Add a Proper Name such as Johannes Gutenberg or François Cézanne and a sentence such as The quick brown fox jumps over the lazy dog.

Figure 13.8: Two Versions of Times

Sources for Typefaces

Which typefaces you use, and what variety of faces, should depend on the range of desktop publishing you plan to do—but it will also depend on your other equipment choices, budget and patience. It may also depend on your final output techniques. If, like most libraries, your final pages (before printing or copying) will emerge from a laser printer, your typeface choices should concentrate on those typefaces that look best at 300 dots per inch. If, on the other hand, you have the budget, time, and requirements to use phototypesetting for your final output, your choices will be based on the need to produce accurate proofs before sending out the files.

If you're fascinated by typography, you will be able to make some of the distinctions discussed here, even though you may disagree with my own judgments. But it is well to remember the crucial point that really makes desktop publishing workable in the first place. It's sad, in some ways, but it's certainly true: Readers don't use magnifying glasses. If the text is not offensive and is easily readable, most readers won't notice minor differences in typeface quality.

It's also important to reiterate a warning that applies to almost all of the software and hardware in this book, perhaps more so to digital-font technology given the current heated competition. Personal computing technology can improve rapidly, particularly when a growing market has more than one major competitor. The drawbacks in some font systems discussed below may lessen or disappear by the time this book appears in print, and it is fair to assume that some companies that currently produce somewhat lower-quality typefaces will, within a year, be producing typefaces that are quite competitive with "the big two," Adobe and Bitstream.

You can basically split high-quality desktop-publishing typefaces into two groups: PostScript typefaces—or, to put it another way, the Apple LaserWriter group—and non–PostScript typefaces—or the Hewlett-Packard LaserJet group. You can modify a LaserJet printer to produce PostScript output, and there are other laser printers in both PostScript and non–PostScript varieties, but the LaserWriter/LaserJet split is both reasonably accurate and includes perhaps 90 percent of all desktop laser printers.

Bitstream Swiss

Fonts vary widely in design and quality. Tests for legibility require not only "character-set runs," e.g. [ABCDE FGHIJ KLMNO PQRST UVWXYZ abcde fghij klmno pqrst uvwxyz 12345 67890 :;?{} !@#$% ^&*()], but also difficult words—such as LITA, Two and Wave or WAVE. Add a Proper Name such as Johannes Gutenberg or François Cézanne and a sentence such as The quick brown fox jumps over the lazy dog.

Glyphix Helvenica

Fonts vary widely in design and quality. Tests for legibility require not only "character-set runs," e.g. [ABCDE FGHIJ KLMNO PQRST UVWXYZ abcde fghij klmno pqrst uvwxyz 12345 67890 :;?{} !@#$% ^&*()], but also difficult words—such as LITA, Two and Wave or WAVE. Add a Proper Name such as Johannes Gutenberg or François Cézanne and a sentence such as The quick brown fox jumps over the lazy dog.

Figure 13.9: Two Versions of Helvetica

PostScript

If you need many different sizes of many different typefaces, if you intend to send your publications out for phototypesetting and use a laser printer for design and proofing, if you use a Macintosh and can afford an Apple LaserWriter IINT or IINTX—in any or all of those cases, you should use PostScript fonts.

The advantages of PostScript fonts are clear enough:

- PostScript typefaces come as outlines; actual fonts are generated only during printing (and, typically, by the printer's internal computer) and can be any size you want—and can take on a number of special characteristics. You don't need to use up disk space for every size of type you might eventually want, and you don't need to make such decisions until the last minute.

- Most PostScript printers come with several typefaces already resident in the printer, saving time and disk space (if not money). The typical contemporary set of typefaces, present in the LaserWriter IINT, includes Times, Helvetica, Courier, ITC Avant Garde Gothic, ITC Bookman, New Century Schoolbook, New Helvetica Narrow, Palatino, and ITC Zapf Chancery, as well as the nonalphabetic typefaces Symbol and ITC Zapf Dingbats. Most typefaces include bold and italic or oblique versions. Many users will never need to buy another typeface—although downloadable PostScript typefaces are readily available.

- PostScript typefaces are device-independent to some extent; the pages that you design and produce on a LaserWriter IINT at 300 dots per inch can be reproduced on a Linotronic phototypesetter (for example) at 1,200 to 2,500 dots per inch, true typeset quality—and, at least in terms of line breaks and page breaks, the design will be identical. (The letters won't be, in practice: good typefaces work somewhat differently at different resolutions.)

When you purchase PostScript typefaces, make sure you see laser-printed samples before you buy. The differences can be noticeable. Dozens of companies sell PostScript outlines. Adobe itself has some 80 typefaces (including 337 variations) available as of late 1989, covering an extremely wide range and including two very fine original typefaces, Lucida and Stone. Typeface packages run from $150 to $400, depending on the typefaces involved and the number of variations in the package.

The disadvantages of PostScript and Adobe typefaces are also fairly clear:

- PostScript printers cost far more than the LaserJet Series II and compatibles, typically some $2,000 more—enough to buy more typefaces than come with the printers, and enough to bust the budget of some desktop publishers.

- PostScript printing is generally somewhat slower than other laser-printing techniques.

- For laser-printer output, Adobe PostScript fonts frequently do not look quite as good as the best LaserJet fonts—they are not as optimized for 300-dots-per-inch output.

Font Cartridges

If you own a LaserJet (original model), you probably own at least one font cartridge—unless you use it entirely for Courier and LinePrinter. A surprising number of font cartridges can be purchased for any of the HP LaserJet models, including some cartridges that include all of the fonts in virtually all of the other ones. There's no faster or easier way to use a LaserJet II than with font cartridges. Unfortunately, the results may not be what you want.

The advantages of font cartridges are quite apparent:

- You don't need any disk space for the typefaces, since they are stored in the cartridges.

- Printing typically begins immediately; no other laser-printing technique is as fast as using cartridges.

Bitstream Zapf Calligraphic

Fonts vary widely in design and quality. Tests for legibility require not only "character-set runs," e.g. [ABCDE FGHIJ KLMNO PQRST UVWXYZ abcde fghij klmno pqrst uvwxyz 12345 67890 :;?{} !@#$% ^ &*()], but also difficult words—such as LITA, Two and Wave or WAVE. Add a Proper Name such as Johannes Gutenberg or François Cézanne and a sentence such as The quick brown fox jumps over the lazy dog.

Glyphix Palatine

Fonts vary widely in design and quality. Tests for legibility require not only "character-set runs," e.g. [ABCDE FGHIJ KLMNO PQRST UVWXYZ abcde fghij klmno pqrst uvwxyz 12345 67890 :;?{} !@#$% ^ &*()], but also difficult words— such as LITA, Two and Wave or WAVE. Add a Proper Name such as Johannes Gutenberg or François Cézanne and a sentence such as The quick brown fox jumps over the lazy dog.

Figure 13.10: Two Versions of Palatino

The disadvantages, particularly for high-end desktop publishing, are equally clear:

- The choice of typefaces and sizes is severely limited; primarily Times Roman, Helvetica, and some monospaced choices, with type size usually limited to three or four even-numbered point sizes.

- Typefaces in the older cartridges are not very good.

- Desktop-publishing support is quite limited.

In the past, another disadvantage was that purchasing more than one or two cartridges was very expensive. The "all-in-one" or "super" cartridges eliminate that disadvantage, although such cartridges can cost as much as $700.

If you don't mind the severely limited choice of sizes and typefaces and you have the modern cartridges with high-quality fonts, you will certainly print faster with cartridges than using other techniques—but, by and large, they're not the best way to go.

Bitstream Zapf Calligraphic Italic

Fonts vary widely in design and quality. Tests for legibility require not only "character-set runs," e.g. [ABCDE FGHIJ KLMNO PQRST UVWXYZ abcde fghij klmno pqrst uvwxyz 12345 67890 :;?{} !@#$% ^ &*()], but also difficult words—such as LITA, Two and Wave or WAVE. Add a Proper Name such as Johannes Gutenberg or François Cézanne and a sentence such as The quick brown fox jumps over the lazy dog.

Glyphix Palatine Italic

Fonts vary widely in design and quality. Tests for legibility require not only "character-set runs," e.g. [ABCDE FGHIJ KLMNO PQRST UVWXYZ abcde fghij klmno pqrst uvwxyz 12345 67890 :;?{} !@#$% ^ &*()], but also difficult words—such as LITA, Two and Wave or WAVE. Add a Proper Name such as Johannes Gutenberg or François Cézanne and a sentence such as The quick brown fox jumps over the lazy dog.

Figure 13.11: Two Versions of Palatino Italic

Soft Fonts

Technically, all other LaserJet (and compatible) fonts are *soft fonts*—fonts that must be downloaded to the printer each time you use them, or at least each time you turn on the printer. That process adds some time to the printing process; there may be a pause of 15 seconds to a minute or more before the printer actually starts to process your text.

A soft font, as it gets sent to the printer, is a series of *bitmaps* describing each character in the font, for a given typeface with a given style and size. For example, a single character in a 10-point font might be stored as up to 1,600 dots—if it was a full 10 points wide and 10 points high. The dots aren't sent each time the character is printed; instead, the complete character set is downloaded, and the printer uses each bitmap as needed.

Soft fonts have one big advantage: they can be the most precisely tuned character sets for the LaserJet and, as a result, can produce the best-quality output.

Soft fonts also have two disadvantages, although there are certain exceptions. First, since each size is stored as a bitmap, soft fonts can consume enormous quantities of disk space. Second, you must decide what sizes you will use before you start to work.

Bitstream Charter

Fonts vary widely in design and quality. Tests for legibility require not only "character-set runs," e.g. [ABCDE FGHIJ KLMNO PQRST UVWXYZ abcde fghij klmno pqrst uvwxyz 12345 67890 :;?{} !@#$% ^&*()], but also difficult words—such as LITA, Two and Wave or WAVE. Add a Proper Name such as Johannes Gutenberg or François Cézanne and a sentence such as The quick brown fox jumps over the lazy dog.

Bitstream Zapf Humanist

Fonts vary widely in design and quality. Tests for legibility require not only "character-set runs," e.g. [ABCDE FGHIJ KLMNO PQRST UVWXYZ abcde fghij klmno pqrst uvwxyz 12345 67890 :;?{} !@#$% ^ &*()], but also difficult words—such as LITA, Two and Wave or WAVE. Add a Proper Name such as Johannes Gutenberg or François Cézanne and a sentence such as The quick brown fox jumps over the lazy dog.

Figure 13.12: Bitstream Charter and Zapf Humanist

Bitstream Fonts

Includes Bitstream Fontware. You see that label on a surprising number of software boxes these days: the major high-end desktop-publishing programs, at least two of the more modest desktop-publishing programs, and most of the advanced word-processing programs. Bitstream has taken the razor-and-blades technique (sell razors cheap, so people will buy the blades) to its logical extreme—but the result is that you may not need to buy any typefaces at all for some applications. Ventura Publisher includes three typeface disks with four styles each of Dutch and Swiss (roman, italic, bold, and bold italic) and a proportional Symbol typeface; some other programs include equally complete starter kits, although some starter kits are as minimal as Charter Roman.

Additional typeface outlines sell for $99–$150 a package; as of early 1990, there are fifty-two packages, each containing either four styles of a single typeface or four different headline typefaces—except for the unique Symbols package, which includes ITC Zapf Dingbats and two different symbol typefaces. The available outlines include many of the most useful and classic typefaces such as ITC Garamond, Bodoni, ITC Clearface, and Baskerville, as well as those illustrated in this chapter. It also includes some of the more distinctive and flamboyant typefaces and a few original typefaces.

Glyphix Baskerton

Fonts vary widely in design and quality. Tests for legibility require not only "character-set runs," e.g. [ABCDE FGHIJ KLMNO PQRST UVWXYZ abcde fghij klmno pqrst uvwxyz 12345 67890 :;?{} !@#$% ^ &*()], but also difficult words—such as LITA, Two and Wave or WAVE. Add a Proper Name such as Johannes Gutenberg or François Cézanne and a sentence such as The quick brown fox jumps over the lazy dog.

Glyphix SWFTE Century

Fonts vary widely in design and quality. Tests for legibility require not only "character-set runs," e.g. [ABCDE FGHIJ KLMNO PQRST UVWXYZ abcde fghij klmno pqrst uvwxyz 12345 67890 :;?{} !@#$% ^ &*()], but also difficult words—such as LITA, Two and Wave or WAVE. Add a Proper Name such as Johannes Gutenberg or François Cézanne and a sentence such as The quick brown fox jumps over the lazy dog.

Figure 13.13: Glyphix Baskerton and SWFTE Century

Bitstream fonts have several advantages:

- They are typographically excellent at all sizes and tuned for good performance on the LaserJet II.

- Generated fonts include complete and effective kerning tables to improve the fit of words (for applications that support kerning).

- Screen fonts can also be generated for most desktop-publishing applications, so that you can see the character of the font as you work on the page.

- Once an outline is purchased, it can stay with you as your needs and equipment change. The installation package will produce fonts for printers as diverse as the Epson MX and FX line and any PostScript device, and screen fonts for an unusually wide variety of monitors, from CGA through full-page displays.

The disadvantages? The same as for all soft fonts, basically:

- The fonts can consume truly massive quantities of disk space—tens of megabytes, in some cases—effectively limiting the number of sizes and faces you will actually use. That's not always true, actually; some add-on devices for the LaserJet now generate fonts on the fly, and this trend may increase in the future.

- The Fontware font-generation routine can take quite a long time to do its work—although, again, that should improve substantially in the near future.

- Bitstream outlines can get expensive if you feel the need for a vast library of typefaces.

Swfte Glyphix: A Low-Cost Alternative

If you want Century Schoolbook, Zapf Calligraphic, Baskerville, and ITC Garamond, you'll spend $400 or more for the Bitstream packages. What would you expect if you got four very similar typefaces for $100 total—with the promise that you could generate the sizes you wanted on the fly?

Swfte was kind enough to send me their Glyphix 3.0 Installation Kit and the six current "business series" font sets (each containing four typefaces) so I could find out the answer to that question. Surprisingly, the answer is that you get good-quality type at a very fair price—but it's mostly intended for use with Microsoft Word 5.0 or WordPerfect 5.0.

Here's how it works, at least as of early 1990. You buy the Installation Kit for either Word or WordPerfect for $80; then, each font set is $100—but, to introduce the fonts, they throw in a second font set free. That's eight typefaces for $180 total—certainly an unbeatable value if the fonts are any good.

After you install the system, which includes setting up new printer-definition files for the LaserJet, you start your word processor by keying **GLYPHIX** instead of **WORD** or **WP**. A special program loads first, before the word processor.

The new printer-definition file includes all the information needed so that you can select the typeface you need and specify any point size from 3 points to 120 points. When you issue a print command, the Glyphix program intercepts the command and carries out its own operations.

Glyphix Garamand

Fonts vary widely in design and quality. Tests for legibility require not only "character-set runs," e.g. [ABCDE FGHIJ KLMNO PQRST UVWXYZ abcde fghij klmno pqrst uvwxyz 12345 67890 :;?{} !@#$% ^ &*()], but also difficult words—such as LITA, Two and Wave or WAVE. Add a Proper Name such as Johannes Gutenberg or François Cézanne and a sentence such as The quick brown fox jumps over the lazy dog.

Glyphix Rockland

Fonts vary widely in design and quality. Tests for legibility require not only "character-set runs," e.g. [ABCDE FGHIJ KLMNO PQRST UVWXYZ abcde fghij klmno pqrst uvwxyz 12345 67890 :;?{} !@#$% ^ &*()], but also difficult words—such as LITA, Two and Wave or WAVE. Add a Proper Name such as Johannes Gutenberg or François Cézanne and a sentence such as The quick brown fox jumps over the lazy dog.

Figure 13.14: Glyphix Garamand and Rockland

Those operations include generating needed fonts on the fly and send the bitmaps directly to the LaserJet—but, if you use large headlines, Glyphix will send those characters as graphic images instead (based on a size limit that you specify). That slows down transmission of the specific characters, but if you're only using one 30-character 60-point headline, it's a whole lot better than sending the definitions for all 220-odd characters!

It gets more interesting. You can specify bold or italic, as you might expect—but you can also specify colors, which translate to a series of special effects: reverse characters, shadow fonts, partially filled outlines, empty outlines, or outlines filled with stripes.

It works—surprisingly quickly and surprisingly well. After using Glyphix fonts with Microsoft Word for several weeks, I erased the Bitstream soft fonts for Word from my system in favor of the more flexible Glyphix typefaces.

Glyphix Oxford

Fonts vary widely in design and quality. Tests for legibility require not only "character-set runs," e.g. [ABCDE FGHIJ KLMNO PQRST UVWXYZ abcde fghij klmno pqrst uvwxyz 12345 67890 :;?{} !@#$% ^ &*()], but also difficult words—such as LITA, Two and Wave or WAVE. Add a Proper Name such as Johannes Gutenberg or François Cézanne and a sentence such as The quick brown fox jumps over the lazy dog.

Glyphix Buckingham

Fonts vary widely in design and quality. Tests for legibility require not only "character-set runs," e.g. [ABCDE FGHIJ KLMNO PQRST UVWXYZ abcde fghij klmno pqrst uvwxyz 12345 67890 :;?{} !@#$% ^ &*()], but also difficult words—such as LITA, Two and Wave or WAVE. Add a Proper Name such as Johannes Gutenberg or François Cézanne and a sentence such as The quick brown fox jumps over the lazy dog.

Figure 13.15: Glyphix Oxford and Buckingham

Glyphix Obelisk

Fonts vary widely in design and quality. Tests for legibility require not only "character-set runs," e.g. [ABCDE FGHIJ KLMNO PQRST UVWXYZ abcde fghij klmno pqrst uvwxyz 12345 67890 :;?{} !@#$% ^ &*()], but also difficult words—such as LITA, Two and Wave or WAVE. Add a Proper Name such as Johannes Gutenberg or François Cézanne and a sentence such as The quick brown fox jumps over the lazy dog.

Glyphix Eterna

Fonts vary widely in design and quality. Tests for legibility require not only "character-set runs," e.g. [ABCDE FGHIJ KLMNO PQRST UVWXYZ abcde fghij klmno pqrst uvwxyz 12345 67890 :;?{} !@#$% ^ &*()], but also difficult words—such as LITA, Two and Wave or WAVE. Add a Proper Name such as Johannes Gutenberg or François Cézanne and a sentence such as The quick brown fox jumps over the lazy dog.

Figure 13.16: Glyphix Obelisk and Eterna

The advantages of Glyphix over Bitstream are fairly clear:

- The typefaces are considerably less expensive—one-quarter as much, if you want the full set of four typefaces.

- You have complete freedom to select type size, as much freedom as with PostScript but at a much lower price.

- You don't need as much disk space—although the disk requirements are hardly nominal. Figure on 800,000 bytes for each set of four typeface outlines.

- The process is generally faster than pre-downloading a set of soft fonts, even if the set does contain everything you need.

The ads for Glyphix invite you to compare the fonts to those of Bitstream, HP, or Compugraphic, and they say "You'll find ours are better and easier to use." Easier to use, yes. Better—well, no.

One problem is not apparent until you try out the fonts, although it actually should be obvious from the copied files. Namely, as figure 13.11 shows rather dramatically, there are no true italics in

Glyphix Business Series typefaces. Look at the lowercase *a* in the Glyphix Palatine paragraph, and compare it to the lowercase *a* in the Zapf Calligraphic Italic paragraph. The Zapf Calligraphic is a true italic, while the Glyphix Palatine is an *oblique*—simply the roman font set on a slant.

Glyphix Avant-Guard

Fonts vary widely in design and quality. Tests for legibility require not only "character-set runs," e.g. [ABCDE FGHIJ KLMNO PQRST UVWXYZ abcde fghij klmno pqrst uvwxyz 12345 67890 :;?{} !@#$% ^&*()], but also difficult words—such as LITA, Two and Wave or WAVE. Add a Proper Name such as Johannes Gutenberg or François Cézanne and a sentence such as The quick brown fox jumps over the lazy dog.

Glyphix Gibraltar

Fonts vary widely in design and quality. Tests for legibility require not only "character-set runs," e.g. [ABCDE FGHIJ KLMNO PQRST UVWXYZ abcde fghij klmno pqrst uvwxyz 12345 67890 :;?{} !@#$% ^&*()], but also difficult words—such as LITA, Two and Wave or WAVE. Add a Proper Name such as Johannes Gutenberg or François Cézanne and a sentence such as The quick brown fox jumps over the lazy dog.

Figure 13.17: Glyphix Avant-Guard and Gibraltar

When you buy a set of four typefaces, that's what you get: four roman typefaces. Bold fonts are simply darkened versions, with no special adjustments; "italic" fonts are simply slanted. Swfte is also releasing Foundry Sets which do include separate italic and bold outlines—but those won't be nearly as cheap, although still somewhat cheaper than Bitstream typefaces.

That's the biggest single disadvantage, and it's a killer for a typeface with an italic as distinctly beautiful as Palatino. But if you're using sans serif faces (some of which come with obliques rather than true italics in any case), or if you rarely use italics, it may not matter all that much. The other disadvantages?

- The dynamic font-generation facility won't work with Ventura Publisher or other desktop-publishing programs. You can generate Glyphix fonts to disk, and convert them to Ventura form, but then you lose the disk savings and size flexibility. Font generation is still faster than Bitstream, to be sure, but the resulting files are just as large.

- The fonts include neither screen fonts nor kerning information, so they are not as useful in Ventura or similar applications. Since Word and WordPerfect don't kern or display actual screen fonts in any case, it doesn't matter for those uses.

- The font generator only works with LaserJet printers—it's not designed for any other purpose.

- All of the fonts are knockoffs—interpretations of other fonts, not licensed versions (thus the odd names)—and, to my eye, the fonts aren't quite as high quality as Bitstream fonts. But the differences are surprisingly small—I would certainly not be offended by these fonts, and most readers would probably never notice the difference.

Glyphix University Ornate

Fonts vary widely in design and quality. Tests for legibility require not only "character-set runs," e.g. [ABCDE FGHIJ KLMNO PQRST UVWXYZ abcde fghij klmno pqrst uvwxyz 12345 67890 :;?{} !@#$% ^ &*()], but also difficult words—such as LITA, Two and Wave or WAVE. Add a Proper Name such as Johannes Gutenberg or François Cézanne and a sentence such as The quick brown fox jumps over the lazy dog.

Glyphix Exchequer Script

Fonts vary widely in design and quality. Tests for legibility require not only "character-set runs," e.g. [ABCDE FGHIJ KLMNO PQRST UVWXYZ abcde fghij klmno pqrst uvwxyz 12345 67890 :;?{} !@#$% ^ &()], but also difficult words—such as LITA, Two and Wave or WAVE. Add a Proper Name such as Johannes Gutenberg or François Cézanne and a sentence such as The quick brown fox jumps over the lazy dog.*

Figure 13.18: University Ornate and Exchequer Script

In short, if you plan to use Word or WordPerfect for word publishing and want to have considerable flexibility in fonts, Glyphix fonts are, as advertised, a genuine bargain. For Ventura or Page-

Maker, their primary virtue is cheapness, and you'll miss the screen fonts.

Look carefully at figures 13.8, 13.9, and 13.10. Each one pairs a Bitstream font and the equivalent Glyphix font. Form your own opinion of the differences in quality—and, more important, whether those differences matter to you.

Notes on the Illustrations

Figures 13.8 through 13.18 should speak for themselves, by and large. They illustrate some of the soft fonts including full alphabets, so that you can see how they compare and which ones you might find useful.

These figures include seventeen different typefaces, representing a wide range of body typefaces and a fairly narrow range of display typefaces. As noted earlier, that's certainly more variety than most library desktop publishers will ever need.

The two typefaces in figure 13.12 make a good combination, at least to my eye. Bitstream Charter offers a clean, contemporary serif font, if a bit more bland than some others; Zapf Humanist is perhaps the most interesting of the highly legible sans serif fonts, and it works extremely well as a headline in combination with Charter.

Figure 13.13 shows Swfte's version of another classic typeface, Century Schoolbook. The only other new Glyphix serif face suitable for body type appears in figure 13.15, together with the marginal Buckingham. Oxford is distinctive, but it is quite workable for body text.

Figures 13.16 and 13.17 show four more sans serif fonts from Swfte. The first two would be considered quite suitable for body text by Europeans and American designers who favor sans serif type-faces. Avant-Guard is a version of Avant Garde, a specialty typeface that can be quite distracting when used for long passages, and the spacing of this version is such that the text becomes unreadable. Gibraltar is another sans serif type that might work well for special situations but seems to have little independent merit.

Finally, figure 13.19 shows the Bitstream Symbol font—a collection of symbols that can be quite useful. It's not quite as flamboyant as ITC Zapf Dingbats, but it serves useful and needed functions in desktop publishing.

Bitstream Symbol (Full Character Set)

[ΑΒΧΔΕ ΦΓΗΙϑ ΚΛΜΝΟ ΠΘΡΣΤ ΥϛΩΞΨΖ αβχδε φγηιφ κλμνο πθρστ υϖωξψζ 12345 67890 :;?{} !≅#∃% ⊥&∗() <>,./ ∴.|~ ‾−_+=] Υʹ≤⁄∞ƒ♣♦♥♠↔←↑→↓°±"≥×∝∂•÷≠≡≈... |—↵ℵℑℜ℘⊗⊕∅∩ ∪⊃⊇⊄⊂⊆∈∉∠∇®©™∏√·¬∧∨⇔⇐⇑⇒⇓◊〈®©™∑⎛⎜⎝⎡⎢⎣⎧⎨⎩⎟⎜⎞⎟⎜⎠⎤⎥⎦⎫⎬⎭

Figure 13.19: Bitstream Symbol

Conclusion

It all comes down to resources, needs, and taste. You should be able to say which typefaces can only be used in special situations and which would see wide use; clearly, the former should either be ignored or purchased cheaply, while the latter deserve closer scrutiny.

Tips and Reminders

- Body type should not call attention to itself.

- Use serif typefaces for body text in almost all cases; it is more readable and legible than sans serif.

- Display type can be more distinctive than body type, but it should be appropriate for the occasion. "Wild West" typefaces don't belong in the typical annual report.

- Monospaced typefaces should be used for illustrations of computer screens, but should rarely be used in other cases.

- Typefaces vary widely in quality, but some subtle distinctions won't be apparent to the average reader.

14

Graphics and Illustrations

 raphics—according to some people, you aren't really desktop-publishing unless you use them. In the broadest sense of the term, that's probably true: good publication design always adds graphic interest to a publication. In a narrower sense, the assertion is nonsense. Still, you will find graphics useful for many of your publications, and one advantage of desktop publishing is the ability to integrate graphics and text dynamically, seeing what you're doing along the way.

I'm basically a text-oriented person—and chronically incapable of drawing a straight line even with a ruler. You will not find me preparing worthwhile illustrations with a paint program or drawing program or with traditional tools: I lack the hand, eye, and imagination for such work. Most likely, that's true of many of you—skill in graphic arts is not a prerequisite for successful librarianship.

This chapter introduces a few aspects of graphics and illustrations as they relate to desktop publishing. Some of the discussion is a bit vague because it deals with programs I've never tried and techniques that would be of no use to me. To my considerable surprise, however, much of the discussion is illustrated with items that I managed to prepare using a few reasonably priced tools. If I can do it, so can you—there is hope for the graphically impaired!

Who Needs Graphics?

You want to produce better subject bibliographies, more readable new-title lists, a staff newsletter, and some directories of local agencies. While you're at it, your library could use bolder, more legible special-hours signs, some effective press releases, and more dynamic quick announcement signs. How many illustrations do you need in order to do these successfully?

None—and you won't improve a directory of local agencies by adding cartoon figures and trumpeters on the title page. You could easily ruin an otherwise effective press release by including a badly drawn illustration or a totally irrelevant piece of clip art; it will detract from the text, not increase reader interest.

Most books lack any illustrations whatsoever within the bound portion; that doesn't seem to make them unattractive or useless. Many newsletters never use illustrations, and most simple signs involve nothing but text.

You can carry out a successful desktop-publishing program without ever using illustrations. But illustrations do have their role, and you are admittedly missing some of the power (and fun) of desktop publishing if you stick strictly to text. For that matter, a fair number of publications almost cry out for illustrations:

- Announcements for programs aimed at children and bibliographies intended for children and juveniles;

- Subject bibliographies when the subject lends itself to illustration;

- Newsletters and publicity specifically reaching out to a wider public, where you need to attract the reader;

- Fliers in general, including calendars of library events;

- Publications that simply need "lightening up" in order to make them more visually interesting.

Illustrations serve two basic purposes. One is to inform, enlighten, or entertain. That can only be done by illustrations that relate directly to the content of a publication. The other is to make a publication more appealing. Here, the primary rules are that the illustrations should be compatible with the content and style of the publication and that the illustrations should not interfere with the image of the library.

Type as a Graphic Element

We all need graphics—but we don't always need illustrations. Some of the strongest graphics consist entirely of type, enhanced only by border lines. The big first letter at the beginning of other chapters in this book is a deliberate graphic element; so are headlines, subheadings, pull quotes, and many other elements.

For most library publications, the way in which type and borders are used will determine the overall graphic quality of the pages; illustrations, if used at all, will be secondary to text. A small number of well-chosen illustrations, used so that each has impact, may improve the design—but proper use of typographic embellishments and typography itself may make or break the design. Don't look for reasons to throw in extra illustrations just for the sake of illustrations, but do look for the cases in which good illustrations will improve your publication.

This chapter does not discuss color. Most of your desktop-prepared publications probably won't use color (except for different-colored paper or a single colored ink). Full-color publications require big budgets and many more production considerations than can reasonably be included here. It may be enough to say that desktop tools can increasingly be used for both *spot color* (where additional colors are used, but not full-color printing) and full-color preparation.

PC Graphic Fundamentals

Before thinking about the kinds of illustrations you might use and how you can prepare them, you should understand a few basic concepts of graphics as supported by personal computers.

Basically, all graphics on a PC are either *line art* (also called *vector graphics*) or *bit-mapped art* (or *raster graphics*). You need to understand a little about the differences between the two types; you also need to understand the significance of halftones and dithering.

Line Art and Vector Graphics

Figure 14.1: Line Art

Vector graphics are graphics composed entirely of lines, curves, and fill patterns. More to the point, a file representing a vector graphic actually consists of a description of the design, rather than an image of the design. Vector graphics are also called *object-oriented graphics*.

If I tell you to start at the Palo Alto City Hall's front door, walk 10 feet forward, turn 90 degrees right, walk one-half block, turn 90 degrees left, walk one block, turn 90 degrees right, walk one-half block, and turn 90 degrees right again, I will have given you a set of *vectors* describing the path from the City Hall to a University Avenue business. Using those vectors, you could draw a sketchy map at almost any scale with equal precision.

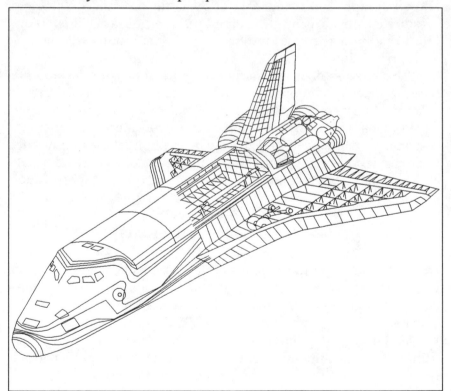

Figure 14.2: Line Art, Enlarged

That's the big advantage of vector graphics. Because the machine-readable file is a description, it can be expanded or contracted without losing precision and clarity. Consider figures 14.1 and 14.2, for example. Both figures represent the same vector-graphic file. There is no loss of resolution as the figure is enlarged, because the computer is actually creating a new drawing based on the same description. It is also the case that, at least for straightforward vector graphics, the disk files tend to be relatively small—and they don't depend on the final size of the illustration.

I've used the term *vector graphics* in this section because the term *line art*, while typically used to mean vector graphics in desktop publishing, is also the proper term for any illustration that does not use color or tones of gray. And, in practice, while it is theoretically possible to convert any piece of line art into a vector graphic, that's not how most line art is actually used.

Bit-Mapped Graphics or Images

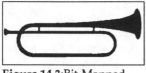

Figure 14.3: Bit-Mapped

A bit-mapped graphic consists of a series of black and white picture elements, also called *pixels* or *bits*; it is a map showing which black and white dots make up the image. The machine-readable file for a bit-mapped graphic does not describe the graphic; rather, it stores the digital equivalent of an image at a certain size and resolution (number of dots per inch).

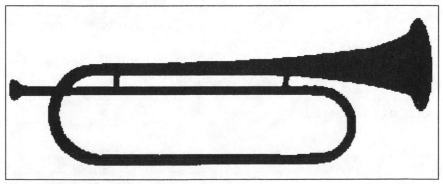

Figure 14.4: Bit-Mapped Art, Enlarged

Figures 14.3 and 14.4 show the significance of this, as compared to figures 14.1 and 14.2. The well-defined image in 14.3 becomes crude and jagged in figure 14.4—because the file does not include enough bits to provide a smooth definition at the expanded size.

If a ¼-inch square from figure 14.1 was printed as an 8-inch square graphic, expanding the original thirty-two times in each direction, it would be precisely as crisp and well-resolved as the original. If a ¼-inch square from figure 14.3 was printed at that large size, it would consist of scattered blots of ink and be unpleasantly coarse: the original 300-dot-per-inch resolution would be down to less than 10 dots per inch.

But you're likely to find that most of your illustrations are bit-mapped. There are several reasons for that:

- Software that can handle the complex descriptions required for good-quality vector graphics tends to be more complex and more expensive than the simpler software required to manipulate bitmaps.

- Widespread graphics on powerful PCs began with MacPaint, a bit-mapped program included free with every early Macintosh. When MacDraw and other vector-graphics programs came along, most people found that they could work more freely and rapidly with bit-mapped programs. Thus, most of the art that appears on bulletin boards, as public-domain software, or as packaged art collections will be bit-mapped art. Also, if vector graphics are available, they tend to be more expensive.

- Illustrations that have been scanned from printed form into electronic form are always bit-mapped, unless complex (and not always successful) methods have been used to convert them to vector graphics.

That last reason may be the most important reason, particularly if you generate your own illustrations and lack artistic abilities: the way you will generate most illustrations inherently produces bit-mapped graphics. All of the figures in this chapter (except 14.1, 14.2, 14.11, and 14.12) and all of the other nontextual illustrations in this book are bit-mapped.

Halftones

You can't print continuous tones of gray—ink is either there or not there. In order to reproduce a photograph in a printed product, it must be converted to a *halftone*—a process that involves breaking it up into a pattern of dots, with the dots varying in size. The varied-size dots simulate tones of gray, creating the visual illusion of continuous tones—assuming that the halftone is fine enough and prints well. You've probably seen badly produced newspapers where the effect begins to fail, with photographs that seem to have only two or three tones from black to white.

It is possible to convert photographic images to machine-readable form at very high resolution while maintaining gray scale, but it isn't possible to print the image back out directly on a typical laser printer. In order to achieve something remotely resembling a halftone, the computer must use a process called *dithering*.

Dithering

Once again, we have a single term that describes two different processes. One form of dithering adds slight intensity variations in a display, in order to make lines and edges appear smooth. But for the computer equivalent of halftones, dithering is the process of treating a single picture element as a group of pixels in order to produce a gray scale. If an element of an image is represented by a pattern of 64 pixels (8 high by 8 wide), it can take on up to 64 different gray levels as more or fewer pixels become black. That is, for each gray element in the image, some number of the 64 dots in a square are black; if only one dot is black, the square is effectively very light gray; if half of the dots are black, the square is medium-gray; if 60 of the 64 dots are black, the square is very nearly black.

That's how you can print photographic images on normal laser printers—but it also reveals the problem with doing so. The resolution of the photograph—the equivalent of the "screen density" in a halftone—is only one-eighth the maximum resolution of a laser printer, or 37½ pixels per inch. That is far too low a resolution to present an effective image. Even newspaper photographs use at least 65 lines per inch (equivalent to 65 pixels per inch).

The easiest advice for most desktop publishers is not to "dither around" with computer-printed photographs; stick to vector graphics (ideal if available) and bit-mapped versions of line art, avoiding the grays.

Categories of Graphics

Graphics that might find a place in your publications generally fall into five categories: logos or logotypes, photographs, graphs and charts, original art, and clip art. Each category involves different considerations for desktop publications, with different problems and possible solutions.

Logos

Your library—or the organization your library is part of—may already have one or more logos. If not, you should consider creating a logo or having one created; it will help the library establish a consistent identity within its publications.

Figure 14.5 shows three different logos, each of them effective as part of many different publications. The first logo identifies the Research Libraries Group (RLG); the second is the informal logotype for the College of Notre Dame; the third, created for this book, is for the fictitious Halltown City Library.

Figure 14.5: Logotypes

You can incorporate logos into desktop publishing in several ways:

- Prepare your original pages on stationery already containing the logo, if that is feasible;

- Paste the logo onto the original page, leaving room during the design process;

- Digitize the logo (usually done by a service bureau), preferably creating a line-art version;

- Scan the logo, creating a bit-mapped file.

All three of these logos were scanned using an inexpensive handheld scanning device, discussed in the section called "Scanners: Graphics for Non-Artists."

Photographs

Don't plan to use photographs unless they carry a specific message that you need. That will be the case, of course, for photographs that specifically illustrate stories in newsletters; sometimes, a photograph is just what you need.

Figure 14.6: Scanned Photograph

Figure 14.6 was scanned in from a black-and-white print using dithering; as you can see, the results are really not acceptable for a serious publication. This is not the highest quality you can achieve with normal desktop publishing, but it is indicative. Figure 14.7, scanned from a printed publication, may be more acceptable, if only because the intent is not photographic—but it is still rather crude. The reasons appear above under the discussions of halftones and dithering.

Figure 14.7: Scanned Printed Picture

The best way to incorporate photographs into desktop-published pages is to add them after you prepare the pages, having a print shop prepare standard halftones to your specifications and adding the halftones to the original pages before making print masters. That's usually an inexpensive process, and it will retain the quality of the photographs.

If you must use photographs frequently and find it unacceptable to sully your pure desktop publications with pasted-in halftones, it is possible to achieve better laser-printed results. The Intel Visual Edge circuit board (and possibly competitive products) can adjust the LaserJet so that it does, indeed, print different-size dots—resulting in fairly good halftone images, with 64 shades of gray and without resolution becoming unacceptably coarse. Since you can also buy full-page scanners that will read 300 dots per inch with 256 gray tones, it is possible to insert acceptable photographs electronically.

The process is not cheap, however—and the expense arises in two areas. First, the scanner and circuit board are both moderately expensive, although cheaper than you might expect (about $1,700 and $500 respectively, advertised prices in mid-1989). That $2,200 will pay for quite a few halftones, probably between 200 and 400 of them. The other cost is disk storage. An 8-by-10-inch photograph, scanned at 300 dots per inch and with 256 levels of gray, can take up as much as six megabytes of disk space—and reducing that to 64 gray levels still means that the picture requires more than a megabyte of storage. You may think type fonts and illustrations take up lots of disk space—and they do—but they are nothing when compared to gray-scale photographs (or, even worse, full-color images).

If you have the kind of publishing program for which this all makes sense, you probably know it. For most of us, where a photograph is an occasional nicety, it does not: the way to handle photographs is to add them manually.

Graphs and Charts

Business graphics can almost always be used in desktop publications, as long as it is possible to send the graph's definition to a disk file in one of several frequently used forms. In many cases, such as graphics prepared by several spreadsheets, the disk files contain vector definitions; that means that you can scale the final image to any appropriate size without being worried about resolution.

If you plan to use graphs and charts, it makes sense to be sure that the software you use to produce the graphics will yield output that your word-processing or desktop-publishing program can read. Chances are, the literature for the business-graphics program will indicate that feature—and the chances are also increasingly good that you will be able to make the conversion, for two reasons: desktop-publishing programs can increasingly import a wide range of formats, and business-graphics programs tend to be written to export in widely useful formats.

Sensible guidelines for using business graphics are usually fairly obvious. Don't use graphs with too much information or information that is not labeled; don't use so many graphs and charts that the point is lost; don't use misleading or ambiguous graphs.

Original Art

If you're lucky enough to have artistic skills or the services of some-one who does, you're considerably ahead of the game. If that rare person who can prepare original illustrations that help to communi-cate a publication's message and enhance the appearance of the publication is also comfortable with computer-graphics tools, so much the better: you will almost certainly be able to use the results directly.

What if you have access to original illustrations, but the illustra-tor has no interest in preparing them in digital form? You have two choices: scan the illustrations into electronic form, or paste the il-lustrations in after you produce the original pages.

If the illustrations involve shadings—if they are "paintings" of some sort, rather than pure drawings—your best bet is to paste them in, for much the same reason as you should paste in photographs. If they are pure line art, scanning may be worth a try—but print out the results and see. If neither you nor the artist is satisfied with the digitized output, compromise: leave a blank space on the page, and paste in photographically prepared illustrations.

Clip Art

Now we come to the heart of the matter: clip art, such as Figure 14.8. Now, I'm not sure why you would want a picture of a clip as part of a publication—but if you do, there it is. Of course, you can get other images as clip art; figure 14.9 shows three pieces of clip art that might be more use-ful for, say, a flier about computer courses, the notice of a staff barbecue, or any pub-lication where you want to show a book.

Figure 14.8: Clip Art

Clip art is camera-ready art that can be cut from a book and pasted onto final pages, electronically copied from a file and included in the desktop publication, or scanned from printed sources and used in desktop publishing. One absolutely critical element of clip art is that it is *copyright-free* or *licensed for use*: this means you can include the image without any fear of being sued for copyright infringement.

Figure 14.9: More Clip Art

There are a number of sources of clip art, in electronic form and in printed form. Several companies sell electronic clip-art collections, either on floppy disks or CD-ROM. If you find collections that actually suit your needs, and the costs are not outrageous, these electronic sources will ensure consistent output quality—if the collections are in a form that you can use. Note that most electronic clip art is still bit-mapped, but much of it comes in Encapsulated PostScript form—which you can't use at all unless you have a PostScript printer.

There is one problem with all clip art that is inherent in its very nature: clip art is "canned" artwork, innocuous images that don't relate specifically to any given topic, because they are designed to relate generally to so many topics.

A second problem for libraries applies mostly to commercial clip-art collections. Most digitized clip art is marketed for use in advertising and related areas, and it is the hard-edged, slick graphic art you see in ads. While it can be used effectively, it is usually quite recognizable as clip art and may degrade the individuality and personality of your publications. If you use it at all, you should use it sparingly.

There is a solution to that second problem, and it constitutes a vast and economically sensible source of clip art: specifically, the *Dover Pictorial Archives* and other Dover publications (and some similar publications from other publishers). These publications are not always copyright-free, but those that are not usually have a sensible 10-image-per-project limit: you can freely use them within a publication, but not to excess.

The wonderful thing about Dover and similar printed collections is that they are not advertising-oriented clip art (although

Dover also sells many collections of contemporary clip art). Rather, they tend to be woodcuts and illustrations from nineteenth-century (and earlier) sources, many of them whimsical and almost all of them lending a gentler and more interesting air to a publication.

Figure 14.10: Dover Clip Art

The Dover collection includes dozens of different books covering a wide range of subjects and sources. Figure 14.10 comes from a Dover collection of nineteenth-century *Punch* illustrations (a veritable treasure trove!). That book includes eleven pages on books, reading and writing with dozens of useful illustrations. The decorative letter beginning this chapter comes from another Dover collection. The rail and children's hour illustrations in chapter 12 are also scanned from Dover books.

Dover books are inexpensive (typically $3.50 to $7.00) and well-made; you could buy six to eight books—each with hundreds of illustrations (sometimes more than 1,000)—for the price of an inexpensive electronic clip-art collection. As with any proper clip-art collection, you can be assured that you will not violate copyright—which brings up the last problem with using art that isn't original: copyright problems.

Copyright

Just because you have access to an image, don't assume you can freely use it. Nonprofit institutions have been sued for violations of copyright, and no library should be in the position of flagrantly violating intellectual property rights.

If you have a publication that predates 1906, you're safe: you can be sure that it is no longer under copyright. Old magazine collections make wonderful sources for graphic images, and legal ones at that.

After 1906, it gets trickier. This is no place to discuss the intricacies of copyright law, but you can generally assume that any contemporary illustration is probably copyrighted, whether or not a notice to that effect appears on the publication. There are exceptions: many governmental publications, including articles written by government employees as part of their employment, are explicitly in the public domain.

If you scan in a copyrighted image and include it in any flier or newsletter, you are violating copyright—and there's no reasonable expectation that the fair use doctrine will shield you. Modifying the image probably doesn't eliminate the violation. The general rule is easy enough: If in doubt, don't.

Of course, you can ask for permission—and I'd be very surprised if, for example, a library vendor was unwilling to have its logo included in a library publication. But remember that owning a scanner does not give you license to use all those images you can scan. It doesn't, and you weaken library arguments in favor of fair use by deliberately abusing copyright.

Drawing, Computer-Aided Design, and Business Graphics

Three varieties of program generate vector graphics: drawing and illustration programs, CAD programs, and business-graphics programs. In each case, you need to know what you want to do and make sure you find a package that suits your needs and taste.

CAD programs range in price from $10 to $3,000 and up. Low-end CAD programs may be the most inexpensive vector-oriented drawing programs you can buy—but make sure that they can export files that your desktop-publishing or word-processing program can import, which may not be the case with the lowest-end software. Take time enough to read reviews and, if possible, talk to users or try out the software; design or drawing software will work for you only if you get along with it.

Drawing and illustration programs tend to range from $200 to $600, adding more power along the price curve. Obviously, it doesn't make sense to lay out $600 for a program unless you're sure that someone on your staff has the talent to use it well and a willingness to work with it. Some of the more expensive programs can import bit-mapped images and attempt to turn them into vector graphics (by tracing the lines in the images); some can use typeface outlines to create a variety of special effects. In the hands of a skilled user, such programs can be enormously effective—but they tend to be designed for skilled graphic artists in the advertising and display fields, not for librarians attempting to produce an occasional illustration.

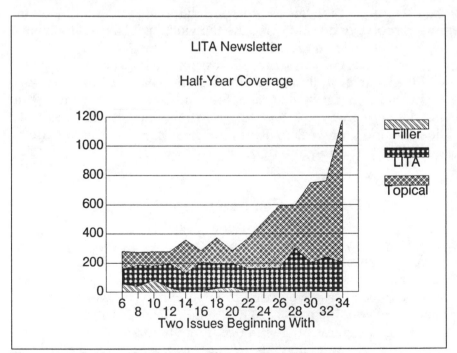

Figure 14.11: Business Graphic (Area Chart)

A limited form of vector graphics may be included in your desktop-publishing software. For example, Ventura provides tools to draw straight lines, rectangles, squares, ellipses, and perfect circles—and you can add arrows to lines, change the thickness of outlines, and provide a background pattern for an area. That's a fairly limited repertoire, useful primarily for enhancing other graphics.

Almost every spreadsheet program will produce business graphs, and it will generally store the graph definitions in a format (such as Lotus's ".PIC" format) that desktop-publishing software can read. Figures 14.11 and 14.12 show two such graphs, created using Borland's Quattro spreadsheet and imported as part of this chapter. Graphs such as these (and others such as bar charts) belong in almost every library's annual report, and they may be useful for many other purposes. The graph was stored as a definition—that is, as vector graphics. As a result, the imported version maintains the highest possible resolution regardless of final print size. In some cases, you will actually find that a spreadsheet-developed graph printed out as part of a desktop-published document will look better than the same graph printed directly from the spreadsheet.

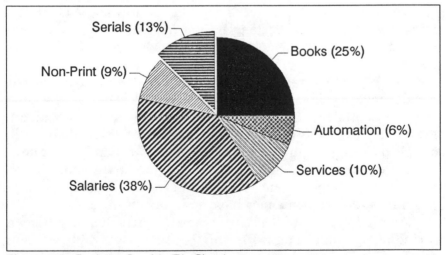

Figure 14.12: Business Graphic (Pie Chart)

Many database programs can also create business graphics that desktop-publishing and advanced word-processing programs can

import, as can other business programs (including programs specifically designed for creating business graphics).

Paint Programs

If you create graphics at all, or modify clip art that you acquire on
disk or scan into your system, you will probably use a paint program.
Such programs range in price from "free" to hundreds of dollars, with
the most popular programs in the $100 range or bundled with hard-
ware.

As discussed in chapter 12, pfs:First Publisher includes drawing
functions in the desktop-publishing program, as do some other
low-end programs. These functions aren't terribly fancy, being designed primarily for touching up the extensive clip-art collection that
comes with the program and the collections that can be added to it.
You can move a graphic, duplicate it (turning one tree into a forest),
rotate or reverse it, invert it (changing black to white and white to
black), or touch it up by erasing portions and adding other portions.
A magnification mode makes it possible to work on one pixel at a time,
by expanding a small portion of the art. You can also add straight
lines of various widths, rectangles, and freehand graphics. It really
isn't a full drawing system, but it provides some rudimentary capabilities.

Since I'm not a graphics person, I haven't attempted to deal with
a wide range of paint programs, and I can't speak to the general range
of features offered. I have had some experience, however, with one
reasonably full-featured paint program because it is automatically
supplied along with the Logitech ScanMan Plus handheld scanner
(discussed later). PaintShow Plus, the program in question, should
serve as an example of what you might expect to find in a painting
program. Other software may have additional features.

Figure 14.13 shows the PaintShow Plus (hereafter PS+) screen,
including a graphic being worked on. The screen was captured using
the "CATCH" screen-capture utility supplied along with PS+. The
left-hand side of the screen shows the tool box, containing twenty
tools for creating and editing pictures. Below that is the line-width
palette. At the bottom of the screen is the pattern palette, showing

thirty-four patterns that can be applied to any enclosed section of a picture.

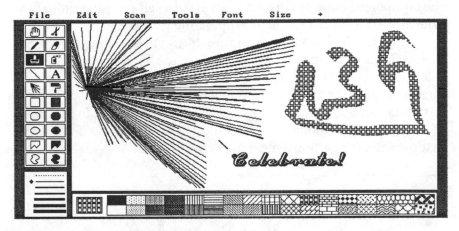

Figure 14.13: Screen from PaintShow Plus

Tools allow you to draw freehand (the pencil); erase portions of a drawing; paint freehand (like drawing, but with brushstrokes and patterns); spray-paint an area; draw straight lines; add text to a picture; create "line fills," fairly dramatic free-form images; fill an enclosed area with a selected pattern; or create specific forms, such as hollow or filled rectangles, rounded rectangles, ovals, polygons, and free-form shapes. (For a polygon, you point out the vertices for a series of connected straight lines; for a free-form shape, you simply draw the edge of the shape.)

Menu choices allow you to load different palette patterns (eight sets of patterns are included, and you can create your own); undo any one editing act (such as when you accidentally fill in the background rather than a particular foreground area); cut, copy, reverse, and rotate; trace the edges of solid objects and leave only the outlines; and magnify a portion of the picture so you can work on individual pixels. Seven different typefaces are included (including Greek and symbols), with six different styles (including underlined, outlined and shadowed) and twelve different character sizes.

Since PS+ is related to the ScanMan Plus, it also includes controls for scanning—setting the resolution, initiating a scan—as well as the usual controls to load and save files, print screens, and the like. You can load an existing picture (or scan a picture) into a portion of a picture you're working on; you can also work in color if you have the equipment for it. Finally, you can build a self-running slide show and convert a limited range of graphic-file formats.

The pointless drawing in figure 14.13 shows some of the features. The large image on the left side is a line fill; the word *Celebrate!* is text in 18-point Script Outline; the large squiggle in the upper right was done with the brush using a wide diagonal brush shape and the pattern shown as a "color." In my hands, this is garbage; in the hands of anyone with a modicum of talent, the tools provide a powerful, fast medium for getting a message across.

Figure 14.14: Example of Fill Patterns

Figure 14.14 shows another graphic created with PS+, in this case using a variety of patterns to fill in large outline roman letters. You would not use that wild a variety in any normal case—but, with the fast, clear letters and the patterns included, you might very well be able to create some worthwhile signs, bookplates and other image-oriented single pages using nothing but PS+. For example, figure 14.15 involved no drawing at all (just text and a pattern used to fill in the background), but it could be a reasonable starting point for a report on the progress of a library building fund.

You may never use a paint program for anything but touching up a scanned or imported image. I can aver to the great danger of spending almost unlimited amounts of time playing with the facilities, a trap that seems inherent in most graphics software—but that's quite a different problem. In general, I can say that a good drawing program will bring the most out of someone with a touch of talent and the willingness to use the program to its fullest—and might even allow a graphics illiterate to produce something worthwhile.

Figure 14.15: Fund-Raising Logo

Screen-Capture Programs

Why do you need a screen-capture program? You don't, except in three cases:

- You want to illustrate your procedural manuals for computer-supported tasks with actual screen images, so that new workers will understand exactly what they're working with;

- You want to make user guides for your online catalog more interesting and pointed by including the occasional screen image;

- You need to publicize a new computer-based service.

If none of those apply, don't bother with a screen-capture program. Unfortunately, you also can't use such a program if the screens to be captured are on terminals rather than PCs, as may be the case with your online catalog. But if you have dial-up options, you should be able to capture the screens.

If you do need screen images, nothing works as well as a capture program. Photographs rarely work well (it is notoriously difficult to photograph a CRT clearly and without reflections), and keying in the information is a time-consuming and error-prone process.

Increasingly, you may find that the software you purchase for some other use includes a screen-capture utility. Microsoft Word 5.0 includes one; so does PaintShow Plus; so do demo-building programs and some other graphics programs. Or you can buy a separate program to capture and edit screens; two of the best-known are Hijaak and HotShot Graphics.

Every capture facility works in a similar manner. A memory-resident program ("terminate-and-stay-resident" or "TSR" in PC jargon) takes up some portion of your computer's memory. You then load whatever application you need to capture—be it a communications program for dialing up your OPAC, a PC-based library support program, or whatever. When you see a screen you need to capture, you press some combination of keys designated as a "hot key"—for example, Shift-PrintScreen for the PS+ capture facility or Microsoft Word capture facility, Alt-p for HotShot. The program saves the screen as a disk file (or, in some cases, as a memory-resident file), possibly prompting you for some information beforehand. (Word and HotShot ask for file names; PS+ provides its own.)

Good capture facilities will handle any normal graphics mode and possibly some unusual modes. The screen, stored as a graphic, can then be imported into other applications. Separate programs will typically include additional features, such as conversion among different forms of image files.

HotShot Graphics

SymSoft provided a copy of HotShot Graphics for my evaluation and use in preparing this manuscript. It was used for all of the screen images in chapter 11 and for some screen images in other chapters. It works very well. You can choose your own file names or tell it to keep incrementing a default file name with each new screen; if it sees that a screen is entirely text (is operating in text mode, e.g., Word), it will save the screen as text and text attributes.

The program itself provides separate editing facilities for captured text screens and captured graphics screens. Text screens can be annotated with text, symbols, and lines; screen segments can be highlighted and inverted; actions can be taken on any block of the screen, and blocks can be moved around, copied, and erased.

Graphics screens can be edited extensively, by adding lines or boxes (hollow or filled), freehand drawing, pixel editing on a magnified screen, and by adding circles, ellipses, arcs, and open and closed curves. Blocks can be moved, copied, saved separately, changed in size, filled with a color, cropped (erasing everything outside the block), flipped, mirrored, and inverted. Text can be added (with four sizes and two typefaces). Unlike PS+, in which text becomes graphics as soon as you finish typing, HotShot retains text as separate information, making it easier to modify. HotShot supports seven different "zoom" levels for looking at more or less of a picture in greater or lesser detail. Finally, HotShot can create catalogs of screen files, print screen images, and convert among a variety of file formats.

Note that HotShot Graphics provides strong tools for editing a screen and more drawing tools than Ventura, but it still offers a far less complete painting toolbox than PaintShow Plus. That's reasonable; HotShot is primarily designed to edit existing files, not to create new ones from scratch. On the other hand, its curve-drawing facilities set it apart from simple graphics editors (and provide facilities not present in PaintShow Plus). Naturally, it works well with a mouse, although some of its features can be used without one.

After some experience with both programs, I can say that both represent intelligent design and workable interfaces—in both cases, with occasional quirks. HotShot Graphics succeeds admirably in achieving its goal; I found it a useful and accommodating tool for capturing screen images. I used PaintShow Plus more than I expected, and frankly I found it delightful. (The manual for PaintShow Plus is a mere 138 pages plus appendixes and index; that seems to be quite enough. The HotShot Graphics manual is much thicker but only slightly longer, at 160 pages plus index. Both are refreshing after the massive Word and Ventura document sets.)

One caution about screen-capture programs: they do take up memory, and some programs want all the memory they can get. I was initially unable to capture Ventura Publisher screens, because my 640K machine did not have sufficient room for both GRAB (the HotShot capture program) and Ventura. By adding a parameter (to tell Ventura to free some printer-support memory), I was able to make it work—but the experience does suggest that you should be wary of capture programs used with "memory hog" programs.

Scanners: Graphics for Non-Artists

You may think of scanners in terms of those expensive, massive objects used to scan in full sheets of paper. Those scanners have gotten less expensive (although most good-quality ones still cost more than $1,000) and your library may have uses for full-page scanners—but there's another option that will serve you well for desktop publishing.

The Logitech ScanMan Plus is one of a small number of hand-held scanners; it sells for around $180–$225 (list $350) and includes PaintShow Plus software, described above. The scanner can read an image just a bit more than 4 inches wide, at up to 400 dots per inch and as either line art or dithered gray-scale.

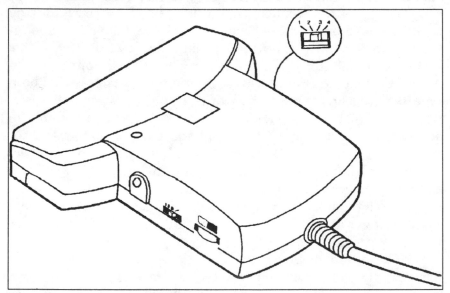

Figure 14.16: Logitech ScanMan Plus

Figure 14.16 is a line-art version of the ScanMan Plus, scanned in with the ScanMan Plus (from the documentation) and touched up in PaintShow Plus. The device is roughly 5 inches wide and 5 inches deep (a little more than 1 inch thick), with a comfortable handgrip and a roller on the bottom. It has a window through which you line up the image you wish to scan. After turning it on (with a software command), you line it up—the window lights up—and, pressing a button on the side of the case, roll the scanner over the image. Pressing any key on the computer stops the scan and turns off the light; the image appears on the PaintShow Plus screen as you scan.

That's it. You need to line up your copy correctly, which may take a few tries, and you need a reasonably steady hand—but, after the first few experiments, you'll find that it goes quite easily. Since you can switch immediately to a view that shows the whole scanned image (PaintShow normally shows an enlarged image), you can rescan if things didn't go quite right. The process is faster to carry out than to describe. You typically cut out the scanned area that you really need; the resulting disk file will be much smaller than a full-page scan.

The ScanMan Plus gives you access to all the Dover clip art, to your library and organization logos, and to anything else you can legally include in publications. For some applications, the four-inch scanning width may be a problem—although you can scan multiple strips and use block moves to line them up.

My reasoned, careful, harsh evaluation of this product is fairly simple: I love it! I also recommend it: I believe that most libraries will find a hand scanner and clip-art collections to be far more useful than software clip art, at a much better overall price. Even though my own desktop publications rarely require graphics, and even though Logitech provided the ScanMan Plus on loan for this book, I concluded after less than a week of use that the ScanMan Plus was worth buying, if only to produce more interesting signs and publications for my wife's library. As you can see in other chapters, it has made a difference: beginning with the scanned-in CND logo, scanned images have been used extensively in this book and for her work.

Do you need a handheld scanner? Possibly not; it depends on your needs. If you're not sure you need one, I would suggest that you not try one out: once you have it and some Dover books, it will be difficult to turn it back in. (One nice thing about MS-DOS computers is that they generally aren't fun; you use them as tools and let it go at that. This device and the PaintShow Plus software are dangerous: they are, indeed, fun to use as well as rewarding.)

To my knowledge, five or six different handheld scanners are on the market in early 1990. I've only tried the Logitech, and can recommend it both on its own merits and on the strength of the company's reputation.

Concluding this chapter, I would reinforce the warning that should be part of any discussion of graphics in desktop publishing: don't overdo it. A few well-chosen graphics will have far more impact than too many graphics—and, in many cases, strong text in a well-designed page will work better without any illustrations at all.

Tips and Reminders

- You don't need illustrations to add graphic interest to a publication; text, borders, and white space make some of the most effective graphics.

- All computer-based illustrations are either vector graphics or raster graphics. Vector graphics will always retain the best possible detail and resolution, no matter what the final output size or medium. Raster graphics, far more common, do not stand up so well to change.

- While it is possible to include good-looking photographs as part of desktop-published documents, it is neither easy nor inexpensive. Unless you need to use many photographs, it's easier and cheaper to add halftones to the desktop-published page—and the quality will be better.

- Good clip art makes it possible for non-artists to add effective illustrations—but much commercial clip art is cliché-ridden.

- Dover publications provide nearly inexhaustible sources of interesting, varied, legitimately copyright-free clip art; all you need is a handheld scanner to use them.

- Just because you find clip art on an electronic bulletin board or in a public-domain collection, don't automatically assume you can legitimately use it. Any illustration that looks almost exactly like a Disney character, for example, is protected by copyright—no matter how you got it.

- Most spreadsheets and many other business programs will prepare graphs that can be imported into desktop publishing. These are usually stored as line art, resulting in the best possible reproduction quality.

- If you're preparing manuals for software or guides for online catalogs, use a screen-capture program to produce accurate illustrations painlessly.

- Illustrations take up disk space—lots of disk space. Be sure to allow plenty of space and get rid of illustrations you won't use.

APPENDIX
Production Details

With the exception of the cover and title page, almost everything in this book was produced using a modest desktop-publishing system. Hardware consisted of the following:

- A 12-MegaHertz 80286-based MS-DOS computer (an "AT clone") populated with 640K of RAM;

- Seagate 251-0 hard disk (40-megabytes 38-millisecond access);

- Hercules-compatible display adapter and Samsung 1252G 11-inch amber monochrome monitor;

- Logitech P7 Mouse;

- Logitech ScanMan handheld scanner;

- Hewlett-Packard LaserJet Series II laser printer with one megabyte of added RAM.

I upgraded this system in January 1990, replacing everything except the printer. Six scanned images were prepared or replaced using the upgraded scanner, a Logitech ScanMan Plus; the final pages were prepared with the new system. While the new system made Ventura Publisher operations much faster and easier, it had no effect on the appearance or content of the book except for the sentences about the effects of disk caching.

Software used to produce the book included the following:

- *Microsoft Word 5.0*, used to prepare the text for all of the chapters and this appendix, and to prepare some of the figures (as discussed below);

- Xerox *Ventura Publisher 2.0*, without the Professional Extension, used to prepare all pages except as noted later in this chapter;

- Software Publishing's *pfs:First Publisher* and Logitech's *Finesse*, two low-end desktop-publishing programs used in chapter 12;

- Pro Tem's *NoteBook II*, used to prepare the entries in the glossary and the book reviews in the bibliographic essay;

- Logitech's *PaintShow Plus* and its *Catch* utility, and SymSoft's *HotShot Graphics* and its *Grab* utility, used to capture screens (*Catch* and *Grab*), control the scanner and edit scanned images (*PaintShow Plus*), modify captured screens (*HotShot Graphics* and *PaintShow Plus*), and create "painted" figures (*PaintShow Plus*);

- Bitstream's *Fontware* and various typeface outlines to create and install fonts for *Ventura*; Swfte's *Glyphix 3* software and typeface outlines, primarily to generate and control fonts in *Microsoft Word* but also to generate and install fonts for *Ventura*;

- Central Point's *PC Tools Deluxe 5.5*, to maintain the hard disk, provide a disk cache during final production, and—blessedly—to locate the captured-screen files hidden somewhere on the hard disk.

All pages were printed out on the LaserJet II using Neenah N.P. 24-pound bond (25 percent cotton fiber, acid-free, specifically designed for laser printers).

The book is set entirely in Bitstream's Zapf Calligraphic except for figures that show other typefaces. The body text is 11 on 13, on a 27-pica by 41-pica body. Chapter titles are 17-point bold; first-level headings are 13-point bold; second- and third-level headings are 11-point bold and italic, respectively; figure captions are 9-point. Bulleted items are 10 on 11.5. The first character of each chapter's first paragraph is 24-point bold.

The notes that follow discuss how figures were created, except for the strictly textual figures that were simply imported as documents into bordered frames and processed entirely by Ventura.

Ventura reads a great many graphics formats, but (as a GEM application) will actually only print from files stored in the ".GEM" format (vector graphics) or the ".IMG" format (bit-mapped). When other files are read, they are immediately converted, resulting in two files for each image. HotShot Graphics captures screens in a proprietary format, but it will convert those screens to any of a number of formats; in all cases for this book, IMG files were created. Paint-Show Plus and the Finesse clip-art collection both use the widely used TIFF graphic interchange format, which Ventura and Finesse convert to IMG. It is possible to delete the original image files once they have been converted; thus, while the short-term disk requirements are as noted in this summary, it was possible to delete a million characters of redundant information for long-term use.

Chapter 4

Figures 4.1 through 4.7 and 4.10 through 4.12 were created separately using Ventura Publisher. The pages were photoreduced to 53 percent of original dimensions to fit into the frames—thus, the framed size represents the complete 8½-by-11-inch page, including margins. Within those pages:

- The rail (bird) in figure 4.1 was scanned from *Treasury of Animal Illustrations*, ed. by Carol Belanger Grafton (New York: Dover Publications, 1988). The children's hour figure (also used in Figure 4.4) was scanned from *Humorous Victorian Spot Illustrations*, ed. by Carol Belanger Grafton (New York: Dover Publications, 1985); the words "Children's Hour" were added using PaintShow Plus internal fonts.

- The Halltown City Library logotype in figures 4.2 and 4.4 was originally created using pfs:First Publisher—taking an image from one of its clip-art libraries, adding the straight line and text, then printing it out—and then scanned into a TIFF file for use in Ventura Publisher.

- The CND logo in figures 4.4–4.7 (and elsewhere) was scanned in from a printed College of Notre Dame document.

- Figure 4.8 is tricky. I specifically wanted to avoid making the text of the letter interesting or particularly legible. The original letter (created using Ventura) was printed, then reduced to 53 percent of its original size, making it narrow enough to be scanned. It was scanned at 100-dots-per-inch resolution, much lower than the normal 300 dots per inch; the recipient and salutation (and portions of the text) were then edited on a pixel-by-pixel basis in PaintShow Plus to make them totally illegible (if you think you recognize characters in those two blocks, you're making them up). The labels were added within Ventura.

Graphics files used in these figures—the children's hour image, the rail, the CND logo, the Halltown logo, and the blurred letter— required a total of roughly 195,000 bytes.

Chapter 5

Figure 5.1 is a reduced (53 percent) photocopy of a brochure originally created using Ventura Publisher; figure 5.2 is a 53 percent reduction photocopy of one page of that brochure.

Figures 5.3 through 5.6 began as Ventura Publisher screens, captured using the Catch utility supplied with PaintShow Plus; in each case, portions of the captured screens were removed to focus on the page or pages directly. The captions, lines, and arrows in figures 5.3 and 5.6 were added using box text and line drawing in Ventura.

Figures 5.7 through 5.11 were created as separate pages in Ventura Publisher—all using the same Microsoft Word text file but different style sheets—then photoreduced at 53 percent. Figures 5.7 and 5.9 use Courier.

The four captured screen portions use roughly 56,000 characters.

Chapter 6

Most figures consist of text files imported into frames and formatted using new tags. The only exceptions are figures 6.6 and 6.7. Both were created as separate documents in Microsoft Word, printed out, and used full-size.

Chapter 7

This chapter uses a variety of techniques for the various figures:

- Figures 7.1 and 7.2 were created using pfs:First Publisher (and the fonts provided with the program), printed out, then reduced to 53 percent for insertion in the frames. Figure 7.1 uses entirely First Publisher internal fonts; Figure 7.2 uses primarily Bitstream fonts.

- Figure 7.3 was created as a separate Ventura Publisher document (using text from a recent *LITA Newsletter*) with the most confused style sheet I could create; it was photoreduced to 53 percent for inclusion.

- Figure 7.4 was created and printed in Microsoft Word and added full-size.

- Figures 7.5 through 7.7 are portions of publications created separately using Ventura Publisher; I scanned in the portions using the Logitech ScanMan Plus (at 300 dots per inch).

- The decorative "S" was scanned from *Decorative Alphabets and Initials*, ed. by Alexander Nesbitt, New York: Dover Publications, 1959. (This letter was originally scanned with the Logitech ScanMan. The Scan-Man Plus makes it much easier for clumsy humans to scan along a straight line; I rescanned the letter to straighten it out. The remaining slanted borders are in the original.)

The four scanned images use a total of roughly 319,000 bytes for the two copies required.

Chapter 8

Figures 8.1 and 8.2 are Microsoft Word screens captured using Hot-Shot Graphics, with the border supplied by HotShot. Figure 8.3 uses an image scanned from Dover's *Humorous Victorian Spot Illustrations*. The thick border was drawn using Ventura's rounded-rectangle graphics tool; the text was added to the frame as box text.

The paperboy image was stored twice, as usual, taking up a total of 34,000 bytes; the two Word screens were stored only once. Total storage requirements for the figures was roughly 77,000 bytes.

Chapter 11

Figures 11.1 and 11.3 through 11.12 are Ventura Publisher screens, captured using HotShot Graphics; that program was also used to capture the Word screens in figures 11.2 and 11.13. Those figures, stored only once, require roughly 280,000 bytes. For reasons that escape me, the simple Microsoft Word screens (originally captured as text) require twice as much space as the complex Ventura Publisher screens (captured as graphics).

Chapter 12

Figures 12.1 through 12.10 are pfs:First Publisher screens captured with the PaintShow Plus Catch utility; figures 12.19 through 12.23 are Finesse screens also captured using Catch.

Figures 12.11 through 12.14 were generated and printed by pfs:First Publisher. The first three pages were reduced to 53 percent; the invitation (figure 12.14) was reduced to 80 percent of its original dimensions. All illustrations in these figures come from First Publisher clip-art collections, and all fonts were supplied with the program. As noted in chapter 12, the footsteps and railroad train in figure 12.11 are actually the Cairo font, not clip art; the image of Mark Twain was extensively modified in First Publisher, but only to eliminate the black background. (These files are not included in the overall space calculation.)

Figures 12.15 through 12.18 were created and printed in pfs:First Publisher (using an imported text file several times) and used full-size.

Figure 12.24 was created and printed in Finesse and used full-size. The car in figure 12.21 is from the clip-art collection provided with Finesse; the text in figure 12.22 is one of the files provided for use in the Finesse tutorial.

The fifteen captured screens were stored twice; total disk requirements are roughly 350,000 bytes.

Chapter 13

Figures 13.3–13.5, 13.7, and 13.15–13.18 were created using Microsoft Word and the Glyphix software driver, printed from Microsoft Word, and used full-size.

Chapter 14

All figures in chapter 14 were printed as part of the Ventura chapter. The images came from various sources:

- The decorative *G* was scanned from Dover's *Decorative Alphabets and Initials*; the TIFF file requires 37,810 bytes.

- The vector-graphics image of the Columbia space shuttle, used in figures 14.1 and 14.2, is included with Ventura Publisher for use in examples and tutorials; it is a GEM file occupying 13,602 bytes.

- The bugle in figures 14.3 and 14.4 is from the Finesse clip-art collection; it was deliberately chosen as one of the smallest files (1,706 bytes in TIFF format), thus presumably having less detail than others (for example, the computer in figure 14.9 is 11,366 bytes in TIFF).

- Two of the logos in figure 14.5 (which, in Ventura terms, is three borderless frames superimposed on the larger, bordered frame) were used in previous chapters; the RLG logo was scanned in from a sheet of RLG logos ready to be used in publications. The logo was scanned at highest possible resolution (400 dots per inch) for eventual use at various sizes; it uses 22,970 bytes in TIFF format.

- Figure 14.6 was scanned from the original photographic print (not a halftone) used for two book-jacket pictures, using a ScanMan Plus "halftone" (dithered) setting; several attempts at various dithering settings and resolutions resulted in this as the best of the trials. (Several trials using the ScanMan resulted in a final TIFF file taking up 48,632 bytes. The second set of trials, using the ScanMan Plus, resulted in the image actually used in the book; the TIFF file takes up an astonishing 164,174 bytes!)

- Figure 14.7 was scanned from the RLG Medieval and Early Modern Data Bank brochure, choosing the best of several different dithering and resolution settings. The TIFF file takes up 79,502 bytes.

- The images in figures 14.8 and 14.9 come from the Finesse clip-art collection—except for the book, which actually comes from pfs:First Publisher. (It is possible to save First Publisher pages or partial pages as MAC files, in the MacPaint format; Ventura Publisher can read MAC files.) The book is one of the rare cases in which the converted IMG file is much smaller than the original, rather than being roughly the same size: the 8,644-byte MAC file becomes a 710-byte IMG file.

- The image in figure 14.10 is scanned from *Humorous Victorian Spot Illustrations*.

- Figures 14.11 and 14.12 were generated using Quattro and saved as ".PIC" files, a Lotus vector format directly readable and convertible by Ventura.

- Figure 14.13 is a screen from PaintShow Plus captured using its Catch utility; figures 14.14 and 14.15 were created in PaintShow Plus and saved as TIFF files. All three screens were created using only the tools, fonts, and patterns provided in PaintShow Plus.

- Figure 14.16 was scanned in from the ScanMan Plus manual.

The total of all file sizes for images in this chapter (excluding those used elsewhere) is roughly 900,000 bytes. In other words, the images used in this chapter alone require more disk space than the entire 100,000-word text of the book.

Summing Up

When people say that "a picture is worth a thousand words," they're grossly underestimating, at least in terms of disk requirements! One of the pictures in this book required as much disk space as 50,000 words—and there were no scanned pictures (and very few images of any sort) that required less than the equivalent of a thousand words.

Total storage requirements for those images comes to more than two million bytes. Of course, it could be much worse: ask anyone who has ever scanned in a full-page, full-color image! (One such image could require much more storage than all of the images used in this book.)

Before you say that these are unrealistic numbers, because this book sets out to demonstrate desktop-publishing capabilities, let me cite one incident. My wife's library (College of Notre Dame) needed a sign announcing a one-day record sale and book sale at the beginning of the new academic year; the library also needed a sign to convince students to buy "copycards" if they planned to use the library's copier extensively. I made a total of six different signs, each using one scanned image: the "copycard" itself for that sign and five different images from *Humorous Victorian Spot Illustrations*, one for the book sale and one each for four different record-sale signs. Total disk requirements—not including the very small Ventura chapters and text files—to make six one-page signs? Just over half a megabyte: 573,613 bytes! Were the results worth it? Yes. Because the illustrations were scanned at 300 dots per inch, the enlarged versions on the signs were still crisp and impressive, and the signs themselves were distinctive. Naturally, I could erase the files once the signs were made; scanning them in once more takes only a few seconds per illustration, plus a minute or two to cut out the specific image in PaintShow Plus.

Those numbers may provide the final argument as to why your library will be better off with a scanner and Dover books than with machine-readable clip-art images. High-resolution images take up a lot of disk space; the only feasible way to distribute large quantities in machine-readable form is CD-ROM or some other form of optical disc. Then again, the CD-ROM collection of Dover art only includes 6,500 images; that's a small fraction of what's actually available. For example, the three books used for this project include more than 5,000 images in all.

The moral to this story is to make sure you have plenty of disk space, and don't plan to keep all your scanned images around. Scan them as you need them; unless you've spent some time modifying the scanned images, get rid of them once the publication is ready—assuming that you have the source material safe and sound.

Glossary

Definitions follow the usage in this book. In most cases, these definitions agree with common usage in desktop publishing and typography.

Ascender: The portion of certain lowercase letters that rises above the body of the letters—for example, the upper strokes in *b*, *d*, and *h*.

Bad break: Any of a number of problems. Specifically, incorrect hyphenation, but also widows, orphans, stranded headings, and hyphenation at the very end of a page.

Banner: The large title running across the top of the first page of most newsletters and similar publications; also sometimes called the flag or nameplate; sometimes called the masthead, but this is confusing (since the box that provides title, frequency of publication, name and address of publisher, copyright, and, typically, staff list is also called the masthead).

Baseline: The line along which the bottom of each character rests, exclusive of descenders (the descending elements in *j*, *p*, *q*, *g*, and *y*). Leading is defined as the distance between the baselines for consecutive lines of text. A badly implemented typeface may not have a rock-steady baseline. On the other hand, some typefaces require that certain letters (for example, the lowercase *c*) deviate from the baseline in order to maintain visual alignment.

Binding margin: Additional space in the inner margin of a page (the left margin of a right-hand page, the right margin of a left-hand page) that is added to facilitate binding or hole-punching.

Bit-mapped: Defined as a series of black and white dots (picture elements or *pixels*), storing a map of an image or character as binary digits (bits). Bit-mapped graphics are sometimes called *raster graphics*, in contrast to *vector graphics* which are stored as descriptions of the lines and patterns of an image. In desktop publishing (using laser printers), all characters are bit-mapped by the time they reach the printing engine—but a distinction is made between fonts that are stored in bit-mapped form on the hard disk and those that are stored as outlines and transformed to bit-mapped form within the printer itself (i.e., using Post-Script).

Block indent: See hanging indent—although a block indent may or may not have the first line run out to the left margin.

Border: Anything serving to define the edges of a frame or page; typically used for decorative borders, rather than rules.

Bullet: Special symbol setting off a paragraph, which is usually indented. The standard bullet is a black circle (as used in this book), but other special characters can also be used as bullets . For example, the character ⇒ makes an effective bullet, as do ◊ and ».

CAD: Computer Aided Design, drawing software that is specifically oriented to drafting and similar uses. The best-known examples are AutoCad and Generic Cadd. All CAD programs use object-oriented drawing methods and produce vector graphics.

Call-out: Labeled element of a figure, with an arrow pointing from the label to the element. Sometimes also used as a synonym for *pull quote*, text from a story repeated, usually enlarged, and accented with distinctive rules, for emphasis and visual variety.

Camera-ready copy: Finished pages ready to be turned into printing plates using a printer's camera. The end result of desktop publishing, even if you don't actually make printing plates from the pages.

Caption: Text identifying a photograph or other illustration, typically appearing directly beneath the illustration. Sometimes called *cut line*.

Clip art: Illustration provided ready-to-use and which is either free of copyright or comes with clearance for use in publications. Frequently banal but also frequently useful. May be digitized (ready to use in desktop publishing) or printed (ready to scan or paste in). Dover Books produces many volumes of clip art.

Crop: Eliminate part of an image by trimming its edges. Typically, desktop-publishing systems provide controls to specify that the displayed and printed portion of an imported graphic should begin at some specified offset (vertical, horizontal, or both) from the actual edge of the graphic. In combination with scaling controls and frame sizes, this effectively crops the image.

CRT: Cathode Ray Tube—or, more loosely, any monitor that uses a "picture tube." That includes almost all monitors except the internal monitors in laptop and portable computers (which frequently use some display technology other than CRT).

Cut and paste: Move. The longer term is a holdover from conventional layout techniques, where material is literally cut from one location and pasted into another location.

Cut line: See *caption*.

Decorative initial: Large, fancy letter at the beginning of a paragraph or section—what you might think of as an illuminated initial letter, except that illumination properly includes painting or gilt as well as decoration. Differs from a drop cap or big initial in that the letter is decorated in some fashion; this book includes two decorative initials.

Descender: The portion of a letter that falls below the baseline. The lowercase letters g, j, p, q and y have descenders in all properly designed typefaces; the uppercase letter J has a descender in a few typefaces.

Device-independent: Not dependent on a specific (output) device. Thus, for example, the width specifications for PostScript fonts are *device-independent*—the letters will have the same width whether printed on a laser printer or a phototypesetter.

Dithering: Within desktop publishing, used mostly to mean the process of simulating halftones (that is, simulating shades of gray) on a laser printer by using clusters of *pixels* to represent a single element of the original. Thus, for example, a four-by-four array of pixels can take on sixteen shades of gray, from white (all pixels off) to black (all pixels on). Dithering trades resolution for gray scale.

dpi: Dots per inch, a measure of resolution for display and printing devices. May be specified as a single number (e.g., the HP Laser-Jet and Apple LaserWriter both print at 300 dpi) or as two numbers (e.g., the Hercules graphics adapter typically displays at 91 dpi by 72 dpi). In the first case, the number applies to both directions. In the second, if horizontal and vertical are not both specified, you can generally assume that the higher resolution is the horizontal resolution, given the nature of text.

Drawing program: Computer software that allows you to create *vector graphics* by direct manipulation. Some drawing programs include functions supported by paint programs; the distinctive aspect of a drawing program is that lines and curves are treated as descriptions, not as pictures. Examples of drawing programs include all CAD programs, AutoSketch, and Corel DRAW!

Drop cap: Large initial capital letter at the beginning of a paragraph; used in this book at the beginning of each chapter. The term is typically used whether or not the capital letter is actually "dropped" below the normal baseline. This book does not drop the drop caps; the *LITA Newsletter* (for example) does.

Dummy file: Also *dummy publication*. A file that shows (and establishes) the style and characteristics of a type of publication and can be used to build an example of that type, by copying the dummy file and inserting real text. Also called *template*.

Em: The width of the letter *m* within a given font; typically equal to the point size of the font, although many typefaces do not follow that rule.

Em dash: True dash—like these—usually represented by two hyphens in typewritten copy. One em wide.

Em space: Blank space one em wide; much wider than a nominal between-word space.

Flush-left: Aligned to the left-hand margin and not to the right; the same as *ragged-right* or *left-justified*.

Flush-right: Sometimes called *right-justified* or *ragged-left*. Type set so that text always ends at the right margin, with the beginning of each line in a paragraph varying. Very unusual and best reserved for special effects: violates normal Western expectations for the look of type.

Font: A single typeface in a single style and a single size. Times Roman medium upright 10-point is a font; so is Times Roman medium italic 10-point. A font includes the full range of characters and symbols defined for a particular character set.

Footer: Text appearing at the bottom of a page such as page number, chapter title, etc. Sometimes called *running footer*. Like header, but at the bottom rather than the top.

Frame: A rectangle in which text or graphics appears. A frame may be any size from a single pixel to a full page; software may allow overlapping and layered frames to handle special needs. A frame may have visible borders, but need not.

Fully justified: See *justified*.

Galley: Typeset text in columns but not yet split into pages, used for proofreading and makeup. In desktop publishing, galleys rarely exist; some desktop publishers may refer to preliminary drafts as galleys.

Grid: Set of row and column marks (visible or invisible) that serve to define and, in some cases, control layouts. Some drawing and painting programs, and some desktop-publishing programs, provide controls so that grids serve as magnets—that is, lines and frames set near a grid edge will automatically move to match the grid.

Gutter: The space between adjacent columns of type. Can also refer to the space between two pages at the binding edge, called the *inner margin* in this book.

Hairline: The finest possible rule: ¼-point for desktop publishing.

Halftone: Photograph converted to different-sized dots so that it can be reproduced by normal printing methods.

Hanging indent: Paragraph style in which the entire paragraph except for the first line is indented. Used in this book for the glossary; thus, this paragraph uses a hanging indent. Also called *outdent*, a term more likely to be encountered in desktop publishing.

Header: One or more lines appearing at the tops of pages carrying information other than that in the body, such as page numbers, chapter names, titles, etc. Also called *running head* or *running header*. This book uses headers on all but the first page of each chapter, and *footers* (q.v.) on the first page of each chapter.

Icon: A small graphic symbol that supposedly communicates the meaning of a command, file, etc.

Insertion mode: Text-editing mode in which, when the cursor is placed within existing text, new text will push old text to the right, rather than eliminating the old text. Every contemporary word-processing program (and desktop-publishing program in text mode) functions in insertion mode unless specifically switched to *overstrike mode*.

Interoperability: The ability of different programs to operate on the same files—more specifically, the ability to create a file in one program, revise it in a different program, then revise it again in the first—without either losing the revisions in the second program or, if the file is again used in that program, losing revisions from the first program. Xerox Ventura Publisher excels in interoperability: when imported word-processing files are modified within Ventura, the modifications are stored with the files; if those files are further modified in the original word-processing programs, Ventura will automatically use the further-modified versions the next time it opens the chapter containing the files. (In most cases, different programs can only import files from other programs, not interoperate.)

Italic: Type in which the characters slant to the right, but properly restricted to those typefaces designed as italic, which usually means a significantly different set of letters. Tip-offs to true italic type are the lowercase *a* and *f*, which are typically entirely different letterforms than the upright "a" and "f." Contrast with *oblique*, simply slanted letters that are not separately designed. Some "italic" typefaces are actually oblique. Many sans serif typefaces lack true italics.

Justified: Lining up at both left and right margin, except for the last line in each paragraph. Also called *fully-justified* (as opposed to left-justified and right-justified).

K: When used by itself in this book (or in most other cases in personal computing), *K* usually stands for *kilobyte*—which is not 1,000 bytes or characters (although *kilo* does mean *thousand*), but rather 1,024.

Kerning: Adjusting spaces between certain letter pairs so that the letters in a word flow properly. Kerning usually results in part of one letter extending over or under part of another letter, and it is only used in those cases where the spacing would otherwise look odd. For example, the "Te" pair in "Technical" is kerned. Good desktop-publishing software used with high-quality fonts will support kerning automatically.

Kicker: Properly, a two-line headline in which the upper line is much smaller than the lower, set to its left, typically italicized and underlined. Informally, the upper line of such a headline.

Kilobyte: Roughly one thousand bytes or characters; actually 1,024 characters.

Landscape: Print or display mode that is wider than it is tall—or, for standard letter paper, "sideways." Compare *portrait*.

Leading: The overall distance from one baseline to the next, usually expressed in points. The body text in this book is set 11/13 or 11 on 13, which means that 11-point text is set on 13-point leading. The name (pronounced *ledding*) comes from the original method of providing additional space between lines, by inserting thin strips of lead. "Whiting" doesn't quite have the same ring.

Left-justified: See *ragged-right*.

Legibility: The ease with which characters can be recognized. Legibility and *readability* (q.v.) are not the same quality; for example, good sans serif type is extremely legible, but it is generally not as readable as good serif type.

Letterspacing: Addition of space between letters within words in order to prevent unreasonably wide spaces between words in justified text. Compare with *tracking*; the difference is that letterspacing (as used in desktop publishing) is an option used by the software only in those lines where blanks will otherwise be too wide.

Ligature: Two characters actually connected as one type element. Typographers sometimes carry the letter pairs *ff*, *fl*, and *fi* as ligatures; desktop publishing can achieve the desired tight spacing through kerning. The only ligatures normally present for desktop publishing are the digraphs œ, Œ, æ, and Æ.

Line art: See *vector graphics*.

Logo: A symbol, frequently (but not always) created from type, that serves to identify an organization or other entity; some publications have their own logos. Short for *logotype*.

lpi: Lines per inch, the equivalent of *dpi* in phototypesetting, also used to specify halftone density and, in some cases, the number of text lines that will be printed on each inch. If a specification says "8 lpi" it is almost certainly referring to text lines per inch; if it says "2,540 lpi" it is certainly referring to phototypeset resolution.

MB: See *megabyte*

Mechanical: Camera-ready copy actually ready for the camera, including instructions for the platemaker as needed. The distinction between mechanicals and camera-ready copy is vague at best when dealing with desktop publishing.

Megabyte: One million characters—either exactly or approximately (in the latter case, a megabyte is 1,024 squared, or 1,048,576 characters). Typical measure of disk capacity or file space requirements. Frequently given as "meg"—which could properly refer to a million of anything.

Megahertz or MegaHertz: Speed rate—or, precisely, frequency rate. Equal to millions of cycles per second. Usually used in the form

MHz or *mhz* to specify computer speed. For example, contemporary "AT-compatibles" usually run at 12 MHz, although the original IBM AT ran at either 6 MHz or 8 MHz.

Megapixel: One million *pixels* (picture elements). Usually used of displays that will show at least one million picture elements—such as the Wyse 700/Amdek 1280, which has a resolution of 1,280 horizontal by 800 vertical.

MHz: See *Megahertz*.

Millisecond: One $\frac{1}{1,000}$ of a second. Typically given as a measure of disk-access time—for example, a good contemporary hard disk can access anything on the disk in an average of 28 milliseconds, usually given as "28 ms random access." (Note: one $\frac{1}{1,000,000}$ of a second would be a microsecond, not a millisecond.)

Monospaced type: Typeface in which each letter occupies the same amount of space. For example, Courier, Pica, and Letter Gothic are monospaced typefaces: the lowercase *i* takes up as much width as the capital *M*. Compare to *proportional type*.

ms: See *millisecond*.

MS-DOS: Microsoft Disk Operating System, the operating system used on almost all "PC-compatibles" or "IBM-compatibles." This book typically uses the phrase "MS-DOS computers" rather than one of the other phrases, largely because most such machines are no longer IBM-compatible in any meaningful sense: they are architecturally compatible with computers that IBM no longer builds, although typically far more powerful.

Nanosecond: One $\frac{1}{1,000,000,000}$ of a second (one-billionth). Usually stated as *ns*, and used to show access times for random-access memory (for example). Typical RAM has access times of 60 ns to 150 ns; high-speed "cache memory" may have 15 ns to 30 ns access time. Note reciprocal relation to speed in MHz or *megahertz*: 12 MHz speed implies 80 ns access, if access is to be achieved within a single cycle. (Note: one-millionth of a second is a *microsecond*, abbreviated μs.)

Object-oriented graphics: Equivalent to *vector graphics* (q.v.).

Oblique: Slanted version of upright or roman typeface—as distinguished from *italic*. An italic typeface is normally an entirely different type design, whereas an oblique typeface can be created within a computer or printer by simply warping the upright typeface. For example, all Glyphix italic typefaces are actually oblique—and the Bitstream Dutch Italic provided with Finesse is actually oblique. Many sans serif typefaces use oblique rather than italic styles.

Orphan: First line of a paragraph appearing at the bottom of a page or column. Automatically prevented (at user option) in the best desktop-publishing and word-processing programs, as are the equally undesirable cases where a heading is orphaned from the paragraph beneath.

Outdent: See *hanging indent*.

Overstrike mode: Mode of text editing in which, if the cursor is placed within existing text, new characters replace old characters rather than pushing the old text to the right. No well-designed contemporary word-processing or desktop-publishing program ever goes to overstrike mode without an explicit command and, usually, an on-screen warning to that effect—since you will wipe out old text that you may not intend to eliminate.

Paint program: Any graphics program that builds and stores images as bit-mapped graphics (that is, maps of the images) rather than as vectors (that is, descriptions of the lines in the images). A paint program may include line-drawing and other drawing tools; the key distinction is the manner in which the screen is manipulated and saved.

Paragraph: In desktop-publishing terms, a paragraph is any segment of text that ends in a carriage return and can be acted on independently. A headline is a paragraph; so is a chapter title, a numbered point, and (in some cases) either one line of a table or the complete table.

Phototypography: Or phototypesetting. Typesetting with a photocomposition machine, which uses one of several electronic technologies to create typeset pages on either film or special typesetting paper. Phototypesetting typically offers much higher resolution than laser printing (1,200 to 2,540 dots per inch), but it is also much slower and more expensive.

Pica: Unit of typographic measurement equal to 12 points or roughly ⅙ inch.

Pixel: Picture element; essentially, the smallest dot that can be displayed or printed. The number of pixels on a screen is a measure of its resolution. For example, a Hercules clone displays roughly a quarter of a million pixels; a full-page display may show more than a million pixels.

Point: Smallest normal typographic measurement, roughly 1/72 inch.

Portrait: Printing or display mode in which the image is taller than it is wide. "Normal" mode for most publications. Compare *landscape*.

PostScript: Page-description language developed and licensed by Adobe. In PostScript printing, type is generated to desired sizes at the point of printing. A PostScript file is a description of the page or document. Although far more flexible than other methodologies for dealing with different sizes of type, PostScript can be excruciatingly slow in dealing with images (since bit-mapped graphics can't be "described" in an efficient manner).

Proportional type: Type in which different characters have different widths. Almost all traditional typefaces are proportional, with the capital *M* being much wider than the lowercase *i*. Early computer-generated text was almost always *monospaced* (q.v.), but desktop publishing almost always uses proportional type. Proportional type is generally considered to be far more readable than monospaced type.

Pull quote: Text repeated in a different location, usually in a larger type size and with special rules, to provide emphasis and visual variety.

Ragged-right: Type set so that the space between words is fixed, with internal lines of a paragraph ending irregularly (ragged). Sometimes called *left-justified*; contrasts with *justified* or *fully-justified*.

RAM: Random Access Memory. The solid-state memory used in computers (and printers) to store information while it is being processed.

Raster graphics: See *bit-mapped graphics*.

Readability: The ease with which a document or page can be read—which can be influenced by the font, the layout, and the content. Differs from *legibility*, the ease with which characters can be recognized; a legible typeface does not imply a readable document.

Reverse type: White type on a black background.

Right-justified: See *flush-right*.

Rule: Line used as a graphic element, as opposed to a hyphen, dash or underline.

Running footer: See *footer*.

Sans serif: Type that does not contain serifs (q.v.). Frequently used for headline type, and frequently used for body type in advertisements and in Europe. There are many sans serif types; the only common element is that they lack serifs. Examples include Helvetica and Optima.

Scanner: Device that converts a printed image to machine-readable form as a bit-map of the image. Personal-computer scanners may be *page scanners* (large devices that scan an entire page) or *handheld scanners* (small devices that are manually moved over the area to be scanned). Many of the images in this book were scanned in using a handheld scanner.

Screen capture: The ability to take an electronic "snapshot" of a screen, for import into desktop publishing or for other uses.

Scroll bar: Bar along one edge of a graphic user interface that shows the relative position of the currently displayed screen in relation to a larger "virtual" screen—or of the displayed portion of a list of files in relation to the entire list, for example. A mouse can be used with a scroll bar in order to change the position in the list or page.

Serif: The thin line or extra element at the edges of characters that characterizes serif typefaces. One of the most obvious serifs is the horizontal slab at the top of Courier's capital "A"—but most characters in this paragraph contain serifs. Serif typefaces can be read more easily than sans serif typefaces; the serifs help to make letters instantly identifiable and connect letters into words.

Shaped text: Text that has changing left or right margins to form a particular shape. Always used as some sort of gimmick; shaped text always interferes with easy reading.

Soft font: Any typeface that is stored on disk and sent to the printer at printing time, rather than being provided as part of the printer itself or on a cartridge.

Soft hyphen: A special hyphen that will print if it appears at the end of a line, but not anywhere else. Also called a *conditional hyphen*, it is a way of letting a program know that a word can be broken at this point.

Spread: In any publication that is printed on both sides and bound in some manner, the *spread* is the combination of an even-numbered and odd-numbered page that appears when you open the publication at any point but the first or last page. Some designers consider the appearance of a spread to be as important as, or more important than, the appearance of individual pages. Some desktop-publishing and word-processing programs will show you how each spread will appear—although you will need a very expensive "two-page monitor" in order to see all of a spread with legible, editable text.

Stranded heading: A heading or subheading that appears at the bottom of a page or column, separated from the beginning of the body text that follows. Controlled automatically by good word-processing and desktop-publishing programs.

Style sheet: Compilation of attributes related to a given document or class of documents—typically consisting of a series of named tags or styles, and ideally capable of being stored as a separate file. A style sheet provides control over the appearance of a document, independent of the text within that document.

Tag: Name for a particular kind of paragraph, in some desktop-publishing and word processing-programs. Thus, the tag for this paragraph is *Un* (short for "undent," a casual form of "hanging indent").

Template: A file that specifies the style of a type of document and can be used as the foundation of a document. Similar to *dummy publication*.

Text block: The portion of a page that contains body text, exclusive of headers and footers. Typically, the text block for a page should occupy around 50–55 percent of the page—except that newsletters and other multicolumn layouts frequently have text blocks taking up 65–75 percent of the page.

Tracking: Setting type tighter (closer together) or looser (farther apart) in order to achieve a desired appearance or fit the text into a certain space. Loose tracking differs from letterspacing, in that tight tracking is always applied uniformly to a section of text (usually a paragraph), whereas letterspacing is applied by the computer only if needed to make certain justified lines fit better. One example of loose tracking is when headlines are expanded to completely fill the column or frame; tight tracking may be used to fit a little extra text into a tight space.

True quotes: Or typographic quotes; distinctly different left and right quotation marks, as compared to *inch marks*, the vertical double-quotes used in most word processing. (The best desktop-publishing programs automatically convert double quotes to "true quotes"—however, Zapf Calligraphic has left and right quotes that differ only subtly.)

Type family: A particular design of type, including all styles and weights. Properly, a Bitstream type package could be considered to be one type family consisting of four typefaces (upright, bold, italic, and bold italic). Most casual usage equates typefaces with type families.

Typeface: Properly, a particular style of a particular type family; also used interchangeably with type family. This book typically follows the latter definition.

Typographer's rule: A special ruler useful in typography and desktop publishing. Several typographer's rules exist; one of the most useful varieties is a fairly large transparent rectangle, with picas on one side, points on another, inches on a third, and various rule thicknesses on a fourth, with guides for measuring leading and point size in the middle.

Typographic fractions: Fractions such as $\frac{13}{16}$, $\frac{147}{256}$ or *distance*/*time* that follow normal typographic style, as compared to the crude fractions (e.g., 13/16) available in most word processing.

Vector graphics: Graphics stored as descriptions of lines, curves, and patterns, rather than as maps of light and dark spots. Also called line art, object-oriented art, draw-type art. Vector graphics retain their visual quality as images are enlarged or reduced, because the stored file actually says how to draw something rather than simply showing what it is.

Widow: The last line of a paragraph appearing at the top of a page or column, separated from the rest of the paragraph. To be avoided, and can be automatically controlled in the best desktop-publishing and word-processing programs. Also, according to some type designers, a short last line of a paragraph.

Width table: A table showing the width of each character in one typeface or in a collection of typefaces. Good handling of proportional fonts depends on width tables: the program must read a width table to determine how characters fit into a line. Width tables should be invisible to most users; if they are prepared or interpreted incorrectly, however, the results can be unfortunate.

WYSIWYG: What You See Is What You Get. Never entirely true, but a goal that desktop-publishing software aims for: what appears on the screen should be a very good prediction of what the printed page will show.

Bibliographic Essay:
Books and Magazines on
Desktop Publishing

Every new use for personal computing generates a small swarm of books, if the use has any real success. Perhaps not surprisingly, uses that are related to writing seem to generate proportionally more books than other uses. That may be why you'll find so many books on word processing, many of them little more than rehashes of program documentation.

Desktop publishing represents an unusual topic with quite a few subtopics such as design and printing techniques. Perhaps not surprisingly, a strikingly large number of books have been published on aspects of the field—and at least four different monthly magazines deal exclusively with desktop publishing, as of late 1989.

What's Out There

A search of the RLIN Books database in early October 1989 using the subject "Desktop Publishing#" (that is, "desktop publishing followed by anything else") yielded 253 clusters—253 different titles and editions. That includes not only published books but Cataloging-in-Publication (CIP) information for books not yet published. Discarding apparent duplicates, cases in which both an American and British edition appear, and "books" that appear to be no more than pamphlets, that total comes down to 200 titles (including later editions of books), still quite an astonishing total. Thirty of these appear only as CIP information. (Incidentally, the total grew by 35 titles between June 1989 and October 1989.)

Those titles fall into four general categories.

- *Books about specific programs or operating systems: 111.* The two best-selling programs naturally dominate this area, with thirty-seven books on Aldus PageMaker and forty on Xerox Ventura Publisher—but there are also three books on Unix-based desktop publishing; seven on Adobe Illustrator (a graphics program); seven on desktop publishing with WordPerfect; three each on pfs:First Publisher and desktop publishing with Microsoft Word; two on the Macintosh desktop-publishing program QuarkXPress; and single books on several other programs.

- *Books about specific computers or other devices: 20.* In addition to those program-specific books that are also computer-specific (roughly half of the total), there were six books on Macintosh-based desktop publishing, three that were IBM-specific, three on the Amstrad PC (all British), three books on PostScript page-definition language, two on the Apple LaserWriter, and one on the Hewlett-Packard LaserJet II.

- *Books for specialized audiences or with specialized purposes: 26.* These include market studies, a legal handbook, books that do nothing other than show fonts, and books targeted to church congregations or other special groups.

- *Books on desktop publishing: 53.* This includes all books that couldn't readily be assigned to some other category, including seven books that specifically concentrate on design issues.

I have either read or skimmed through most of the design-oriented books and roughly half of the general books on desktop publishing. I have also glanced at perhaps one-third of the books on Ventura Publisher and PageMaker. Between the fifty or sixty books that I've looked at briefly, and the dozen or so that I have read from cover to cover, I have formed some fairly strong opinions on the state of the literature.

The next portion of this appendix is based on those opinions and includes some advice on choosing other books and magazines to suit your own needs. Your needs won't be the same as mine—but you may find some of these comments useful. That discussion is followed by a series of reviews of the books I have read from cover to cover and brief notes on the four magazines that I have been following for at least a year.

Selecting Books on Desktop Publishing

How should you go about selecting additional books on desktop publishing? That depends on your own needs, preferences, and budget. For most desktop publishers, the books you might need will fall into three general categories: books on general aspects of desktop publishing and, more specifically, design questions; books that relate specifically to the software you use; and books that provide reference or special information. The guidelines below apply to all three categories.

I should stress that these are my own opinions—and that I am deliberately pointing out defects you're likely to find. Out of all the books I have read or skimmed, I can only point to two or three (not reviewed here) that were completely useless and a total waste of money—and those were obvious from quick examination. Most of the others, unless they were program-specific or machine-specific books for programs and machines I would never use, had enough useful information and commentary that some readers would find them worthwhile. While I do believe that a fair number of "quick-and-dirty" books have been published in the desktop-publishing area, as in almost every other area, there's very little outright trash, at least in my experience.

Length and Title

First, look out for obvious warning signs. The word *complete* in the title of any desktop-publishing book is almost certainly misleading. When the claim is for the entire field of desktop publishing and the book is shorter than 300 pages (or shorter than 120 pages!), the claim is clearly "complete" nonsense. Even for Daniel Will-Harris's book, reviewed later in this appendix, the claim for completeness in the subtitle overstates the case considerably.

Length can certainly be a clue. You can't cover the whole field adequately in 100–200 pages. You really can't provide good coverage for one of the high-end programs in 200 pages (although that might be enough for one of the more modest programs). On the other hand, a shorter book may provide a good overview, introduction, or specialized perspective.

Layout and Production

Is the book attractive—are the pages well designed? That's an important criterion, particularly for any book that purports to deal with design issues. That criterion alone eliminated two generally well-regarded books on desktop-publishing design that I might otherwise have purchased and reviewed. The books were so annoying to look at and difficult to read that I immediately distrusted any advice from the writer/designer (who had clearly designed the books). A good book on design will include examples of bad design—but those examples should be clearly labeled as such. That wasn't the case with these books.

Is the book easy to read—is it clearly laid out, with good choices of typeface? Some books that deal with typography seem to show little real understanding of it—or, more likely, suffer from the fact that what works well for short magazine articles or advertisements does not work as well for a book.

Was the book produced using desktop-publishing techniques? That's a more difficult criterion, and there may be good reasons not to use desktop techniques for some books in the field. I would not expect a writer to use pfs:First Publisher to produce a book on that program—the program simply is not designed for book-length projects. But it certainly lends an air of credibility when a book was produced using the techniques discussed therein. Most (but not all) of the better books in the field have been produced using desktop techniques. The final copy may or may not be produced on a desktop laser printer; that's really a different question. (All but two of the books reviewed here were produced using desktop methods.)

Quality

Is the book well written and properly edited? After all, desktop publishing isn't really publishing—but some desktop publishers become self-publishers and fail to see that their books are properly copyedited. As a writer and as a reader, I appreciate the work of good manuscript editors and copy editors; you may appreciate it more after you encounter the unfortunate results of some self-edited projects.

Is the book properly done? Does it have a meaningful table of contents? Does it have a good index? Does it have a glossary—and, if not, is that a problem? Personally, I'm a little uneasy about any single-author nonfiction book more than 150 pages long that doesn't include an index, but you may not be so demanding.

Does the author appear to know what he or she is talking about? That's a subjective call, and the background of the author(s), if it appears in the book, may not help all that much. A chiropractor might be an authority on an aspect of desktop publishing and capable of communicating his or her knowledge magnificently; a full-time desktop publisher may be hopelessly biased, ignorant of everything outside a narrow area of the field, and wholly incapable of clear, straightforward writing.

Currency

Some reviewers say that any book on desktop publishing needs to be revised annually. That's nonsense—but it's fair to say that a program-specific book that is more than two or three years old may be hopelessly out of date.

The need for up-to-the-minute currency depends on the focus of the book. Elements of style and design don't change all that rapidly; I would expect most of Roger Parker's *Looking Good in Print* to be quite useful five years from now. Certainly, aspects of page layout, typography, and the other operations facilitated by desktop publishing aren't in any rapid state of flux; a book on desktop publishing that concentrates on issues more than on specific products may still be quite useful even if it is four years old—and even if it does discuss programs to some extent.

Usefulness and Need

Will the book be useful? Do you need it? That latter question is particularly important when you consider books about specific programs. Before you rush out and buy any program-specific books, try reading the most authoritative book on the program: the documentation. Don't buy other books until you've at least tried to read and use the book(s) that come with the program.

My guess is that many of you will find that the program documentation works very well, if you give it a little time and approach it in a reasonable manner. I found that to be true for Xerox Ventura Publisher, and Version 2 has significantly better documents than Version 1.

Still, you may find that you can't cope with the program documentation, and that you really must read some other book to make sense of the program at all. In that case, you'll have a number of choices; quite a few of the program-specific books seem to be little more than rewrites of the documentation. If you prefer the author's style to that of the documentation writers, so be it; $20–$25 is not a lot to pay in order to make more sense of a $500 program.

If you do find the program's documents satisfactory, that does not mean that you should never buy any book related to that program. Some books go beyond the documentation, or explicate minor (but useful) points somewhat hidden in the documentation. *Ventura Tips and Tricks* (discussed later) is a classic of this type; there are others for Ventura and other programs. These are the books that will help you move to more fluent use of a program and serve you well as references.

Summing Up

The notes above suggest some things to consider, but you must make the final judgment based on your own needs and preferences. Only you can determine which books will prove useful to you. You may want different perspectives on design and examples of techniques for improving publication design. You have presumably almost finished reading one overview of desktop publishing, admittedly from a special perspective; you may or may not want another overview from a different perspective. Some books concentrate on typography; some offer particularly good advice on graphics. I'd be surprised if you didn't find that at least four or five books in the field were worth reading and, quite possibly, buying.

Book Reviews

The books reviewed here are ones that I have read from cover to cover—either borrowed from public libraries, received for review, or purchased. They are arranged alphabetically by author; the arrangement carries no implications as to quality or preference.

Bonura's Dictionary

> Bonura, Larry S. *Desktop Publisher's Dictionary*. Plano, Tex.: Wordware, 1989. 435 p. Bibliography. ISBN 1-55622-406-1: $19.95.

The vocabulary includes not only desktop publishing but typesetting and publishing-related areas in general, including definitions for some of the older typeface sizes such as agate. There are some odd inclusions (a definition for *acquisitions librarian*) and some padding (*advertisement*). There are also a few errors—for example, the first definition for *Cataloging in Publication* is "pre-designated reference numbers provided by the Library of Congress and included in the front matter of a book as well as on the spines." I could only find a few omissions, one of which is most peculiar: a book prepared using Ventura does not define *tracking*, a concept known in typesetting and called by that name in Ventura!

That's nit-picking, however. The book contains an interesting range of information in its well-written definitions, appears to have a relatively small number of errors and typos, and—at $20 for a 435-page, attractively produced hardbound—is well priced. *Recommended*, if you feel the need for such a dictionary.

The Pleasures of the Mac

> Johnson, Harriet H., and Richard D. Johnson. *The Macintosh Press: Desktop Publishing for Libraries*. Westport, Conn.: Meckler, 1989. 180 p. Bibliography, index. ISBN 0-88736-287-7: $24.50 (paper).

This is not a full review and does not include a recommendation. For several reasons, one of them that Dick Johnson is an acquaintance of long standing, I choose to disqualify myself from doing a full evaluation. The book is readable, enjoyable, generally sensible, and quite well done, although also quite short. It offers many illustrations and is, itself, an example of what you can do with the Macintosh, PageMaker, and an Apple LaserWriter Plus. Don't expect this to be a complete introduction to desktop publishing. Do expect to enjoy it, and quite possibly get some useful ideas.

The Big Picture

> Kleper, Michael L. *The Illustrated Handbook of Desktop Publishing and Typesetting.* Blue Ridge Summit, Penn.: TAB, 1987. 770 p. Bibliography, indexes. ISBN 0-8306-2700-6: $49.95 (hardbound); ISBN 0-8306-0700-5: $29.95 (paper).[1]

This massive 8½-by-11-inch book is as much about typesetting as about desktop publishing. It offers a great deal of good information in both areas, together with a certain amount of padding. While certainly not flawless, it is one of the best early books dealing with desktop publishing.

The first chapter, "TYPE!", offers a fast-moving, thirty-six-page blend of history and good advice on typography and page design—more good advice than many of the other books on desktop publishing offer in their entirety. The second chapter, "Word Processing as a Part of Typesetting," also includes much that is useful in its twenty-six pages, although some of the material is now outdated.

The next eleven chapters—550 pages—combine discussions of issues with profiles of particular programs and pieces of hardware. The chapter subjects include word- and text-processing programs; text creation, generation, and reformation [sic] tools; telecommunications methods; data manipulation and conversion; typesetting hardware tools (e.g., keyboard enhancements); professional typesetting software; specialized typesetting languages; desktop typesetting (98 pages); desktop publishing (200 pages); and output devices.

---

1   These notes are based on my review of this book in 1988 for *Information Technology and Libraries*, augmented by recent reexamination of the book itself.

Two brief chapters (twenty-four pages combined) discuss type-setting decisions and business applications, and they appear to be intended exclusively for traditional typesetting operations. The last chapter consists of lists of possible applications for desktop publishing and typesetting, along with a number of brief user profiles. An eighty-four-page appendix lists various suppliers and offers brief profiles of programs; the book ends with a brief bibliography and what appears to be an appropriate index. There is no glossary.

The book is weakest in its program profiles and reviews. Kleper includes too many shots of Apple II menu screens; quite a few outdated programs for no-longer-available computers; too many very obscure programs; too many "fancy" but ugly dot-matrix type-faces for the Apple II; and a lot of strange headline fonts for the LaserWriter and collections of mediocre clip art. Kleper also, in more than one case, includes fairly lengthy profiles of two different versions of a program, older and newer. That doesn't make any sense, unless he really expects readers to consider buying versions of programs that are no longer on the market. Many of the reviews are seriously outdated, and too many simply list menus and functions rather than discussing what the programs are all about. There are surprisingly few negative comments about programs.

This book was one of the basic early works on desktop publishing, and it also includes at least a book's worth of information on typesetting and related programs and techniques. Should you buy this book for your personal library if you're interested in desktop publishing? You could do a lot worse, and you could spend more money without getting as much useful information. It isn't perfect, but it's well worth the money.

One of Many on PageMaker

Kramer, Douglas, and Roger C. Parker, with Eda Warren. *Using Aldus PageMaker 3.0*. 2d ed. Toronto and New York: Bantam, 1988. 356 p. Index, bibliography, glossary. ISBN 0-553-34624-5: $22.95 (paper).

I chose this out of several books on PageMaker based on cursory inspection. After reading it carefully, I'm not sure it was the best choice—but, since I don't use PageMaker, it's hard to say. The book is sloppy, both in terms of copyediting and, sometimes, simple fact. It includes the NeXT as one of the computers that runs PageMaker (as an example of "any computer that runs Windows"), which is sheer nonsense; it includes miscaptioned illustrations and some nonsense about bit-mapped graphics (suggesting that they will look better if set at typesetting resolution, which is true of vector graphics, not bit-mapped graphics); it regards "normal" paragraphs as un-indented, and it essentially defines pull quotes as being completely boxed.

As a book on PageMaker, it appears to be acceptable, although I'm not the best judge. As a book on desktop publishing—which it purports to be, with several chapters on issues not directly related to PageMaker—it is seriously flawed, and it is not itself an example of good design. I found the widely spaced lines of relatively small type (Times Roman 10/15) very tiresome; that's not a good use of white space, and the book would be far more readable with larger type and less leading.

It does appear to be a fairly coherent introduction to PageMaker. To my mind, all the chapters, except one on "Tips & Techniques," represent the sort of thing that the program's documentation should handle, but I'm well aware that many users would rather read other books than actually read a program's documentation.

Design Principles: Yes, But. . .

Lichty, Tom. *Design Principles for Desktop Publishers*. Glenview, Ill.: Scott, Foresman, 1989. 201 p. Bibliography, index. ISBN 0-673-38162-5: $19.95 (paper).

This is a "yes, but" book. Is it a good book? Yes, but. . . Does Lichty have worthwhile things to say? Yes, but. . . Would I buy the book? Yes (in fact, I did), but. . .

Lichty does stick to design issues for most of the book, and he avoids program specificity. He writes well; the book is a pleasure to read. All of his points are worth thinking about, and many of them are worth following. On the other hand, Lichty frequently overstates his points, makes absolute statements that should not be more than advice or opinion, makes a number of questionable or simply incorrect statements, and doesn't really provide as complete a discussion of typographic and design issues as seems to be claimed.

Part of the problem may be that, while the book was desktop-published, he didn't do the work himself (which is unusual for this sort of book). Another part is that, although he avoids program specificity, he seems totally unaware of the key virtues of the most typographically powerful desktop-publishing programs, particularly Ventura Publisher. Thus, for example, he talks about defining boxes around headings so that you can be sure that a given level of heading always has the same spacing before and after, in relation to text. Well, yes, you could do it that way—but why would you, since a proper style-sheet-driven program allows you to define the heading level and automatically provides the proper spacing? He omits any discussion of tracking, and his discussion of kerning is defective (for example, his "kerned" version of **WAVE** is not well kerned).

Lichty is an absolutist about some aspects of design. For example, he says that the proper choice of typeface for body text can "make or break" a publication—and he's talking about, for example, the choice between Times Roman and Palatino! Given that, many of his design choices—for example, his excessive use of Avant Garde (the figure captions, which tend to be long and are eight- or nine-point Avant Garde, are almost painful to the eye), his bizarre right-justified blurbs at chapter heads and long centered statements in margins, his use of only one level of heading, and the generally heavy style of the book (particularly the first page of each chapter)—all indicate that Lichty may not be the ultimate judge of good style. And, in fact, in his sequential examples of "how to improve a design," I frequently found his "best" examples to be overdesigned, sometimes to the point of being irritating.

The best example of that, because it's the first lengthy example and he spends so much time on it, appears in chapter 2. He gives five different versions of a newsletter including a graph. The first is, admittedly, clumsy—with an enormous single column of type. But by the time he gets done, he has reduced the publication's name to the size of a story headline; eliminated the numbers and labels that give the graph meaning and added clip art that simply doesn't communicate; reduced the type size "to improve readability" (!); and strewed the page with lines and boxes. He justifies eliminating all actual meaning from the chart because "our readers already know the information provided by the axes." Then why include the chart at all? If I had opened the book to this discussion before buying it and read both his examples and his justifications, I would not have purchased the book. In particular, I can't buy the principle of throwing away information to make the design more "interesting."

Lest this sound all negative, the truth is that Lichty says a lot of sensible things—and a few silly things. He flatly says that you can't do desktop publishing without the equivalent of PostScript, which is untrue. He oversells the virtues of special laser paper; he oversells the need for a desktop publisher to invest in pasteup equipment; and he seems to be unaware of typography outside the Adobe PostScript catalog. For example, he flatly states that there are no black-letter fonts for laser printers. Bitstream has included Cloister Black in a headline-font package for quite some time; Figure 14.5 in this book shows a Glyphix black-letter font. Bitstream fonts can all be installed as PostScript outlines; his statement is simply wrong. He reverses the meanings of widow and orphan; he seems to think scanning is terribly expensive and assumes that it will be done at low resolution; he stacks the deck in some comparisons. (For example, a comparison of "material with and without display type" shows the "without" side typewritten edge to edge in a single huge column with no margins; the "with" side is proportional, in columns, with good spacing. The use of display type is a relatively minor part of the differences. That's deck-stacking.)

Well, now, what am I really saying here? I skimmed through the book, liked what I saw, and paid good money for it. The writing is very good, and many of the points are well taken. I've concentrated on the negatives above because Lichty seems to be so absolute on certain points, including points where he's simply wrong. Overall, I found the book interesting and worthwhile—but it would be a good deal better if it showed a wider knowledge of the field and a little less absolutism.

LaserWriters Are Not The Universe!

McClelland, Deke, and Craig Danuloff. *Desktop Publishing Type and Graphics: A Comprehensive Handbook.* Boston: Harcourt Brace Jovanovich, 1987. 265 p. ISBN 0-15-625298-8: $29.95 (paper).

The subtitle says "comprehensive" as does the blurb on the back cover. It doesn't say "extensive sample of Macintosh/LaserWriter type and graphics done in total ignorance of the rest of the world"—that might not sell quite as well, but it's a better description of the book. What we have here is almost entirely type samples and clip art (photoreduced, thus looking better than it should) with a very small amount of text; it has little or no relevance to anyone not using a LaserWriter and Macintosh. At $30, I don't think a book of type samples is much of a bargain. As a writer and reader, I don't think this book would be a bargain at any price.

The most astonishing aspect of the book is the inclusion of any number of "body-copy typefaces" that would be absolutely appalling for any copy meant for serious reading. Their concept of "maximum readability" includes not only typefaces such as Fritz Quadrata and Eras that are difficult to read, but also typefaces such as Monterey, Tipe, Venezia, and Fina that could never seriously be meant for copy outside a fashion magazine or advertisement. A page of Fina will give you an instant headache! The commentaries on type, apparently supplied by manufacturers, are uniformly favorable and, while perhaps interesting historically, are useless for selecting type.

A section of "non-laser typefaces" is really the Macintosh screen fonts and has no meaning in a PC environment—which can also be said for page after page of Mac keyboard-and-symbol charts. A font usage chart is truly remarkable: for example, it shows Palatino as ideal for books and magazines, but as a bad choice for newsletters!

What text there is, is not very good. They offer some awful examples of letterspacing; they barely touch on kerning. They offer 6 to 12 points as suitable body-text sizes, going 3 points smaller than most writers. Their recommended line lengths include incredibly narrow columns (maximum columns as little as 30 characters wide). They say that 85 percent of people who see an article never read beyond the headline—an extreme statement offered without any reference or proof.

The sample documents shown are generally busy, hard to read, misspelled, and certainly not examples of readable, coherent design. They say that toner is "magnetically" attracted to paper in a laser printer, which must be quite a revelation to the engineers at Xerox and Canon, who thought they were using electrostatic charges. If you do have occasion to look at this book, your best bet is to ignore the text altogether; I regard it as generally untrustworthy. The book itself is a waste of paper. (Adobe, Bitstream, and other type companies will be happy to send you catalogs of their typefaces.) *Not recommended.*

Ventura Expertise

> Nace, Ted, with Daniel Will-Harris. *Ventura Tips and Tricks*. 2d Ed. Berkeley: Peachpit Press, 1989. 760 p. Glossary, 40-page small-type index. ISBN 0-938151-03-7: $24.95 (paper).

When I first purchased Ventura Publisher (in 1988), I checked the few Ventura-related books then on the market and talked to some other users. My conclusion was the same as their advice: Ted Nace's *Ventura Tips and Tricks*, published in 1987, was an essential companion to Ventura—and, if you could deal with Ventura's manuals, it was the only other book you needed. I purchased the book and used it extensively for the useful tips and commonsense advice. At $16 for 286 pages, it was a genuine bargain.

This second edition is almost three times as thick, about 50 percent more expensive, and just as useful as the first one was—although there's so much here that it can be overwhelming. Ventura's own documentation improved considerably with Version 2.0, but the program also does a lot more, and there are more related products. My quick cut on this book, then, is simple: *If you buy Ventura Publisher, buy a copy of this book.* You may not want to read it cover-to-cover, but the excellent index and deep table of contents (seventeen pages!) will allow you to dip into it as you need it.

Ventura Tips and Tricks is a mixture of software and hardware profiles (short reviews) and commentaries, discussion of parts of Ventura and how to use the program effectively, and several "tips and tricks" chapters. There are some copyediting lapses, although relatively few for a book of this size. There are some shortcomings—for example, the chapter on scanners lacks any profiles of inexpensive handheld scanners—but, overall, the book is honest, carefully done, not biased too strongly in any given direction (except in favor of Ventura, of course), and extremely useful. For example, even though Nace uses PostScript, he recognizes that Bitstream's non-PostScript typefaces are the highest-quality laser-printer typefaces available. Nace and Will-Harris dismiss the use of special paper a bit too readily, but that's no worse than saying that special paper will vastly improve output; the truth lies somewhere in between.

There are too many topics in this book to summarize easily; the authors cover essentially the whole field of Ventura-related topics. The most essential chapters, in some ways, are in section 6, including tips on speed, safety, printing, and "voodoo" (things to try when nothing else works). That section may well be worth the cost of the book.

This guide is not perfect—but then, nothing is. It is well done, worthwhile, pretty much authoritative, and a really basic purchase for anyone who wants to get the most out of Ventura Publisher. *Strongly recommended* for Ventura users.

Looking Good

Parker, Roger C. *Looking Good in Print: A Guide to Basic Design for Desktop Publishing.* Chapel Hill, N.C.: Ventana Press, 1988. 221 p. Bibliography, index. ISBN 0-980087-05-7: $23.95 (paper).

The subtitle accurately describes this book, prepared by one of the better-known desktop-publishing advisers. Parker intersperses bits of advice with a basic course in the elements of graphic design, goes through fourteen make-overs as examples of thinking through design questions, and concludes with discussions of design principles for each of several categories of publication. You don't have to agree with all of Parker's own preferences. He writes clearly enough and in such a manner that you will profit from the discussion even if you don't. In short, this is a worthwhile book, although certainly not flawless.

Parker sets out to deal with design issues, not specific software and hardware combinations, and he succeeds admirably. Although some of his advice on building a consistent design will work much better with Ventura than with PageMaker, he really avoids mentioning either program except in the introduction.

The first eighty-seven pages, "The Elements of Graphic Design," include five chapters: beginning observations, tools of organization, building blocks, tools of emphasis, and common design pitfalls. He stresses coherence, consistency, restraint, and the use of design as an extension of content and purpose. He stresses that there are no universal rules and that good design involves experimentation and your own good taste, not simply following a set of rules. In most cases, he offers reasons for his own preferences; even if you disagree (as I do in some cases), at least you know why suggestions are made, which will help you think through the design process.

The section on common design pitfalls is particularly useful, although his definition of *widows* (short lines at the ends of paragraphs) is different than the usual definition (used in this book). Unlike many modern designers, his suggestions on column width are within the traditional mainstream: width should be based on size of type, and a 12-point face will work well in a 24-pica column (for example). In those terms, the book's own column is at the wide edge of optimal, 24 picas for 10-point type—almost exactly equivalent to this book's 27 picas for 11-point type.[2]

The section of make-overs includes enough annotation to show why he has made changes. Once again, even if you don't agree with all of his decisions, you will learn from the thinking process that is revealed in the commentary.

The third section, "Getting Down to Business," deals with developing formats and styles for various categories of publication. Much of this is very much business-oriented and promotion-oriented, but most of it is nonetheless valuable advice.

---

2   Note that some modern designers would call for no more than 13 or 14 picas for 11-point type!

The book lacks a glossary, but his writing is clear throughout; terms are explained as they appear. He uses *masthead* where this book uses *banner* (both uses are legitimate), but there is never any question as to what he means.

I've read a number of articles by Parker; sometimes, in short pieces, he comes across as adamant about things like ragged-right text. After reading this book, I ascribe that to the pressures of writing to fit and making an impact. Parker has good things to say and says them well, even in those cases where I might disagree. The book is accessible, easy to get through, and never bogs down in detail. *Recommended:* a keeper.

Transitional Perspectives

Seybold, John and Fritz Dressler. *Publishing from the Desktop.* New York: Bantam, 1987. 299 p. Index. ISBN 0-553-34401-3: $19.95 (paper).

Seybold has been involved with photocomposition and publishing systems for many years, and this book frequently says more about how things have been or are done in larger and older systems than it does about desktop publishing. I would estimate that less than half of the text focuses directly on desktop publishing, but the other text is certainly interesting, even if it's not very useful.

It's hard to say whether or not this is a good book. On its own terms, it is interesting; I just don't find that it includes much useful content specifically related to desktop publishing or to the actual task of preparing publications. It is not, I would say, a book you would keep and refer to; while there is some specifically useful information, that really doesn't seem to be the point of the book. I found myself wanting more information in several places and frequently having trouble digging out the information relevant to desktop publishing from extended discussions of coding and other techniques used in early professional photocomposition systems. My sense is that the authors cobbled together a book from existing material, putting a little desktop slant on it.

A book about publishing should itself be carefully edited and published—and this one isn't. Some words are misused, there are misspellings, and one nonexistent word ("quantitizing") is used consistently in place of the perfectly good word ("quantizing"). One page includes a horrendous composition error, making it very difficult to follow a paragraph that begins on the previous page. Not that the book is riddled with errors; it isn't. But composition errors should surely be avoided in a book on publishing, and some of the spelling errors could have been caught by a spell-checker (e.g., "acronymns").

In the end, a mixed bag. Fairly good writing by authors who clearly know the details of professional composition systems, but little useful content for contemporary desktop publishers. Read it as history.

The "Bible"?

Stockford, James, ed. *Desktop Publishing Bible.* (The Waite Group, Inc.) Indianapolis, Ind.: H. W. Sams, 1987. 470 p. Index. ISBN 0-672-22524-7: $24.95 (paper).

If you aren't turned off by the name, you will find this to be a curious mixture of excellence, mediocrity, and irrelevance. The book consists of twenty-six essays by several different authors, grouped into four sections: Traditional Underpinnings (86 pages); Systems and Hardware (154 pages); Software (130 pages); and Techniques and Special Applications (82 pages).

I found most (but not all) of the first section interesting and worthwhile, but I have little good to say about the other three sections—particularly for readers who are not Macintosh zealots and don't buy the big lie that only Postscript printers can achieve typographic excellence.

The first section discusses print production (offering some good notes on working with a printer), copyright law, conventional typesetting, design for desktop publishing, and situations when desktop publishing makes sense. There are some problems even here. For example, one author says (probably correctly) that the ideal line width is seven to ten words—but then goes on to say that this equals 35 to 40 characters, which is nonsense! In fact, seven to ten words will average 45 to 70 characters. An essay comparing desktop costs to costs for traditional methods assumes that both methods are farmed out at high hourly rates, which rather misses the whole point of desktop publishing! The essay says flatly that long documents will be cheaper to produce if typeset rather than desktop-published, which is absolutely not true under most circumstances. Still, there's lots of good advice and comments in the first section.

After that, the book goes downhill. An essay by an obvious Macintosh zealot shows a sample screen in which most of the icons are identical, then tells us that it shows the superior communication bandwidth of icons over text. An essay on PC desktop publishing says flatly that it absolutely requires an EGA monitor and adapter at $1,500 to $3,000 in addition to the computer—which is sheer nonsense, since a Hercules clone at $150 combined cost (even in 1987) offers higher resolution. An essay on graphics cards says that the Wyse 700 has 1,280-by-400 resolution, which should have been recognized as absurd (the right figure is 1,280-by-800).

Several essays don't really seem to lead anywhere and seem to be rather offhand efforts. An essay on Unix is simply a sales pitch, and it's not a very good one at that. An essay on high-end workstations begins with the absurd statement that "dedicating a single PC or microcomputer to an expensive laser printer and disk drive is a waste of resources" and offers workstations as an alternative—but a low-end workstation costs more than a PC, hard disk, and laser printer combined!

The third section includes some useful information but also some surprisingly wrong and inadequate information; I came away unwilling to trust anything I read in the section. Once again, an author asserts that you need "the most advanced video boards with the latest enhanced color and high-resolution monochrome monitors" to "come very close to" the Macintosh for desktop publishing. In simple fact, the standard Mac screen has 512 by 300 pixels and the standard Hercules screen, the cheapest display subsystem you can buy for a PC, has 720 by 348 pixels on a larger screen. What we have here is truly offensive—people that are committed to the Macintosh offering deceptive descriptions of the PC in order to make it look bad.

What else can I say? A chapter that discusses Donald Knuth's landmark TEX consistently calls it "TeX".[3] A surprisingly large number of essays say that desktop publishing isn't really that good—largely because they ignore the fine typographic control that Ventura offered even in 1987. An essay extolling the superior control of JustText is curious, since Ventura does everything listed while permitting interactive control. One essay says that the LaserWriter appeared in 1976, roughly a decade earlier than it actually did.

Overall conclusion? *Not recommended*—which is a shame, because much of the first section is really quite good. But $25 is too much to pay for fifty pages of good information, particularly when the rest of the book is so flawed that you must distrust what is said. The main flaws are: misinformation about PCs; too many essays that have nothing to do with desktop publishing; and too many essays trying to say why you really shouldn't use it.

Not Complete, but Interesting

Will-Harris, Daniel. *Desktop Publishing with Style: A Complete Guide to Design Techniques and New Technologies for the IBM PC and Compatibles.* South Bend, Ind.: and books, 1987. 444 p. Bibliography, glossary, index. ISBN 0-89708-162-5: $19.95 (paper).

This large-format (8½-by-11-inch) book was prepared using Ventura Publisher and HP-compatible laser printers. Will-Harris brings an informal, somewhat Peter McWilliams-ish tone to the book, which can be tiresome at points. The book's subtitle is somewhat misleading: only one chapter deals with aspects of design (about thirty pages of text), with another chapter offering thirty different examples of how Will-Harris might design specific products.

This review covers two different versions of the book—what may have been the original 1987 edition (but was not the first edition) and a version released in the summer of 1989—which, although it

---

3 The discussion of production methods used for the book extols the superior typographic control of the software used; if it can't handle subscripts and manual kerning, it's certainly not superior.

has a different-color cover and a slash on the cover saying that it is "Fully Updated," still carries the 1987 copyright and original ISBN. I'm sure that the second version dates from 1989; I can't be sure whether the earlier version is really a 1987 version or something in between.

Will-Harris starts out being very clear, but starts tossing in terms like *deckhead* with no immediate explanation. He offers quite a bit of good basic advice in the one real design chapter; on the other hand, I find most of his examples to be less than convincing. For one thing, he has a weakness for sans serif body type; for another, several of the examples are overdesigned to the point that you see the "look" more than the content. One comparison of laser-printed to typeset output is misleading, as he compares half-density (150-dpi) laser printing to very high density (2,540-dpi) typesetting.

Most of the book is reviews—of page-composition programs, graphics programs, printers, fonts, word-processing software, and utilities. Some of the reviews are quite useful; some are difficult to deal with, as they tell more about Will-Harris's own biases than about the product. The current version is significantly better than the earlier version in this regard.

It would appear that almost the only changes between the two versions are in the reviews—and these are somewhat inconsistently handled. I don't have the sense that anyone read the revised version through from beginning to end, checking for internal consistency. The book also has problems with copyediting—particularly habitual confusion between *it's* and *its*, but also a number of other problems that a good copy editor should catch.

The lack of a complete update is more apparent in the examples (which appear to be completely unchanged) than the text, but it does show there as well. For example, he spends some time on scanners—but completely fails to mention $200 handheld scanners as a lower-cost alternative to $2,000 page scanners, although such scanners do get one sentence later in the book. His discussion of low-cost alternatives to laser printers seems unchanged from two years previous, and he does not mention the HP DeskJet—although, again, it turns up in a later discussion of system prices! Apparently, some sections were actually rewritten while others were simply incorporated without change or inspection.

Generally, I like the book—but it could be considerably better with proper copyediting, a little more time spent on the supposed emphasis of the book, and a clearer sense of the actual date of the current version.

Desktop-Publishing Magazines

Of the many newsletters and other publications made feasible by desktop publishing, several have been devoted to desktop publishing. There are expensive newsletters in the field; there are program-specific newsletters and magazines, as well as publications that come as part of membership in an organization.

I've been reading four monthly publications in the field for the last year or so (somewhat longer in two cases). These include the two most widely circulated general magazines on the field, one PC-specific magazine, and a Ventura-specific publication that began as the newsletter for a users' group.

The brief notes below try to give something of the flavor of each magazine, but that can be difficult to do. Naturally, a monthly magazine represents a number of different viewpoints and includes articles at different levels of quality.

None of these magazines approaches the sheer bulk of *PC Magazine*; these are all relatively slender publications. None has the extensive, authoritative review capabilities of *PC Magazine* or *Info-World*; when comparative articles do appear, they are usually fairly brief and not backed up by extensive testing.

You will probably want to subscribe to at least one desktop-publishing magazine, if only to keep track of new products that may improve your own capabilities. But you should deal with the editorial content of these magazines with a good deal of skepticism: you may not be the audience they are apparently written for.

The notes are arranged alphabetically.

PC-Specific, Lightweight

> *PC Publishing*. ISSN 0896-8209. Monthly; $36/year ($3.95/issue).
> (Offered at full price; renewed at $54/two years.) Published by
> Hunter Publishing. Also offered as part of membership in
> National Association of Desktop Publishers.

Slender (1989 issues range from seventy-four to eighty-eight pages), about the same age as *Publish!* (1989 is volume 4), and more specialized (coverage is limited to PC-compatible computers), this magazine is heavy on "how such-and-such company uses desktop publishing" and seems light on useful content. Editorial content is about 50 percent of the total; most of that seems to be departments. I'm not sure just what it is about this magazine, but it seems to be the least useful of those I read.

PC Publishing is produced using desktop methods (and set on a medium-density phototypesetter). Unlike the others, this one uses entirely PC-compatible equipment (explained in great detail). Body type is Times Roman; heads are Helvetica. Yawn.

There's some good information here, but I find that most issues are heavy on fluff; articles that do have a point rarely include the level of detail or illustrations needed to make them satisfactory. In general, there doesn't seem to be much here. While never as garish as *Publish!* can sometimes be, *PC Publishing* is also not as useful as either competitor mentioned below.

I know that PC-based desktop publishing can be quite as interesting as Mac-based publishing—but you can't tell that from this magazine. That's too bad.

The Generalist Perspective

> *Personal Publishing*. ISSN 0884-951X. Monthly; $24/year
> ($3/issue). (Offered as low as $12/year; renewed at $15/year.)
> Published by Hitchcock Publishing, a division of ABC Publish-
> ing.

This magazine has been around for a while: the October 1989 issue is volume 5, number 10. Issues during 1989 were eighty-two to ninety pages long, almost exactly half advertising and half editorial. Produced using desktop techniques (but output on a phototypesetter), the magazine is relatively conservative (body text is mostly justified New Baskerville, a very readable serif type) and quite readable. Editorial content is split between ongoing columns, reviews, and feature articles, with quite a wide range of topics in all areas.

Personal Publishing has several positive virtues as compared to other magazines in the field. It is far less oriented to professionals than other magazines; it deals with the realities of 300-dot-per-inch final output in a nonpatronizing manner, and it does not implicitly assume that all serious desktop publishers use the Macintosh and PostScript. It does not include make-overs on a regular basis, but instead it discusses how people have carried out specific original publication designs.

Naturally, some nonsense appears in the pages—but quite a few different writers appear, and I find more common sense and diversity than nonsense and uniformity. Personally, I find one of the newer columnists almost uniformly annoying and wrong-headed—but I still read the column.

This magazine isn't perfect, by any means, but I do find that it stands up well to reference and rereading. You may find it useful and less irritating than some alternatives.

Big, Brash, and Biased

> *Publish!* ISSN 0897-6007. Monthly; $39.90/year ($3.95/issue). (Actual offered rate varies considerably, but no higher than $24/year. Renewed at $22/two years!) Published by PCW Communications (*PC World*).

Publish! is the biggest (96–120 pages per issue in 1989) and probably most widely distributed desktop-publishing magazine. It may also be the most annoying and frustrating, with its orientation toward professional graphic artists, its frequent disdain for anything but the Macintosh, and its assumption that lasers are only suitable for proofing.

Most body type is justified New Baskerville, set on a phototypesetter. *Publish!* layout can be quirky, with alphabets popping up in various places and lots of graphic tricks that sometimes, but not always, make sense. It's not the oldest magazine in the field; 1989 is volume 4. Content is roughly half editorial, half advertising, with editorial space split between departments, reviews, and feature articles. *Publish!* is strong on page make-overs, allowing its designers to show just how much they will distort content in order to achieve a "look" that they like.

While *Publish!* has more content than its competitors, I find that I rarely go back to an issue. That may be personal taste. On the other hand, what do you say about a feature of "hot tips" that includes the quite sensible note that text should be set in lines that are 45 to 75 characters wide, with the note itself set in a 6-pica column (about 20 characters to the line)! (The "hot tips" feature was one of those articles that was so infuriating in its design and, sometimes, content that I was tempted to discard the issue on the spot.)

Chances are, you'll want to read at least two or three issues of *Publish!*. Although it is frequently maddening, it also tends to include more up-to-date information than the other magazines in the field.

Ventura-Specific

> *Ventura Professional!* ISSN 1046-9885. Monthly; $36/year
> ($65/two years), which is actually membership in the Ventura
> Publisher Users Group (VPUG); not discounted. $5/issue. Pub-
> lished by Ventura Publisher Users Group. Also available auto-
> matically as part of Xerox's customer support programs for
> Ventura Publisher.

Here we have a truly specialized magazine—or newsletter, depending on how you look at it. This is an independently published, full-size (8-by-10½-inch), substantial (sixty-four to seventy-two pages for 1989 issues) monthly devoted entirely to Xerox Ventura Publisher. VPUG, the San Jose users' group that is also the central agency for some fifty Ventura users' groups in the United States (and eight in other countries), is one of the most successful recent users' groups. I've never been to a meeting, but I find the magazine well worth its $36 subscription rate.

Since April 1989, this magazine has been a curious hybrid: it is still independently published, but it is also the technical communications medium for the Xerox Desktop Software Division Customer Support Group, replacing their former *Pipeline* (a thin quarterly newsletter). The name *Ventura Professional!* began in September 1988. The publication goes back a bit further, as the magazine *Ventura*

Publishes . . . since April 1988 and as a newsletter for fifteen months before that. In other words, it's been around just about as long as Ventura itself.

There's a lot that you don't get in this magazine, compared to the three more generalized magazines reviewed in this appendix. The only color is on the cover (and sometimes inside full-page ads); the range of advertisements is smaller; obviously, there isn't much discussion of the Macintosh, PageMaker, or any other desktop-publishing systems. There are relatively few photos and relatively little dazzling graphic design. The paper isn't slick. There are also a lot fewer advertisements—each issue has close to fifty pages of editorial space, not including house ads and contents.

What you do get, then, is content—and lots of it. Content is split between features and departments; each issue has a theme for the features, and articles are long enough to be informative, with good examples as needed. They do have a substantial preference for Post-Script printers, but not at the expense of editorial balance. I could do without their almost uniform use of ragged-right body type, but that's my own taste. The magazine isn't slickly done, by and large, but it is frequently quite useful.

The narrow focus of the magazine makes it worthwhile reading for almost any Ventura user—and, of course, essentially useless for anybody else.

Conclusions

It's important to state once again that the books and magazines that suit my needs may not be the ones that work best for you. I don't do much in the way of promotional brochures or advertising, so some of the design-oriented publications aren't very useful for me—but for some libraries they could be extremely worthwhile. I haven't felt any urge to adopt canned style sheets for publications, but I can surely see why many desktop publishers would find them worthwhile. I appreciate books and articles that deal with type and layout within a historical perspective, not as something newly invented in 1985—but others may have had their fill of history.

That said, which books do I expect to go back to, and which ones would I buy if I had time enough and money enough?

The most obvious case is Ted Nace's *Ventura Tips and Tricks*. The first edition saw heavy use alongside my Xerox Ventura Publisher manual; the massive second edition now sits right next to the new Ventura manual, and I expect it will also be heavily used over the years to come.

The *Desktop Publisher's Dictionary* was quite useful in writing this book, mostly to check on my own understanding of words; I'm not sure that it will see much use in the future, however. I thoroughly enjoyed Will-Harris's book when I first read it a year or so ago—and it might get some reference use.

Tom Lichty's book sits next to the dictionary, and I do expect to go back to it from time to time. I certainly don't agree with everything Lichty says, but there's still quite a bit of useful material here.

I borrowed Roger Parker's book (reviewed above) from the City of Mountain View Public Library. If I were planning to design a number of new publications, or if I were a little earlier in my own use of desktop publishing, I would probably buy it; it's a good one. There are other design books that I've considered, off and on; to date, none of them has called out to my wallet.

Once this book is published, I will no longer feel obliged to subscribe to all four monthly magazines reviewed above. Which ones will I keep? I'm not quite sure, just yet—*PC Publishing* will probably be the first to go, but *Personal Publishing* seems to have earned a warm spot in my heart. *Ventura Professional!* continues to be useful. Right now, I might or might not renew *Publish!*—but that may change by the time my subscription expires, and the renewal is so cheap that I'll probably keep subscribing.

Other Subjects

There's more to a publications program than desktop publishing itself, and you may find books in some other fields useful. You can certainly find interesting books on type design and the principles of good typography, worthwhile books on writing and editing, and useful guides to editorial practice. *The Chicago Manual of Style* (Chicago: University of Chicago Press) is a treasure trove of good advice, as well as being the most widely used standard for copyediting; I've used the 13th edition (the first to actually have *Chicago Manual of Style* as its title; issued in 1982) for some years, and I find it an accessible, reliable guide—even if I don't always follow its advice.

Index

About the Author

Walt Crawford works in the Development Division of The Research Libraries Group, Inc. (RLG). He is active in the Library and Information Technology Association (LITA) of the American Library Association (ALA), serving on the LITA Board of Directors from 1988 to 1991 and as editor of the *LITA Newsletter* since 1985. Mr. Crawford converted the *LITA Newsletter* from traditional typography to desktop methods in 1986 and to full desktop publishing (Ventura Publisher) in 1988. He is also the founding editor of *Information Standards Quarterly*, a publication of the National Information Standards Organization (NISO) that began in 1989 and is also prepared using Ventura Publisher. Mr. Crawford has written several books in the Professional Librarian series; this is the second such book to be produced using Ventura Publisher.